ESSAYS ON
RELIGION AND EDUCATION

ESSAYS ON
RELIGION AND EDUCATION

R. M. Hare

CLARENDON PRESS · OXFORD

1992

Oxford University Press, Walton Street, Oxford OX2 6DP
Oxford New York Toronto
Delhi Bombay Calcutta Madras Karachi
Petaling Jaya Singapore Hong Kong Tokyo
Nairobi Dar es Salaam Cape Town
Melbourne Auckland
and associated companies in
Berlin Ibadan

Oxford is a trade mark of Oxford University Press

Published in the United States
by Oxford University Press, New York

British Cataloguing in Publication Data
Data available

Library of Congress Cataloging in Publication Data
Hare, R. M. (Richard Mervyn)
Essays on religion and education / R. M. Hare.
p.   cm.
Includes bibliographical references and index.
1. Moral education.   2. Ethics.   I. Title.
LC268.H265   1992   370.11'4—dc20   92-2862
ISBN 0-19-824997-7

Typeset by Pentacor PLC, High Wycombe, Bucks

Printed in Great Britain by
Biddles Ltd, Guildford & King's Lynn

PREFACE

This, the third of my present series of volumes of essays, is concerned with two closely related topics. For myself, I have found it impossible to discuss education for long without bringing in religion, if only to forestall claims by some religious people to a monopoly of moral education. One's attitude to religion will impinge powerfully on one's approach to education. This is because the irrational side of our nature, from which none of us can escape, needs to be educated, and religion, interpreted broadly to include humanistic beliefs, is the only way of doing this. In that sense, religion is a necessity. Some might call it a necessary evil—and it certainly can be very evil. Others will retort that it need not be an evil if we are careful to choose good kinds of religion. But we can hardly avoid having some kind. If the devil is driven out, seven devils at once take his place.

My own views have changed somewhat since I wrote 'The Simple Believer'. I am still confident that the ideas in it are a possible approach to a viable religion. But I am less confident now even than I was then that this approach will find favour. On the one hand we have the growth of fundamentalisms and fanaticisms in all or most religions, leading in some to extremes of cruelty and violence. On the other we have 'advanced' theologians who think that by minor reinterpretations of the creeds, accompanied by a lot of vagueness and evasion, they can square them with the real beliefs of most educated people. They seem not to have absorbed the lessons they should have learnt from the disputes, now quite old, which engendered the first two papers in this volume. The arguments of philosophers like Wisdom and Flew cannot just be dismissed; the failure to confront or even to understand them condemns many present-day theologians to inanity.

Moral philosophy, if intelligently pursued, can shed a flood of light on both topics, as I hope will be shown by the essays which follow. As before, it has proved impossible to avoid a great deal of repetition (though I have done my best), simply because, whatever topic one takes from these fields, the same moves are crucial. This produces a conflict between the interests of two sorts of readers: those who want to read the whole volume through, and those who want only to read particular papers in it. I have preferred to make it easier for the second sort, because they are likely to be in the majority. I have done this by leaving in many of the repetitions, without which the papers could not be read independently. To have substituted cross-references would have shortened the book by only a few pages. If readers get tired of hearing about *agapē* or about the two levels of moral thinking, I ask them to be patient, because these ideas really are essential to an understanding of almost any moral problem, and cannot be repeated too often.

The paper on euthanasia could have been included in a forthcoming volume, *Essays on Bioethics*; but I put it into this volume because it illustrates very well the bearing that religion should have, and that which it should not have, on practical moral issues. Likewise, the paper 'Why Moral Language?', which is more theoretical than the others, could have gone into my *Essays in Ethical Theory*; but it is so germane to the problems of education that this is a good place for it.

I have to thank the original publishers of these essays for giving permission, where this was necessary, to reprint them. The original sources are given at the foot of the first page of each essay. My thanks are also due to Angela Blackburn and her colleagues at the Oxford University Press for their instruction in how to prepare a computer disc for use in typesetting—a task in which, together with much library work, my kind assistants at the University of Florida, Rory Weiner and Marin Smillov, have proved most helpful. But above all I have as always to thank my wife, without whose encouragement and active help I would never have got the volume together.

R.M.H.

Ewelme, Oxford
May 1991

CONTENTS

I

The Simple Believer

I

I must start with an apology. The philosophy of religion is not a speciality of mine. It is, indeed, a subject which fastidious philosophers do not like to touch. This is not merely because it is a confused subject—that could be said of other branches of philosophy—but because the whole atmosphere of the subject is such as to put a premium on unclarity of thought. The confusion is not of philosophical origin; nor do the problems with which I shall be dealing belong to the class sometimes confidently called 'pseudo-problems'. They have been generated, rather, by the quite genuine perplexities of those who want to call themselves Christians, or at least theists, and yet cannot bring themselves to believe what theists are supposed to have to believe. These people have been appealing for help to the theologians for a long time; they have received a great deal of comfort but not much clarification—because the issues have not been faced in the clear light which only a thorough understanding of the concepts involved could give. The philosophers, for their part—those few of us who have cared to soil our fingers—have contributed, perhaps, a little towards this understanding; but our failure to make any decisive progress has prompted in some the thought that the concepts are inherently confused and can never be clarified. For the rest —the non-philosophers—hardly anybody has any interest in achieving clarity; it would be too harsh and unpleasant. And such philosophical work as has been done on these questions has not (or so it would appear) made much impact on those who are most troubled by them.

There thus remains a cleavage between philosophically sophisticated people who have (or think they have) some

From *Religion and Morality*, ed. G. Outka and J. Reeder (Anchor/Doubleday, 1973).

understanding of the issues, but do not care very much about them, and the unsophisticated, who care (or think they care) very much, but are in a complete muddle. This may explain what usually happens—at any rate in England—on the rare occasions on which these matters are discussed at professional meetings of philosophers. There are three main parties to these discussions—if we exclude those who, either because of lack of interest, or because of lack of confidence that they know their own mind, stay silent. The first party consists of the orthodox Christians; the second of the downright no-nonsense atheists. The third party is made up of those courageous people who, like Professors Braithwaite and van Buren, want to be Christians and yet to hold a faith which is defensible against the attacks of the philosophically well-armed atheist. A member of this third party produces some version of the Christian faith which he thinks is both defensible and genuinely Christian; the other two parties then at once form a holy–unholy alliance and have no difficulty at all in making him look silly. 'How could you possibly pretend', they say in chorus, 'that you are a Christian, when all you believe is *that*?'

When I refer to these three parties, I do not mean to imply that there are no other voices which are or ought to be heard, but only that these are the loudest. The predominant impression that one receives from any gathering in which the orthodox and the atheists are present and speak their minds is that they are united in ridiculing my third party, whom I shall call the Christian empiricists. As I shall be saying again later, the reason why the atheists ally themselves with the orthodox in this way is that they have an obvious interest in making the Christian religion as absurd a faith as possible, in order the easier to justify their rejection of it. The reason why the orthodox ally themselves with the atheists is harder to see. It would be merely mischievous to suggest that they have taken the old Greek proverb 'Everything noble is difficult' and, by a familiar logical fallacy, converted it into the proposition that everything difficult is noble, and think that because it is so very difficult to believe the things which they say that Christians have to believe, peculiar merit is acquired by those few elect who manage to do it. Though some do seem to believe *quia absurdum*, a more likely explanation in most cases is that they do not believe *quia* anything at all. This is not to say that they lack arguments to defend their beliefs once acquired.

It is to be hoped that the orthodox Christians, who have, with the help of the atheists, thus easily made fools of their supposedly Christian brethren, are not so pleased with their victory as to ignore its consequences. It can safely be predicted that, if the third party were finally and decisively eliminated, and the orthodox and atheists were left to fight out the clear issue remaining between them, the orthodox would find themselves in a tactically much less defensible position than that in which they now are. For, once the issues are seen clearly—once, that is, the condition is firmly laid down that in order to be called a Christian one has to believe all the things that the orthodox say they believe, and believe them literally —then nobody with any claim to rationality is going to say that he is a Christian.

The orthodox appear so strong a party only because they have the support of a very large number of Christians— probably the huge majority of educated ones—who have so far been able to avoid the issue just because it has not been put to them clearly. Theologians have produced a succession of devices for concealing from Christians the starkness of the choice which, if the orthodox and the atheists are right, they have to make. Even the orthodox will often make use of these evasions if hard pressed. The reason why the vast majority of educated Christians are people who have evaded the issue is that those educated people who have not evaded it have ceased to be Christians. If there is no third alternative besides orthodoxy, strictly and clearly interpreted, and atheism, it is likely that most thinking people will choose the latter.

I now come back to the apology which I said I had to make. The position has been as I have just described it for at least fifty years. Near the beginning of this period I wrote a little piece on the subject (pp. 37 ff.) which has become so notorious that I have many times wished that I had never published it. I wrote it within the compass of twenty-four hours because I liked the face of the man who wanted it for his new magazine, and was too good-natured to refuse. This was the article in which the word 'blik' first got into the literature. Very shortly after that I wrote a longer article which I never published, but, after reading it to one or two student societies, put it away in a file and forgot about it. Then, much later, all the fuss started about God being dead. Thinking that my old paper might be of interest, I took it out of its box and was astonished to find that it had suddenly become topical. Indeed, I thought that if the issues in that old controversy had been properly understood, much that has since been written would either not have been written at all, or would have been written more clearly. Since I myself have never been able to state the issues any more clearly than I did in that paper, I expanded it into two lectures I gave in Oxford as part of one of my courses as Wilde Lecturer in 1963. This paper is a revised version of those two lectures.

I am going to set the scene, as I see it, by telling a story. There was once a Simple Believer—too simple to be classified as one of the orthodox I have spoken of, for he was unacquainted with those disputes, and as innocent of theology as philosophy. If you asked him 'Is there a God?' he would reply, 'Of course'. And if you then asked him 'What is he like?' he would say 'He is something like a man (for it says in the Bible that God made man in his own image); and he lives in Heaven, which is a place far up in the sky; and he made both Heaven and Earth in six days in the year 4004 BC, as you can find by doing some calculations based on the information given in the Bible. He made it in the manner described in Genesis, and he continues to rule the world by causing things to happen in it according to his will; and especially he causes things to happen which are for the good of those that believe in him; for God is loving, etc.'

This sort of belief satisfied the Simple Believer until, at an impressionable age, he met another person, whom I will call the Simple Unbeliever. The Simple Unbeliever said 'Surely you don't believe *that* any more? We know now, for it has been established by science, that a being like a man couldn't possibly live up in the sky.' (The conversation took place before the days of space travel.) 'If you know any science at all, you know that he couldn't survive for a moment; and in any case, if he did exist on some star, how could he intervene from that distance in our affairs? And as for him making the world in 4004 BC, we know that the world is much older than that. And he couldn't intervene in the world, since we know— for science tells us—that the world proceeds on its way by immutable scientific laws; so how could he make any difference to what happens in the world?'

The Simple Believer's faith was considerably shaken by all this; for he found on reflection and enquiry that most people believe that what science says, is true, and in his heart of hearts he believed so too. The picture that the Simple Unbeliever gave of the findings of science was, indeed, crude and over-simplified; but that could be remedied without altering its impact upon his former simple beliefs. Fortunately, while he was in this state of incipient doubt, he met a third person, whom I will call the Sophisticated Believer. The Sophisticated Believer set the Simple Believer's doubts at rest by saying 'You have been taking the Bible too literally. Of course, if you have these "literal and low conceptions of sacred beings" (as Hogarth called them in the text under one of his engravings), your beliefs won't stand up against the latest scientific discoveries. If you want to survive the advance of empirical science, you must at all costs *keep out of the way* of the scientists; and this isn't at all difficult. Of course God (God the Father, that is) isn't like a man to look at—the Thirty-nine Articles say that he has neither body, parts, nor passions. And of course Genesis is only legend, although it is of deep symbolical significance. The Creation certainly wasn't like it says in Genesis, and there's no need to believe that it happened in 4004 BC. You have been taking much too literally the statement that God made the world in six days—"day" here is to be interpreted as meaning an epoch of very great but unspecified length, so that the Genesis story (so far as chronology goes, at any rate) can be reconciled with whatever science discovers about the age of the universe. This is an example of what I mean by "keeping out of the scientists' way"; you must be careful to say nothing that they can ever disprove. And in the same way to say that God rules the world is not to say anything that science would contradict. Aren't the laws of science the very best evidence that the world is ordered by a master-mind? For everywhere we turn we see things happening, not just by chance and haphazard, but according to the most precise laws. In believing in God, you aren't asked to believe anything about the world except what common sense and science (which is organized common sense) would allow. Religion is not about material things but about the things of the spirit.'

This sort of comfort satisfied the Simple Believer, until he met the Simple Unbeliever again. This time the Simple Unbeliever had been reading Freud, and all about Pavlov's dogs. When he heard what the Sophisticated Believer had said about the things of the spirit, he exclaimed 'But that won't do either now, you know. The distinction between the spiritual and the material is nothing but a Cartesian category-mistake, or myth. [He was alluding to Ryle 1949: 18.] Scientists don't only find out the laws that govern what you call the material world, but also those that govern what you call the things of the spirit. We can often give very good explanations of people's religious beliefs, for example, in terms of their early upbringing. No doubt if I knew more about *your* early upbringing I could account for your religious beliefs. The phenomena which you call spiritual and those which you call material are all just phenomena; science will explain them all in the end by the methods which have been so successful hitherto. Of course not everything has been explained yet; but that is a stimulus to us to go on looking for the true scientific explanations of things. Your talk about the things of the spirit is just an impediment to our researches, because it makes people think that there is something in the way people behave which is out of the reach of scientific enquiry. The Sophistic-ated Believer was quite right to tell you to keep out of the way of the scientists—I only wish you would; but to succeed in doing so you will have to move faster and farther than he thinks.'

The Simple Believer was of course troubled by this; so he went hurrying back to the Sophisticated Believer, who had been of such assistance to him before, in the hope that he would provide an answer. And he did provide an answer; for if a believer is sophisticated enough, he can provide an answer to anything. He said 'You mustn't be upset by this kind of thing. When I said, the last time we met, that religion did not contradict science, I didn't mean to confine myself to what are called the physical sciences. I included the biological sciences; and, now that psychology has become respectable, I have no hesitation in including that too. Of course the religious believer doesn't want to contradict the psychologist, any more than he wants to contradict the physiologist. Come to that, he doesn't want to contradict *anybody*. Even when the religious person and the psychologist are talking about the same sort of phenomena, they are talking about them in a quite different way. When St Francis gets swellings on his hands, the psychologist calls it "hysterical stigmatization"; but the Christian will call it a miracle. And both will be perfectly right. In general, science is concerned with counting, measuring, observing, and predicting; religion is concerned with worship. Therefore it is quite impossible for the statements of the two to contradict one another. Statements about God creating and loving the world are statements of a different logical category from those about nebulae or atoms or bacteria or neurones; and so a person can go on making both kinds of statement without being in any way inconsistent. That is to say, it is perfectly possible to be a scientist and a religious believer at the same time—why, look at all the people who do it!'

While the Sophisticated Believer was offering this comfort, and the Simple Believer was on the way to being comforted, they did not notice that a friend of theirs was standing nearby and listening to what they were saying. He was there quite by accident, and had not meant to join in the conversation at all. But what he heard was too much for him, and he burst in 'But I don't see what the devil is left of your religion after you have said this. Your religious utterances used to consist of plain assertions about the existence of a Being about whose character, though exalted and mysterious, you had at any rate some idea. But now, in your determination to say nothing that anybody could disagree with, you have been surreptitiously whittling down your religion until there's nothing left of it but words, and a warm and womblike feeling that still sometimes comes over you when you utter them. Surely you must have heard of the invisible gardener!'

The two Believers both said that they had not heard of the

invisible gardener; so the Sophisticated Unbeliever (as I will call him) went to the library and got out *New Essays in Philosophical Theology* (Flew and MacIntyre 1955: 96), and started to read from Flew's article (from which, by the way, I stole the example about St Francis which I have just used). He chose Flew's version of the parable, not Wisdom's original one (1944), because it made the point more clearly.

Once upon a time two explorers came upon a clearing in the jungle. In the clearing were growing many flowers and many weeds. One explorer says, 'Some gardener must tend this plot.' The other disagrees, 'There is no gardener.' So they pitch their tents and set a watch. No gardener is ever seen. 'But perhaps he is an invisible gardener.' So they set up a barbed-wire fence. They electrify it. They patrol with bloodhounds. (For they remember how H. G. Wells's *The Invisible Man* could be both smelt and touched though he could not be seen.) But no shrieks ever suggest that some intruder has received a shock. No movements of the wire ever betray an invisible climber. The bloodhounds never give cry. Yet still the Believer is not convinced. 'But there is a gardener, invisible, intangible, insensible to electric shocks, a gardener who has no scent and makes no sound, a gardener who comes secretly to look after the garden which he loves.' At last the Sceptic despairs, 'But what remains of your original assertion? Just how does what you call an invisible, intangible, eternally elusive gardener differ from an imaginary gardener or even from no gardener at all?'

By the time he had finished, the Simple Believer was in a bad way; for the point was only too clear to him. He had started off by thinking that he was making perfectly good assertions about the existence of a being called God, and had in his imagination some sort of idea about what this being was like. Then, when he met the Simple Unbeliever, he came to see that what he had been saying was literally false. At first, when he discovered that a being of the sort he had been imagining could not live in the sky, he was comforted by the Sophisticated Believer's telling him that of course he had the wrong ideas about God; God did indeed exist, but he was not quite the sort of being that he had been imagining, and his location was not spatial in the way that he had thought; that in a sense he was everywhere and yet nowhere; that his hand was visible where no hand (no literal hand, that is to say) was visible; that God's love was manifested even in events which, in our normal use of words, we should not regard as manifestations of love, nor even of hate, but just as things that happen in the world. But as the process went on, it had begun to be a bit beyond him. He did at least understand the old literal ideas about God, even if they were false; but these new ideas—well, even if they were true, it was so very hard to say what they meant, and they seemed so far removed from the God he used to worship. True, he still got the old warm feeling when he thought about religion; but even that was beginning to fade away a bit.

And then he thought of another thing. His father was a clergyman, and his grandfather had been a bishop; and so he had naturally sometimes had occasion to try to persuade people whose faith was going or gone to come back into the fold. He had heard his father doing this in the pulpit, and he had tried in his private conversation to reproduce, and indeed to improve on, his father's arguments. But it did not seem to work, somehow. The trouble was that the people he was trying to reconvert (quite ordinary people) did not seem to understand what it was they were being asked to believe in. They would say things like this: 'You tell us to go to church; but why? We understand you when you say that a certain man at the beginning of the ADs, whom we can agree was a very good man if all that you say about him is true, was wrongfully and painfully executed; but we don't see what this has got to do with our enduring even much less discomfort and a great deal of boredom by going to church now. When you start talking about God our mind somehow shuts up—and all the bright new liturgical gimmicks that your father is so keen on don't help. We don't know what it is you are saying. You say God answers prayer. But when somebody prays to God and the thing prayed for doesn't happen, you say "God has thought it better not to answer this one; and of course he knows best." But in that case what do you *mean* when you say God answers prayer?'

They just did not seem to understand what it was they were supposed to believe; and he found it hard to explain to them. He could have explained to them the things he believed in before he met the Simple Unbeliever; but he didn't really

believe in *them* himself any more. And these new things that
the Sophisticated Believer told him he ought to believe were
somehow so difficult to explain, or even to understand. And
after he had heard about the invisible gardener, the frighten-
ing thought occurred to him that the reason why he found it so
difficult to explain what he was saying was that he wasn't
really saying anything.

The Simple Believer's grandfather, as I have said, was a
bishop, and he wrote a book about fossils that was a best seller
among the faithful. In it he proved conclusively, in his own
opinion, that fossils were of very recent origin, and certainly
more recent than 4004 BC; that they all dated from round
about the biblical date for the Flood. And so he thought he
had proved the literal truth of the Genesis account, and saved
the faith from the attacks of the scientists who were trying to
subvert it. The Simple Believer had read his grandfather's
book, and very good hard-hitting stuff it was; but it did not
seem to help him in his present difficulty. His grandfather had
thought he was having a real battle: it said in the Bible that
the world was made in 4004 BC, and here were all these
geologists and palaeontologists saying that it was much older:
and it was his job as a bishop to refute them. But what was it
the job of his grandson the Simple Believer to refute or prove?
For the worrying thing was that he did not believe any longer
the things his grandfather was trying to prove—good solid
assertions like 'The world was made in 4004 BC.' No; *he*
believed the scientists that his grandfather was attacking; his
grandfather had lost that battle, for all his hard hitting.

But that would not have mattered if there were something
substantial left now to fight about; the trouble was that, as a
result of the Sophisticated Believer's qualifications, the faith
had become so insubstantial that it was hard to see what one
was supposed to defend. That perhaps explained why
Christians were, taken all in all, so very like other people; in
all the things that mattered they seemed to think just like
anybody else. In his grandfather's day, if you were a Christian
you thought one thing, and if you were not you thought
something very different. You disagreed, for example, about
the date and manner of the beginning of the world. But now,
what are the Christian and the non-Christian disagreeing

about? For the Christians have, on the advice of sophisticated believers, conceded all the points to the scientists that the scientists required. And so it came about that, while in his grandfather's day those who attacked Christianity were saying that its affirmations were false, in the Simple Believer's day, which is our own, the most dangerous and up-to-date attack comes from those who say that they are meaningless, that they assert nothing. And a great deal of public opinion has come round to the attackers' point of view.

So it is easy to understand why the Simple Believer was unhappy. What was he to do? He did not feel that he could go back to the simple assertions of his grandfather, which the scientists had overthrown; but yet he did not any longer see much substance in the consolations of the Sophisticated Believer. If he went back to the views of his grandfather, he would be saying what he believed to be false; but if he said what the Sophisticated Believer wanted him to say, he would be uttering words without meaning.

It was when the Simple Believer was in this dilemma that I first got to know him. I understood his predicament very well, for it was one I had been in myself, and to a great extent was in still. He came to me for philosophical advice; but I was at a loss to know what to say to him. Would it be best, perhaps, to seek out some simple, slick way of comforting him? The philosopher always has in his armoury plenty of snap refutations that will readily deceive the inexpert. He does not always like to use these devices; but in defending what you think really matters, all's fair. The trouble is that, even if I could outwit the Sophisticated Unbeliever by any logical trick, I should not think that I had thereby helped the Simple Believer much. It would be like proving that the evidence of fossils was no good; it might deceive the layman for a time, but sooner or later the truth would prevail. After all, the God the Simple Believer believed in was a God of Truth; and it would be odd to try to defend faith in him by spurious arguments.

Nevertheless, I did very much want to help the Simple Believer—I will call him from now on the Believer, for he is simple no longer. There seemed to me to be something about his faith that put me to shame—something whose loss would make the world a worse place. And in so far as I had a little

(though perhaps only a little) of this something myself, I
wanted to strengthen it rather than destroy it; and for this
purpose the Believer, for all his philosophical difficulties and
perplexities, was a great example and source of strength to
me. He might get into a muddle in his thought when
sophisticated people tied him into knots; but to know him was
to know that these knots somehow did not matter. Anyone
who knows any people of the type I am describing will know
what I mean.

So in the end I hit upon this method. Instead of trying to
teach the Believer what he ought to believe, I sought instead
to learn from him what he really did believe. This is a thing
that cannot be done entirely by kindness. It entails preventing
the victim getting away with any evasions and confusions; and
so sometimes I seemed to be trying to undermine his faith. I
kept on dinning into him the arguments of the Sophisticated
Unbeliever, and had sometimes even to appear a Sophisticated Unbeliever myself. But I felt that the brutality was worth
while; for what I was trying to do was no less than to find out
what it was about his faith that really made him different—
and believe me it did make him different—from other men. It
was this that I wanted to find out, and if possible imitate.

I soon came to the conclusion that what the Believer
believed in were not *assertions* in the narrow sense, as the term
was used by the Sophisticated Unbeliever. At least, though he
may have believed some assertions in this narrow sense, they
were not central to his faith. By this I mean that they could be
abandoned or modified without his losing that whose basis I
was seeking to discover. This much was shown by his
readiness to abandon these assertions when Unbelievers cast
serious doubt upon them in argument. Of course, in a sense,
what the Believer believed in were assertions. But I did not
want to perform the usual philosophical trick of saying 'It all
depends what you mean by an assertion.' This is often a useful
thing to say—but only as a prelude to taking each of the
things that might be meant in turn, and examining its
consequences. So to start with I saw no harm in accepting the
Sophisticated Unbeliever's criterion of what were and were
not assertions—the criterion was that if the utterance were to
express an assertion, there had to be something which, if it

occurred, would constitute a disproof of the assertion. But I did not want to admit that all meaningful utterances expressed assertions in this sense; for after all there are plenty of utterances which are quite meaningful and yet do not in this sense express assertions—for example, imperatives, questions, expressions of wishes, and so on. There are, moreover, beliefs which are not beliefs in the truth of assertions, in this narrow sense, and yet which are fundamental to our whole life in this world, and still more to our doing anything like science.

Let me explain this last point. Suppose we believed that everything that happens happens by pure chance, and that therefore the regularities that we have observed so far in the phenomena around us have all been quite fortuitous; that the world might start behaving tomorrow in a quite different manner, or in no consistent manner at all. Then it is obvious that we should not be able to make any scientific predictions about what was going to happen, and our science would become quite useless. It is only because we believe that there are some causal laws to be discovered that we think it worth while to set about discovering them. But what sort of belief is this? Is it a belief in the truth of an assertion, in the Sophisticated Unbeliever's sense? Let us apply the test to it (Flew 1950, *s.f.*). 'Just what would have to happen, not merely (morally and wrongly) to *tempt*, but also (logically and rightly) to *entitle*' the scientist to stop believing in or looking for causal laws? The answer to this seems to be, as in the case of the religious believer and his God, that nothing that could happen could have this effect.

Suppose that a scientist has a hypothesis which he is testing by experiment, and the experiment shows him that his hypothesis was false. He then, after trying the experiment again once or twice to make sure there has been no silly mistake, says 'My hypothesis was wrong; I must try a new one.' That is to say, he does not stop believing in, or looking for, regularities in the world which can be stated in the form of scientific 'laws'; he abandons this particular candidate for the status of a law, but only in order to look for another candidate. Thus, *whatever* happens, he still goes on looking for laws; nothing can make him abandon the search, for to abandon the search would be to stop being a scientist. He is just like the religious believer in this; in fact, we may say that the belief of the scientist is one kind of religious belief—a kind, moreover, which is not incompatible with what is called Christian belief, for it is part of it (see e.g. Hodgson 1969).

I want to emphasize this point, because it is the most important that I have to make. When the scientist refuses to give up his search for causal explanations of things, even when any number of proposed explanations fail, he is acting in an essentially religious manner. Therefore, for anyone who wants to know what religion is, this is one of the very best illustrations to take. When the scientist says 'There must be an explanation of this, although none of the explanations that we have thought of so far works', he is manifesting just that refusal to doubt which in religious contexts we call *faith*. And indeed it *is* faith; for the scientist does not *know* that there is an explanation. For all he knows there may be no explanation. Indeed, even when he thinks he has found the explanation, how does he know that it is an explanation? For what is and what is not an explanation of something is not a question that can be settled by any sort of proof or appeal to the facts. To say that something is an explanation of something else is to hold just the kind of belief that the Sophisticated Unbeliever said was not belief in the truth of an assertion.

So then, to be a scientist is to be a kind of believer. And the Sophisticated Believer was quite right—perhaps it was the only thing he was right about—when he said that religion did not contradict science. But this is not, as he thought, because religion and science are different kinds of thing; it is because, though different in many respects, in this one crucial respect they are the same kind of thing. And, as I said, scientific belief is not incompatible with Christian belief. It is rather a *part* of Christian belief. It is a part of Christian belief to believe in the possibility of explaining things by means of scientific laws.

But scientific belief is not the whole of Christian belief. There are whole fields of human conduct outside the laboratory where scientific belief does not give us the answers to the questions we are (or ought to be) asking. It does not give us these answers, not because it is wrong, but because it does not apply in those fields. I will mention only one of those fields, that of morality. We cannot decide by experimental methods or by observation what we ought to do. That I ought to do this or that is another of those beliefs which I have to accept or reject (for what I do depends on this decision) but which are excluded by the Sophisticated Unbeliever's test from the realm of assertions. It is only if he ignores such questions that the scientist is able to make do with so limited a faith.

II

It has been an extremely common move in these controversies to say that religious belief is a kind of moral belief or attitude. This is the suggestion which I am now going to explore. I shall not accept it as it stands; but I think that a great deal is to be learnt from it.

In order to avoid misunderstandings it is necessary to make it clear that I am not going myself to advance any thesis about the qualifications for being called a Christian. That is a terminological question which I am prepared to leave to others. I am going, rather, to explore a possible system of beliefs, which I think it reasonable to hold, and which I am myself inclined to hold. Whether these are to be called Christian or even religious beliefs is of less importance; for what serious students of this question ought to be troubled about is what they can believe, and not what they can call it. And whether the Christian imagery is an appropriate expression of such beliefs is a highly subjective matter which is to be settled by whoever has something to express and does or does not find the Christian language an adequate and fitting vehicle for what he is trying to say. I do not think that very many Christian church-goers would like to be held to the letter of all that they say in church; they go because there is enough that they can sincerely (though not always literally) say, and that cannot be said at all succinctly in any other way, to make it more appropriate for them to be inside than outside. If, when I have published my views, it still seems unscandalous for me to go on going to church, I shall do so.

The best-known recent statement of the proposal to reduce religion to morality is that of Professor Braithwaite, whose Eddington Lecture (1955) struck me, at the time I heard it delivered, as by far the best thing on this subject that I had ever heard or read; and I have since then seen no reason to revise this opinion. His sincerity, and his refusal to take refuge in the evasions and the obscurities that are the occupational disease of those who write in this field, compel admiration. It is therefore distressing that, since the lecture was published, it has received almost no support either from Christians or from non-Christians, and has come to be regarded as a rather ridiculous attempt to do what cannot be done. It may be that, if Braithwaite had wrapped up his views in the almost impenetrable darkness that is fashionable in this sort of writing, he would have got away with it. Perhaps he and not Tillich would have been the hero of Bishop John Robinson's book *Honest to God* (1967). For in many ways the views of Braithwaite and the bishop are highly congenial to one another. It is the same lumps of orthodoxy that stick in the throats of both of them: and the motives of both go back to the difficulties which I discussed earlier—in particular the difficulty of assigning to statements of religious belief a logical status which will leave them saying something that is, first of all, meaningful, and, secondly, not obviously false.

Braithwaite sums up his position as follows:

A man is not, I think, a professing Christian unless he both proposes to live according to Christian moral principles, and associates his intention with thinking of Christian stories; but he need not believe that the empirical propositions presented by the stories correspond to empirical fact. (1955: 246)

Thus, to adopt a slogan, religion could be described, on Braithwaite's view, as morals helped out by mythology. This crude description is, however, unfair to Braithwaite. For he includes under the summary term 'moral principles' a great deal which, I am sure, he would distinguish from them if he were expounding his view more fully. Perhaps the term 'way of life' would represent more fairly what he means; but even so we shall have ourselves to go into more detail before we can do justice to his position.

I think that the clearest way of doing this will be to take what we may call the minimum Braithwaitian position (corresponding to an over-narrow interpretation of the passage that I have just quoted) and to ask how Braithwaite might meet the objections to it that would be made by an old-fashioned Christian believer, whether simple or sophisticated. There is, however, one style of criticism to which I shall offer no reply, since an entirely devastating rebuttal of it has already been given by Mr J. C. Thornton (1966). This is the style of those who by a palpably circular argument assume that the traditional interpretation of Christian belief is the only admissible one, and then think that they have refuted Braithwaite by showing that he does not conform to it. Such a manœuvre will not strengthen the faith of anybody who is in serious doubt about the acceptability of the traditional interpretation.

Of the objections which I shall consider, I will start with the smaller ones. First, it may be objected that merely to have certain ideas about what our duties are, even if we then go on to act accordingly, is hardly to practise even the Christian virtue of charity—let alone faith and hope. Christian charity or love (*agapē*) is not, it may be said, a kind of behaviour, but a state or attitude of mind (loving my neighbour as myself). This Braithwaite can easily concede, and does concede:

The superiority of religious conviction over the mere adoption of a moral code . . . arises from a religious conviction changing what the religious man wants. It may be hard enough to love your enemy, but once you have succeeded in doing so it is easy to behave lovingly towards him. (1955: 243)

So evidently the *agapē* to which Braithwaite is referring is, unlike Kant's 'practical love' (1785: BA13 = 399; cf. 1797: A119 = 448), a state of mind or attitude, and not merely the obedience to a moral code.

Nor need he limit himself, as in his lecture he largely does, to the morality which consists in loving our neighbour as ourself. If he did, it might be objected that there is also the love of God to be considered (see pp. 62, 74). Before we can understand what could be meant, by one of Braithwaite's views, by 'loving God', we shall first have to explain in what sense, for Braithwaite, God can exist to be the object of love. Here I want only to point out that, even for a humanist, and *a fortiori* for a Braithwaitian Christian, there can be more to morality than the love of neighbours; there is the whole sector of morality to be considered which is concerned with moral ideals, and which may have nothing to do with our neighbours. Since I said a lot about this in *FR*, ch. 8, I will not repeat it here.

Nor need Braithwaite confine himself to morality in the narrow sense. It may be that not only our moral attitudes, but all our desires, aspirations, and ideals should be included in that total attitude to life which Braithwaite wants to call religious belief. To be a Christian, then, is not merely to acknowledge certain duties, nor even to aspire to certain virtues; it is also to have an entirely different idea of what is prudent or sensible. For if our desires become different, what is prudent—i.e. what is likely in the long run to conduce to the fulfilment of our desires—will radically change. Thus we are bidden not to take thought for what we shall put on, but to seek first the Kingdom of God.

There is no reason why Braithwaite should not incorporate these modifications into his theory. For what he is trying to do is to get the better of the Sophisticated Unbeliever, who said that statements of religious belief are not falsifiable, and therefore say nothing. Braithwaite's manœuvre consists in assimilating statements of religious belief to a class of utterances which can be unfalsifiable without lacking content. This class includes moral judgements, on Braithwaite's and my view of them; but it includes much else besides. The important thing for Braithwaite is, not to admit that religious statements are any kind of factual assertion. For if he admits that, it is open to the Sophisticated Unbeliever to place him in the dilemma we explored earlier: he has either to open his statements to factual refutation, in which case they get refuted; or else he has to acknowledge that in uttering them he is not really doing what, in a factual assertion, one is supposed to do.

It is time now to consider another objection which an old-fashioned Christian might make against Braithwaite's view. He might say 'Surely religious assertions *are* factual. For the Christian does not merely follow a way of life; he has the *hope* that this way of life is not vain or pointless. And this hope would be futile if the world were not ordered in a certain way.'

Here we get very close to one of the traditional moral arguments for the existence of God. The old-fashioned Christian would, indeed, surely put his objection in terms of the existence of God; he would say 'To be a Christian is not merely to be disposed to follow a way of life; it is to believe that God is there to *sustain* one in this way of life. Otherwise it would be pointless and stupid to follow, or try to follow, the way of life.'

What can Braithwaite make of this objection? I think that he can go a long way to meet it. To begin with, he might say that the Christian may, indeed, be committed to certain factual assertions about the world, but that these are all empirical ones, and so are not at the mercy of the Sophistic-ated Unbeliever. Suppose that the Christian has certain desires, aspirations, ideals, moral principles, etc. which, on this view, constitute his religion. And suppose that, as he must, he believes that it is not futile to act in pursuit of these aspirations etc. He need not believe that the aspirations are certain to be fulfilled, but only that there is a reasonable hope that they will be. Since the aspirations themselves are not very determinate—but sufficiently determinate to be meaningful—the empirical propositions to which he thus commits himself are not very determinate either. But they are far from being contentless. The easiest example to take is that of the effects of our actions on people. Do we not often hear it said that if only we behave towards people in a Christian way—if we have the faith and trust to do this—they will respond in ways that would surprise an unbeliever. This is often expressed in terms of the working of the Holy Spirit in men's hearts. Now, it may be that if I have certain Christian aspirations which cannot be realized without the co-operation of other people, the proposi-tion that it is not pointless to pursue these aspirations is one that can be called, in a sense, a factual one.

But we need not confine ourselves to the responses of other people. A Christian may believe that the inanimate world also is so ordered as not to make his endeavours pointless. Earlier I said that the attitude of the scientists was like this, and I said that this scientific attitude was a part, though only a part, of Christian belief. Now we are in a position to understand this better. Both the scientist and the religious believer can claim that among their beliefs are two classes of affirmations, both of which escape the Sophisticated Unbeliever's dilemma, but in different ways. The first, and philosophically less interesting, class is the one I have just mentioned. Both the scientist and the religious believer will find themselves making some assertions which, though they are assertions in the narrow sense, are sufficiently indeterminate to escape refutation by single or even by quite numerous counter-instances—they contain enough *ceteris paribus* clauses to look after the counter-instances, in all of which it will be claimed that other things were not, after all, equal. The scientist does not give up his claim to be able in principle to predict natural phenomena just because of the notorious failure of the Meteorological Office to predict the weather accurately. And the religious believer does not give up his belief that, on the whole, if you behave Christianly towards other people, they will respond accordingly, just because he has had one or two disappointments.

The more interesting class of beliefs consists in those which are not in assertions, in the Sophisticated Unbeliever's narrow sense, at all, though they may be in assertions in some less restricted sense. These are the beliefs I was referring to earlier. The scientist believes that there is scientific truth to be discovered in the form of natural laws to which the processes of the world conform. This belief is not itself testable in the ordinary way (though the hypotheses which the scientist frames as candidates for the status of natural laws are testable). If a scientist has thought up some hypothesis, and when he tries it out by experiment it turns out to be false, he gives up the particular hypothesis, but does not give up the belief that there are laws to be discovered. This belief, therefore, is not a belief in the truth of an assertion in the narrow sense. Yet in another sense the belief is surely factual; it is 'about the world'. If the scientist, after repeated failures, did lose faith, not merely in his own abilities as a researcher, but in the possibility of anybody ever discovering laws which governed a certain range of phenomena, we should say that his beliefs about the character of those phenomena had changed, and not merely that he had adopted a different way of life.

If this is true of the scientist's belief that his researches are not pointless, may it not also be true of the Christian moralist's belief that his morality is not pointless? The scientist does not know that even the most long-established hypothesis may not be refuted by new evidence tomorrow. All that has been written about the problem of induction has not altered the fact that belief in the future regularity of the universe is an act of faith; and yet we base all our actions on this faith. The faith might be represented as faith in a prescription: 'Don't give up hope'. But this would be misleading if we did not at the same time emphasize that the hope which the scientist is not to give up is a hope that he or some other scientist will find answers to questions which are not prescriptive but, in any ordinary sense of the word, factual.

Similarly the moralist has to have the faith, not that he has found, but at least that it is possible to find, moral 'policies' (as I am sure Braithwaite would call them) which are not pointless. It is not enough to be convinced that some kind of act is a duty. Without going now into the tangled and, I think, unnecessary controversy between the teleologists and the deontologists, I will merely record my conviction that what it is our duty to do must depend on what we should be doing if we initiated a certain train of events; and this depends on the consequences of alternative courses of action. But in this world consequences must always be to a large extent a matter of conjecture and of faith. We have to have faith and hope that our actions will turn out for the best; they are hostages to the world, and no practical morality could do without an ample faith that events will not frustrate its ends. It is extremely natural to express this faith in religious terms.

Here again we might be tempted to say that the faith is not factual but prescriptive. The prescription is, not to give up hope of finding a moral policy that is not futile. But here again we must reply that, though the faith is not faith in an assertion in the narrow sense, abandonment of it would entail a radical change in our view about what the world is like. We should not merely be ceasing to look for non-futile moral policies, but be doing so because we thought that the world was such that we would never find any.

When I speak of 'non-futile moral policies', I shall certainly be misunderstood unless I add an explanation. I am not talking about the presence or absence of rewards for virtue. Sometimes a 'moral argument' for God's existence is put in the following terms: there must be a sanction for morality; it must be shown that, in the end, the virtuous are rewarded and the wicked punished, or at least that for some other reason honesty is the best policy. That is not what I am talking about at all. I do as a matter of fact believe that, as the world is ordered, honesty is the best policy—in the sense that if one were asking how to form the character of a child (or of oneself), considering solely his own selfish interests, one would be wisest to seek to implant in him the traditional virtues. In the actual world, *pace* Plato (*Rep.* 359c), there are no reliable rings of Gyges (*MT* 194)—and that there are none might also count as part of our religion. But that is not what I am talking about. Although virtue is the surest recipe for happiness, occasions undoubtedly arise on which the path of virtue leads to great suffering. On these occasions the virtuous man will, like Hermeias in Aristotle's poem (1583^b8), accept the suffering as the price of virtue; just because his character has been formed in virtue, he will want the ends of morality to be achieved more than he wants to avoid the suffering. But even if this is what he above all wants—even if he totally disregards his own selfish interests—he still needs to have the kind of faith that I am speaking of. I am not advocating the view that the virtuous man will do the virtuous thing and disregard the consequences; for what is the virtuous thing depends in part on the consequences, if not for himself, for others. A man might stoically cultivate his own perfection by doing an act which he thought virtuous, even though it led to disaster for everybody; but I would not call virtuous a man who could deliberately do such a thing.

What I am saying is that, granted that the good man wishes above all to realize the ends of morality—moral ideals—he can hardly pursue this object unless he has faith in the possibility, as things are, of realizing them. That is why faith and hope are virtues as well as charity. And I must confess that faith in the divine providence has always seemed to me to be one of the central features of the Christian religion, and one to which it is possible to cling even when much else is in doubt. This faith that all shall be well is matched by a feeling of thankfulness that all is well.

So, then, I want to say that religion cannot be reduced to morality even in an extended sense, unless we include also the faith in something that saves moral endeavour from futility. But it is obvious that in saying this I shall not have done very much to appease our old-fashioned Christian objector. It is, indeed, evident that for a long time he has been wanting to say that I have left out God from my account (or rather from my tentative expansion of Braithwaite's account) of religion. However, this objection cannot be made clear until we have discovered what it would be to bring God in. I think that matters may become clearer if we discuss something which I certainly have left out, and that is what is called 'the supernatural'. Recently the idea has been put forward more than once that religion can do without the supernatural; and so in leaving it out I do not feel so isolated as in some other things that I have said. But first we must ask what the supernatural is.

One absolutely crucial distinction that needs making here is between two different senses of 'supernatural'. I shall use, to stand for these two senses, the words 'contranatural' and 'transcendental'. An event may be said to be *contranatural* if it is contrary to the ordinary natural laws. Miracles, for example, are, on the usual interpretation, contranatural. It has been said, of course, that if a miracle were established to have happened, then we should revise our ideas about the natural law in question, and so there would be no breach of natural law. But there is an understandable sense in which a miracle is contrary to natural law—i.e. to those natural laws in which, after much experiment and observation of phenomena, we have considerable confidence.

It is a distinguishing feature of the contranatural that propositions stating that a contranatural event has occurred are perfectly meaningful empirical propositions. The controversy is about their truth, not about their significance. Thus it is an empirical proposition that the sun stood still for Joshua; what we quarrel about is whether it actually did stand still, or whether the story in the Bible is the result of credulity.

The *transcendental* is quite different. Let us suppose that someone alleges that there is a god in the fire who makes it burn; it would not burn without him, it is said, and to get him to make it burn you have to perform the right ritual, lay the sticks correctly, not put too much big stuff on top, etc. My wife can always perform this ritual correctly, and I cannot; my fires always go out. But, it may be asked, what is the difference between the statement that there is a god who, if we perform the right ritual, makes the fire burn, and the statement that the fire will burn if we do the specified series of operations? I call this fire-god 'transcendental' because his existence or non-existence makes no difference to observable phenomena. He is, as Wittgenstein might have said, idling—doing no work.

The Sophisticated Unbeliever's main point could be put in terms of these two words. What the Simple Believer had been doing was that, when he came to think that his contranatural beliefs were false, he substituted for them beliefs in transcendental entities and events, with the results that we saw. I do not believe myself that religion can last much longer, among educated people, unless it rejects both the contranatural and the transcendental. This is going to be very repugnant to old-fashioned believers; but I think that it is inescapable.

It is escapable, indeed, by the uneducated—and I must explain what I mean by that. I am going to call that kind of religion which relies on the supernatural, in either of its senses, *superstition*. If anybody does not like the implications of this word, or thinks it offensive, he need not disturb himself, because I shall not use these implications in my argument. Now, there are three things, I want to say, which cannot, all three, coexist in the present state of knowledge. They are superstition, science, and philosophy. By 'science', I mean not merely the practice of science, but the acceptance of its results by non-scientists. By 'philosophy', I mean the ability to reason logically about these and other subjects with enough familiarity with the verbal traps that lie in one's path not to fall into them—the ability, that is to say, to see the issues clearly and not to be deceived by sophistries, whether intentional or inadvertent.

Now, there is no difficulty in science co-existing with superstition. There are many scientists who achieve it. All that is necessary is to be philosophically naïve; it will then be possible to construct systems of belief which are essentially superstitious, but not to notice that they involve elements which are either contranatural, and therefore incompatible with scientific beliefs, or transcendental, and therefore idle. It is likewise not difficult to be a superstitious philosopher, if one is not concerned about science. If one is willing boldly to deny facts which nearly all scientists would accept, one can easily suppose, for example, that the nether regions are just as Dante describes them, and one's system of the world need not fall into any *logical* errors. But when we try to put together all these three things, science, philosophy, and superstition, one of them is bound to succumb. That is what I meant when I said that an educated man has to abandon superstition, i.e. the belief in the supernatural. It is wrong of me, I know, to say all this without arguing for it; but this ground has been gone over so often by abler expositors than I am (Mackie 1982, for example), that I do not feel like entering upon it now, even if there were time. If any Christians do not, when they have understood the issues clearly, feel the overwhelming force of these arguments, I envy them, but address myself rather to those who do feel their force, and to whom, therefore, I may be able to say something helpful.

The problem for me, therefore, as apparently for some more august people, is, Can religion do without the supernatural? In facing this question we ought not to be put off by a move which is often made. It is sometimes said that, if we banish the supernatural from religion, we leave no difference between Christianity and humanism. This notion that Christianity has got to be *different* is a very difficult one to overcome. But, I ask, suppose that someone produced an interpretation of Christianity that could be accepted by the best humanists; would this necessarily be a bad thing? We have, at present, in our civilization, a very absurd state of affairs. I constantly meet people who evidently share my outlook on life quite as much as my fellow Christians do, and who yet call themselves humanists. It is a source of scandal to me that I am supposed to have to make myself different from these people, some of whom I very much admire. Of course there are differences between us; but so there are between me and a great many

Christians. And it is no use saying that the reason why I can say this about the humanists is that I am not a very solid Christian; I am quite sure that the same could be said by a great many extremely solid Christians. Anyone who thinks that he is a solid Christian can verify this for himself. So I should not be at all sorry if it could be shown that there is a type of Christianity which is compatible with humanism. I know I said earlier that the Believer's faith made him different from other men. But the point is, Was it faith in the supernatural that made him different, or was it a faith that could be had by somebody who did not believe in the supernatural? That really is the crux of our whole problem.

We must, however, face the fact that in abandoning the supernatural we shall have to abandon some things which have been thought to be very central to traditional Christianity. This is, of course, why left-wing theologians, when they get on to these topics, are apt to become impenetrably obscure.

> So well-bred spaniels civilly delight
> In mumbling of the game they dare not bite
>
> (Pope 1734)

I will take two of these topics which I think are among the most difficult, namely prayer and the after-life. The problem of prayer arises mainly from the rejection of the transcendental; that of the after-life from the rejection of the contra-natural. But, as we shall see, there is an overlap. In thinking about prayer, it will be as well to have particular examples in mind. In preparing this lecture, I had especially two. The first is from Arthur Bryant's *The Turn of the Tide* (1957: 266). This book is a history of the Second World War based on Lord Alanbrooke's diaries and recollections. Lord Alanbrooke is writing, in retrospect, about the day in November 1941 when Churchill asked him to become Chief of the Imperial General Staff.

I am not [he says] an exceptionally religious person, but I am not ashamed to confess that as soon as he was out of the room my first impulse was to kneel down and pray to God for guidance and support in the task I had undertaken. As I look back at the years that followed I can now see clearly how well this prayer was answered.

The second example is more extended; in a book called *Fire in Coventry* (1964), Canon (now Bishop) Stephen Verney describes the prayers of clergy and people in the diocese of Coventry in preparation for the consecration of the cathedral, and the remarkable way in which these were answered. He is convinced that something powerful, which he calls the Holy Spirit, took hold of the diocese and that observable effects happened which would not have happened unless there had been prayer and it had been answered. Both these books are well worth reading by anybody who wishes to study this question. Another is *Miracle on the River Kwai* (1963), by Ernest Gordon.

When a prayer is answered, what to the naked eye happens is this. A person conceives of or imagines a being more powerful than himself, to whom he makes certain requests, or whose guidance he simply awaits. Afterwards, certain ideas for action come into his head, and certain external events take place which are conducive to the success of the actions, and which are interpreted as the answer to the prayer. We have to ask what part the transcendental has to play in this. My answer would be, None at all. For what is the difference between there being a transcendental God who listens to the prayer and directs events accordingly, and it just being the case that the events take place? Braithwaite would no doubt speak of what the person praying imagines or conceives as a 'story', and would say that it makes no difference to his being a Christian or not whether it is thought of as a true story or a myth. But this really misses the point. The point is that, where the transcendental is concerned, there is no difference between a true story and a myth; it is therefore wrong to speak of the person who prays having an *illusion* that there is somebody that he is praying to. If prayer is important in religion—and I am convinced that it is—it cannot be that its importance rests upon the existence of a transcendental being whose existence could not, in principle, make itself felt in the world as we see it.

Since Bishop Verney's book is called *Fire in Coventry*, may I recur to what I said earlier about fire. I said that, in making an ordinary fire, we might think of what we did as a ritual to propitiate a fire-god who then, if propitiated, caused the fire to burn; but that there is really no empirical difference between this story and the chemist's account of the matter, namely that if certain prior conditions are carefully created, a certain chemical reaction will take place. The transcendental 'god' is really idling. And I venture to suggest that the same is true of the larger-scale spiritual conflagration which took place, according to Bishop Verney, in Coventry, and that this does not in the least diminish its importance for good or its significance for religion. Surely we do not want to relegate God to a position of logically guaranteed ineffectiveness.

The question of the after-life is an even more difficult one. I was struck, in reading *The Turn of the Tide*, by the fact that Lord Alanbrooke (in spite of his protestations, a devout man, who was often in situations of extreme danger), says almost nothing about the after-life. Nor, in my conversations with most clergymen, have I been able to obtain from them any clear idea of what they believe on this question. My impression is that belief in the after-life does not now have the importance for Christians that it once had—perhaps because they have become convinced by scientists and philosophers that it is not very plausible to believe in personal survival in a literal sense. I am not myself a follower of those philosophers who allege that no sense can be given to the statement that we shall survive the death (the literal death) of our bodies. I believe that this statement is meaningful, but unbelievable. This is so, whether what we are required to believe is that the soul can exist without any body, or (more orthodoxly) that the body will rise again at the last day, and that we shall then again have experiences, including memories of what passed before our deaths. I think that symbolic significance can be given to either of these doctrines, on the lines advocated by sophisticated believers. But I think it would be better if this stumbling block in the way of belief were removed by some entirely plain speaking on the part of Christians, making clear what is the substance which this shadow veils.

If that necessitated a revision or reinterpretation of the Creeds, this should be accepted. The Creeds are not scriptural, and were written a very long time ago in the light of philosophical and cosmological ideas which nobody would now accept. Even if they were scriptural, this would not be so important; for in the same way as we are not bound to believe, just because St Paul says that the seed has to die in the earth before the corn can come up (1 Cor. 15), that this is in fact what happens, so we are not bound to believe, just because Jesus spoke in terms of theological and philosophical ideas and terminology different from any to which we can attach truth or significance, that this is the way in which the Christian religion has now to be expressed. A lot has changed about the Christian religion in the course of the centuries; and, just as change in other matters is now faster than it has ever been, we must expect religion to change faster too. Either that, or it will cease to be practised altogether; but I am confident that Christians will prove at least as adaptable in the future as they have been in the past.

Since I know that the orthodox, who are still numerous, will disagree with nearly everything that I have said in this paper, I must end with a warning. Changes in the intellectual climate can be divided into two classes. First, there are the quick and superficial ones—fashions in thinking. The ebb and flow of these fashions signifies nothing for the future. We have religious revivals; Oxford Movements; Moral Rearmaments; and so on. And on the other side we have equally transitory humanist movements. This has been going on at least since the sixteenth century; and very similar things happened in ancient times before the rise of Christianity. There are those who fix their eyes on these relatively superficial movements, and, because they ebb and flow, think that underneath nothing has changed.

But there is a second kind of intellectual movement, which goes on all the time, and mostly in the same direction. It is a function of the increasing education (or should we say 'sophistication'?) of the bulk of mankind, and of our increasing knowledge of, and control over, nature. Though the movement goes on almost continuously, there are certain steps or stages in it which can be marked. And at certain times it does move faster than at others. Those who have the required intellectual penetration ought to discern the signs of the times, and be guided by them. At the present time, we can see clearly that the movement is accelerating—just because education has fairly suddenly become more widespread. And we can see also that a clearly marked stage in the process has been reached.

Let me now try to explain these rather prophetic remarks. At most times in past history the orthodox have been able to rely on a vast reservoir of uneducated people. Whatever the ebb and flow of intellectual fashions among the sophisticated, they have been only on the surface, because, even where there is an educated class, its little enlightenments can never compete on equal terms with the superstitions of the masses. But when people start to be educated—or even half-educated —in really large numbers, a quite different stage is reached; and that is where we have got to now.

Another very important factor in our present situation is a new attitude to morality. Ever since Kant (indeed, ever since Hume, and perhaps ever since Protagoras) it has been *possible* for people to insist on the autonomy of morals—its independence of human or divine authority. Indeed, it has been *necessary*, if they were to think morally, in the sense in which that word is now generally understood. However, few people up to the present time have entirely cut themselves free from the kind of pre-moral, heteronomous thinking which previously sufficed. But now their numbers are increasing dramatically. One is seeing a symptom of this every time one finds a teenager asking 'But why *should* I behave in the way you—or anybody else—calls morally right?'

This situation would be extremely dangerous, were it not that the remedy has arisen at the same time. This too we owe to Kant. To replace the more or less socially effective, though basically irrational, disciplines of heteronomy, we now have available a way of moral thinking which can do the same job within an autonomous, rational framework of thought. This means that the God of the orthodox, who was never competent to provide us with the basis of our morality, can now be seen to be unnecessary for this purpose. And the realization of this fact by an increasing number of people can only present the gravest threat to the orthodox position. I was therefore not surprised to see Professor Flew (1964) hailing my book *Freedom and Reason* (which is in spirit Kantian) as a step on the road to a viable humanist morality. That would make it a nail in the coffin of much orthodox Christianity.

Once people realize that they can have a rational morality without the orthodox God, and cannot have one with him, one of his chief props (indeed, perhaps, his only surviving prop with any strength) will have disappeared. And it is this situation for which Christians ought to be preparing. I will now discuss various strategies which they might adopt.

The first is to ignore what educated people are saying, and concentrate on ministering to the wholly uneducated, to whom the old stories can still seem true. In some parts of the world it is possible to do even better, and actually prevent the spread of education, or confine its content to topics thought to be harmless. But the result of such a strategy would be to make the Church into the Church of that diminishing minority of mankind which education had not reached.

The second possible strategy (which is not incompatible with the first) is to fight, at the intellectual level, what is bound to be nevertheless a losing battle. I think that it is as impossible that a fully educated population should believe in the God of the orthodox as it is that the present-day population of England, or New England, should believe in witchcraft. Still, at this high intellectual level there is scope for unlimited spoiling manœuvres. For to be clear about these matters is exceedingly difficult; whereas anybody whose intentions are mainly polemical has an easy task. These discussions have reached a degree of subtlety which is beyond the attainment of most people; therefore, when a new argument is produced—or often an old and discarded one revived in a form that is more intricate and whose invalidity is therefore harder to detect—the only possible courses are either to ignore it (and this can be dangerous) or else to spend a great deal of time taking it to pieces. Those who are trying to make things clearer are thus at the mercy of those who are not; either they leave themselves defenceless, or they abandon hope of advancing the subject and devote themselves to polemics. This, I think, is one of the reasons why the philosophy of religion has in recent times attracted relatively few first-rate philosophers.

However, I do not think that these intellectual delaying actions are going to do the orthodox much good in the long run, because I believe that *magna est veritas, et*—in the long run—*praevalebit*. Therefore I think that Christians—and by this I mean not just the orthodox but all those who are ready to profess and call themselves Christians—are bound to consider what they should do in the situation, which must come in the end, in which the orthodox have plainly lost the intellectual battle. But I am inclined to think that the question of what they are to do turns into one which has more terminology than substance about it. What it comes down to is really this: if the position for which I have been arguing is acceptable, are we to *call* it a Christian or a humanist position? Now this, as I said earlier, is a less important question than whether it *is* acceptable; but nevertheless, since I am sure that a great deal of breath is going to be spent in the next few decades on this terminological question, it is worth giving a little attention to it.

While orthodoxy held the field among those who call themselves Christians, there seemed to be no two ways about it. The position which I have been defending could be said to be obviously a humanist one, and incompatible with Christianity. But I wonder whether this is still the case. We must reflect that there was a time when it was thought—and that there are people who still think—that you cannot be a Christian (at least not a non-heretical one) unless you believe in transubstantiation, or in the Immaculate Conception, or in the Genesis story of the Creation, taken literally. We have to allow that ideas about what is requisite for being said to be a Christian can change, and may change radically and, in the present circumstances, rapidly.

Therefore I would say that at present, though it is certainly possible for a person who holds views like mine to be called a humanist, it is not necessary. And perhaps it might be misleading. For 'humanist' is an even vaguer term than 'Christian' (it often means 'non-Christian, non-Muslim, non-Jew, non-Hindu, etc.', and has no positive content of its own); and on the other hand it is sometimes used to describe positions from which I should strongly dissent (for example, the view that humanity is the only proper object of worship). My differences from even orthodox Christianity are, however, less important than they might seem. For, first of all, I agree on all prescriptive matters—that is to say, on everything that concerns what we should do, whether it is morals or prudence or science or whatever it is—I agree with Christians, or at any rate with a highly representative group of them, about everything that could determine our conduct.

Secondly, I agree with Christians, or at any rate with a fairly typical group of them, about all ordinary empirical matters of fact. In a sense, for example, I expect prayers to be answered—in the rather weak sense, that is to say, in which most Christians expect them to be answered, which is compatible with them not being answered in the way that we were thinking of when we prayed. And I do believe in divine providence (that, incidentally, is the main reason why I have such a firm conviction that the truth will prevail in philosophy, despite all the manœuvres that are available to falsehood). I believe, that is to say, that matters are so ordered in the world that there is a point in trying to live by the precepts to which Christians subscribe.

My differences with those who can perhaps still be called typical Christians concern, of course, the supernatural. And I am obviously not alone in this; for it is becoming quite fashionable among Christians to reject the supernatural. The supernatural, as I said, is divided into the contranatural and the transcendental. As regards the transcendental, I cannot believe that the differences between those who accept it and those who reject it have the slightest substance. For really they are both believing the same thing, but saying it in different words—even if the words are different, which they are not always. I have, I hope, argued convincingly that the transcendent God is bound always to be an idle element in our religious life. His existence or non-existence cannot possibly make any difference, either to what we ought to do, or to what is going to be the case. His transcendence logically rules this out.

On the other hand, the differences between those who accept and those who reject the contranatural are of substance. But I think that it is legitimate to ask Christians who say that they differ from me about this to cross their hearts and declare whether they themselves really do believe in the contranatural (when it has been freed from transcendentalist 'interpretation'). I am certain that a great many Christians— Modern Churchmen, for example—do not; and I am convinced that still more would not, if they had become

sufficiently clear about the distinction between the contranatural and the transcendental, and were therefore more
aware of what is happening when we say 'You are not bound
to take this doctrine literally.' They are able to cling to the
contranatural only because, when the belief seems to be
threatened, they at once take refuge in the transcendental,
without realizing that they have entirely altered, and indeed
trivialized, their position. The danger once past, they emerge
from their hiding places and think that they can go on as
before believing in the contranatural. But these manœuvres
cannot long survive the serious study of philosophy.

I conclude, therefore, that not very much separates me even
from what would now be called typical educated Christians;
and I think that in a fairly short time my views will not seem
so unusual as perhaps they do now. Not that *my* views are
important; I have only spent so long discussing them because
I am convinced that the dilemma in which I now find myself is
one which, in the near future, very large numbers of
thoughtful Christians are going to have to face. The dilemma
is really this. If we call ourselves Christians, we run the risk of
being thought dishonest, because to call oneself a Christian is,
at present, to create in the minds of many people the
impression that one believes in the supernatural. But perhaps
since *Honest to God* this danger has become more remote. On
the other hand, if we call ourselves humanists, we run, I am
convinced, much greater risks. For we shall be thought to be
abandoning, possibly the prescriptive principles which I said
were essential to Christianity, and most certainly the other
beliefs which I said were also part of it—beliefs in the
ordering of the world so as to give morality a point. I think
that there is still some danger that if one says that one is a
humanist, one will be thought to be embracing, if not some
kind of moral nihilism, at any rate a morality without visible
means of support. And this I do not want to do.

How this dilemma will work itself out is a matter for
uncertain speculation. It may be that the orthodox will
succeed in capturing for good and all the name 'Christian'.
This may not make very much difference to what anybody
actually believes; for, as I said, the dispute that I am now
discussing is a terminological one. But it will have the result

that the name 'Christian' is reserved for a diminishing body of people, composed in varying proportions of the ingenuous and the disingenuous. Then most of us will be (suitably qualified) humanists, and we shall reserve the names 'religion' and 'Christianity' for positions that we have left behind, in much the same way as we now reserve the name 'superstition'.

I cannot believe that this is the best outcome. What I should like to see happen, and what I think shows some signs of happening, is that the name 'Christian' is extended to cover positions like that which I have been defending; and that people who think as I do, or in more or less similar ways, will still think—as is indeed the case—that they have enough in common with typical Christians to make it less misleading to call them Christians than to call them anything else.

It has been maliciously said of Professor Braithwaite that he may have given a true account of the faith of King's College Cambridge Senior Combination Room, but not of that of the saints and martyrs. But it needs to be asked (given that we obviously do not believe, and do not, in order to be called Christians, have to believe, everything that was believed by every saint and martyr) what it was in their beliefs that made them into saints and into martyrs, and whether mankind in the future can be got to go on believing this. I should regard the opinions of any fellow of King's who was prepared to call himself a Christian as of great relevance in answering both these questions.

Braithwaite once came to talk to a college society in Oxford, and told us the story of his religious life, and how he came to be baptized, and about his religious beliefs. At the end of the meeting, he bravely asked if he might take a vote on the question whether he was a Christian or not. Unfortunately I cannot remember the exact figures; they were distributed fairly evenly between 'Yes', 'No', and 'Don't know'. But what was more significant was this. I had a strong impression (which could not have been made any more than an impression without lengthy and possibly embarrassing researches) that, on the whole, the people who said he was a Christian were the Christians, and the people who said he was not were the non-Christians. The reason is obvious. If one is a Christian, and is trying to hang on to one's Christianity, one does not want to set up for oneself unnecessary hurdles; therefore it is in one's interest to admit that a man of Braithwaite's left-wing views is, after all, a Christian. These people, I am sure, showed a very sound feeling for what is essential to Christianity and what is not, and were not merely displaying Christian charity.

The non-Christians, on the other hand, were in the opposite position. What they were trying to do was to justify their rejection of Christianity; and therefore it suited their book to make it difficult to be a Christian, in order that, in arguments with Christians, they could saddle the Christians with as absurd views as possible. Therefore it was in their interest to insist that Braithwaite was not a Christian; for, if he *was* a Christian, a lot of very promising arguments against Christianity go by the board. I hope that by telling this story I have succeeded in my object of showing how trivial, really, is the terminological question, once the matter behind it is made clear. The important thing is what one believes, and not what one calls it.

Appendix: Theology and Falsification

I wish to make it clear that I shall not try to defend Christianity in particular, but religion in general—not because I do not believe in Christianity, but because one cannot understand what Christianity is until one has understood what religion is.

I must begin by confessing that, on the ground marked out by Flew (1950, see pp. 38 below and 8 above), he seems to me to be completely victorious. I therefore shift my ground by relating another parable. A certain lunatic is convinced that all dons want to murder him. His friends introduce him to all the mildest and most respectable dons that they can find, and after each of them has retired, they say 'You see, he doesn't really want to murder you; he spoke to you in a most cordial manner; surely you are convinced now?' But the lunatic replies 'Yes, but that was only his diabolical cunning; he's really plotting against me the whole time, like the rest of them; I know it I tell you.' However many kindly dons are produced, the reaction is still the same.

We say that such a person is deluded. But what is he deluded about? About the truth or falsity of an assertion? Let us apply Flew's test to him. There is no behaviour of dons that can be enacted which he will accept as counting against his theory; and therefore his theory, on this test, asserts nothing. But it does not follow that there is no difference between what he thinks about dons and what most of us think about them—otherwise we should not call him a lunatic and ourselves sane, and dons would have no reason to feel uneasy about his presence in Oxford.

Let us call that in which we differ from this lunatic our respective *bliks*. He has an insane *blik* about dons; we have a sane one. It is important to realize that we have a sane one, not no *blik* at all; for there must be two sides to any argument—if he has a wrong *blik*, then those who are right about dons must have a right one. Flew has shown that a *blik* does not consist in an assertion or system of them; but nevertheless it is very important to have the right *blik*.

Let us try to imagine what it would be like to have different *bliks* about other things than dons. When I am driving my car, it sometimes occurs to me to wonder whether my movements of the steering-wheel will always continue to be followed by corresponding alterations in the direction of the car. I have never had a steering failure, though I have had skids, which must be similar. Moreover, I know enough about how the steering of my car is made to know the sort of thing that would have to go wrong for the steering to fail—steel joints would have to part, or steel rods break, or something—but how do I know that this won't happen? The truth is, I don't know; I just have a *blik* about steel and its properties, so that normally I trust the steering of my car; but I find it not at all difficult to imagine what it would be like to lose this *blik* and acquire the opposite one. People would say I was silly about steel; but there would be no mistaking the reality of the difference between our respective *bliks*—for example, I should never go in a motor car. Yet I should hesitate to say that the difference between us was the difference between contradictory assertions. No amount of safe arrivals or bench-tests will remove my *blik* and restore the normal one; for my *blik* is compatible with any finite number of such tests.

It was Hume who taught us that our whole commerce with the world depends upon our *blik* about the world; and that differences between *bliks* about the world cannot be settled by observation of what happens in the world. That was why, having performed the interesting experiment of doubting the ordinary man's *blik* about the world, and showing that no proof could be given to make us adopt one *blik* rather than another, he turned to backgammon to take his mind off the problem (1739: I. iv. 7). It seems, indeed, to be impossible even to formulate as an assertion the normal *blik* about the world which makes me put my confidence in the future reliability of steel joints, in the continued ability of the road to support my car, and not gape beneath it revealing nothing below; in the general non-homicidal tendencies of dons; in my own continued well-being (in some sense of that word that I may not now fully understand) if I continue to do what is right according to my lights; in the general likelihood of people like Hitler coming to a bad end. But perhaps a formulation less inadequate than most is to be found in Psalm 75: 'The earth is weak and all the inhabiters thereof: I bear up the pillars of it.'

The mistake of the position which Flew selects for attack is to regard this kind of talk as some sort of *explanation*, as scientists are accustomed to use the word. As such, it would obviously be ludicrous. We no longer believe in God as an Atlas—*nous n'avons pas besoin de cette hypothèse.* But it is nevertheless true to say that, as Hume saw, without a *blik* there can be no explanation; for it is by our *bliks* that we decide what is and what is not an explanation. Suppose we believed that everything that happened, happened by pure chance. This would not of course be an assertion; for it is compatible with anything happening or not happening, and so, incidentally, is its contradictory. But if we had this belief, we should not be able to explain or predict or plan anything. Thus, although we should not be *asserting* anything different from those of a more normal belief, there would be a great difference between us; and this is the sort of difference that there is between those who really believe in God and those who really disbelieve in him.

The word 'really' is important, and may excite suspicion. I put it in because, when people have had a good Christian upbringing, as have most of those who now profess not to believe in any sort of religion, it is very hard to discover what they really believe. The reason why they find it so easy to think that they are not religious is that they have never got into the frame of mind of one who suffers from the doubts to which religion is the answer. Not for them the terrors of the primitive jungle. Having abandoned some of the more picturesque fringes of religion, they think that they have abandoned the whole thing—whereas in fact they still have got, and could not live without, a religion of a comfortably substantial, albeit highly sophisticated, kind, which differs from that of many 'religious people' in little more than this, that 'religious people' like to sing psalms about theirs—a very natural and proper thing to do. But nevertheless there may be a big difference lying behind: the difference between two people who, though side by side, are walking in different directions. I do not know in what direction Flew is walking; perhaps he does not know either. But we have had some examples recently of various ways in which one can walk away from Christianity, and there are any number of possibilities. After all, man has not changed biologically since primitive times; it is his religion that has changed, and it can easily change again. And if you do not think that such changes make a difference, get acquainted with some Sikhs and some Mussalmans of the same Punjabi stock; you will find them quite different sorts of people.

There is an important difference between Flew's parable and my own which we have not yet noticed. The explorers do not mind about their garden; they discuss it with interest, but not with concern. But my lunatic, poor fellow, minds about dons; and I mind about the steering of my car; it often has people in it that I care for. It is because I mind very much about what goes on in the garden in which I find myself that I am unable to share the explorers' detachment.

2

Religion and Morals

The recent history of moral philosophy has been the history of the impact upon it of that philosophical movement which is usually referred to loosely as Logical Empiricism or Logical Positivism. From the point of view of moral philosophy the most challenging thing the Logical Empiricists did was this: they directed their attention to a certain type of language, namely to those sentences which express 'scientific propositions' and other statements of fact, in the narrow sense; and they examined the conditions under which we are prepared to allow that such sentences are meaningful. They claimed that the criterion which we employ is this: to know the meaning of such a sentence is to know what would have to be the case for the statement which it expresses to be called true, or false. There are various ways of formulating this criterion; but I will not here discuss their relative merits, nor whether the criterion *can* be formulated in a satisfactory way. It is enough to say that this criterion, when it was first propounded, aroused much enthusiasm among empiricist philosophers. For here, they thought, was a way of eliminating from the pages of philosophy, once for all, those sentences (of which there are, it must be confessed, too many) that do not carry any weight of meaning. Philosophical books, it was said, are full of statements or so-called statements to which, when we examine them in the light of this criterion, we cannot assign any significance at all; we cannot think what would have to be the case for us to call them true, or false. Such books the empiricists, following Hume's prescription (1748, sect. 12, pt. 3), were prepared to commit to the flames as containing nothing but sophistry and illusion.

The result of following this prescription was to sweep

From *Faith and Logic*, ed. B. G. Mitchell (Allen & Unwin, 1958).

language too clean. At the time, the impact on both moral philosophy and the philosophy of religion was startling; for by this criterion it was thought that both moral statements and statements of religious belief could be shown to be only 'pseudo-propositions' and the sentences expressing them 'literally senseless'. But it later appeared that all that had been done was to isolate *one* kind of use we make of language, and to give a criterion of meaningfulness for statements made in this field. If we confine ourselves to what are ordinarily called statements of empirical fact, the criterion is enormously useful. Indeed, it might be said that the criterion provides us with a way of ascertaining, not whether what somebody says has meaning *of any sort*, but at least whether it has empirical meaning. For to call a statement an empirical one is perhaps to include it in the class of those statements of which we can say or show what would have to be the case in our own experience or somebody else's for us to call them true, or false. What we have here, then, is not really a criterion of meaningfulness (a way of separating wheat from chaff) but a criterion of empiricality (a way, as we might say, of separating wheat from oats, or barley, or rice). Or, to use St Paul's metaphor, our language

is not one member, but many. If the foot shall say, Because I am not the hand, I am not of the body; is it therefore not of the body? And if the ear shall say, Because I am not the eye, I am not of the body; is it therefore not of the body? If the whole body were an eye, where were the hearing? If the whole were hearing, where were the smelling? But now God hath set the members every one of them in the body, as it hath pleased him. And if they were all one member, where were the body? But now they are many members, yet but one body. (1 Cor. 12: 14)

Anatomy and its related disciplines (physiology, pathology, etc.) are the study of the several parts of the body to see what they are like, how related to one another, what the function of each is, and how it can go wrong. The more these sciences have progressed, the less inclined people have become to despise or depreciate parts of the body whose use they do not yet know. It has often been discovered that some insignificant-looking piece of the body, to which nobody had paid any attention, is in fact so important that we could not live without it—that some small organ, which seemed to be only a part of a larger one, has in fact its own peculiar function, without which the whole body would perish.

Logic, as it is being studied in many of the most important philosophical schools at the present time, is the anatomy of language. Since among the functions of language are thought and communication, the physiology of language, which goes along with its anatomy, is the study of the different ways in which we think and the different sorts of things that we communicate to each other. The most important result of the challenge made by the Logical Empiricists has been to stimulate an intensive study of these various uses of language. We have been forced to recognize that there is a very large number of different things that we do with words, and that they all have a vital part to play in our thought and discourse. The logician who thinks that he can confine his attention to one of them and ignore the rest is not doing the whole of his job.

About some kinds of words quite a lot has been discovered; this applies, I think, to various kinds of words used in scientific discourse, and also to moral words. How much has been discovered about any kind of discourse has depended first of all on the amount of time and interest philosophers have given to it; but more on the relative complexity and difficulty of the kind of discourse in question. Religious discourse has come off badly on both these counts. For in the first place few philosophers nowadays are interested enough in religious questions to make them their main study; not many are even sufficiently conversant with the use of religious language to succeed in such an enquiry. And secondly, religious language is, as I hope to make clear, a very difficult subject; there are a great many different kinds of things that we say which are all part of religious language; and some of these things can be said or listened to with comprehension only by people whose experience of the religious life has gone much further than that of most of us modern philosophers. But, on the other hand, many of the logical problems raised are not such as can be dealt with by logical amateurs. For this reason some who know very well how to use religious language have not been able to give a very convincing *account* of its use, just as some gardeners can grow very good vegetables without being able to tell us clearly or even correctly how they do it.

The present essay is intended only as a first attempt to explore part of this field. I wish first of all to draw attention to some points of similarity between moral language and some sorts of religious language. At the very least it will, I hope, be agreed that all or nearly all religions have what may be called a moral aspect. By this I mean not merely that the adherents of a particular religion have in fact usually adhered to a particular set of moral principles, but that the moral principles are linked in some intimate way with the religious belief. Thus we find religious teachers, as part of their religious teaching, uttering moral precepts. The most tangible way (if I may so put it) of distinguishing between different religions is to see how their adherents behave. What was it that happened to St Paul when he stopped being an ordinary Jew and became a Christian? There may be a more recondite answer to this question; but at any rate there is this obvious answer, that he stopped doing one sort of thing (persecuting Christians) and started doing another (converting new Christians). Thus one obvious thing that happened to him was that his ideas about what he ought to do (his principles of action, or, in a wide sense, his moral principles) changed radically. And this is also true of lesser converts. Part of what it means to stop being a drunkard or a cannibal and become, say, a Methodist, is that one stops thinking it right to consume gin or human flesh. That religion is very intimately linked with morals, so that one cannot be said to adhere to or accept a religion unless one accepts and at least tries to act on its moral precepts, is implied by St James:

If any man thinketh himself to be religious, while he bridleth not his tongue but deceiveth his heart, this man's religion is vain. Pure religion and undefiled before our God and Father is this, to visit the fatherless and widows in their affliction, and to keep himself unspotted from the world. (Js. 1, *s.f.*; cf. 2: 14 ff.)

This may afford some comfort to the Christian empiricist; for the logical character and significance of moral judgements can by this time, I think, be stated in a way that ought to meet with fairly general acceptance among empiricists. To realize, therefore, that what religious people say in the course of their religious activities is in part moral is to realize that at any rate not all religious discourse is senseless. But this will be regarded, perhaps, as only a small contribution to the solution of the problem; for, it will be said, the *distinctive* character of religious discourse is not thereby illuminated. We may admit that part of this discourse consists of moral judgements; but not the central part. The moral judgements, as we may say, arise out of the religious belief; they do not constitute it. St Paul thought that he ought to stop persecuting Christians because he had changed his belief about a specifically religious matter which was not itself a matter of how one ought to behave, but more like a matter of fact; he had come to believe that Jesus was the Christ, the Son of God.

I do not think that it is possible to sort out this question without a more thorough investigation of the way in which factual beliefs and principles of action are related to each other, and the way in which both are related to our actual conduct. There is a famous doctrine of Aristotle's which, I am convinced, offers the key to a great range of problems in this field, namely the theory of the practical syllogism (see p. 185). Aristotle said, roughly, that when a man does anything, there are two things that lie behind what he does. He calls these two things the two premisses of the practical syllogism. The major premiss is some kind of precept or aim or prescription. The minor premiss is a statement of fact. The conclusion of the syllogism is an action. Thus, if I accept the principle that one ought always, if one has a streaming cold, to stay away from public places, and if I know that I have a streaming cold, I do stay away. Aristotle includes among major premisses of this sort of syllogism everything that can be called, in a phrase that Professor Braithwaite has used, 'springs of action'. That is to say, he includes both desires, and purposes, and principles. Since what I wish to say can be said without discussing the important though troublesome distinctions between these different things, I shall adopt Braithwaite's phrase. I shall also from time to time use the particular expression 'moral principles', although I should more correctly express what I have in mind if I used some more general and cumbrous expression such as 'principles governing conduct'. That is to say, I do not wish here to raise, any more than did Aristotle, the important and difficult question of what distinguishes moral principles from other principles of action.

I have said elsewhere that a man's moral principles are most reliably ascertained by seeing what he *does* (*LM* 1). This view has been strongly attacked; but I still hold it. For I think that if a man consistently breaks a moral principle which he professes, this inclines us to say that his professions are insincere. But it has also been commonly held that the way to find out about *any* of a man's beliefs, factual or otherwise, is to study what he does. And this must be true, provided that the word 'does' is given a sufficiently wide interpretation. For the only thing that we *can* study about a man is what he does. We cannot take his mind out and look at it (even if such an expression is meaningful); and, therefore, if we are to find out anything about his thoughts, we can do so only by studying his actions (including, of course, those actions which consist in his talking to us). I need not now raise the question whether the actions are merely *evidence* of the thoughts, or whether, as some have held, thinking *consists* in acting in a certain way. But at any rate it follows from what I have said that if believing something is a kind of thinking, we can only find out what a man believes by studying his actions; and likewise, if holding a moral principle, or desiring something, or having a certain purpose, are in a wide sense kinds of thinking, we can only find out about a man's principles or purposes or desires by studying his actions.

An example will help to illustrate the view which I am presenting, and some of its difficulties. If we see a visitor from another town, who has no other means of conveyance than the train, looking at the clock, which says 10.25, and going on talking unconcernedly, we may conclude either that he *believes* that the last train leaves after about 10.30 or that he does not *want* to get home tonight. The possibility of drawing *either* of these two conclusions presents us with a problem. If we assume that he wants to get home tonight we can conclude from his behaviour that he believes that there is a train after 10.30. If, on the other hand, we assume that he believes that there is no train after 10.30, we can conclude from his behaviour that he does not want to get home tonight. What we cannot do is to draw both these conclusions at once without making any assumptions. In Aristotelian terms, from the premisses 'Let me do whatever is necessary to get home tonight' (major) and 'To get home tonight it is necessary to catch a train at or before 10.30' (minor) there follows the conclusion 'Let me catch a train at or before 10.30'; and this conclusion would be expressed in action by catching the train. So if the man does not catch the train we can conclude that he does not accept one of the premisses, if we assume that he does accept the other. In short, actions are evidence for springs of action, if we assume beliefs; or for beliefs, if we assume springs of action; but they cannot be evidence for both at the same time. This, it may be noticed in passing, presents a very real, though perhaps not insuperable, difficulty for those who wish to analyse statements about *all* mental states, including both desires and beliefs, in terms of statements about behaviour.

Let us now return to St Paul. He had always believed that he ought to follow the Christ when he appeared. Thus, it might be said, his conversion was not an alteration in his moral principles; they did not change at all. What was altered was the minor premiss—his factual belief. For whereas he had previously believed that Jesus was a pretender, he now came to believe that he was the Christ. This altered his actions, not through altering his moral principles, but through altering his opinion about a matter of fact.

Yet I find it very difficult to accept this view either. For when a man says 'Jesus is Christ' or 'Jesus is Lord' is he stating a fact (in the ordinary sense) at all? I think it would be agreed that of the people who were familiar with Jesus in his earthly life, some were ready to make this affirmation, and some were not. St Paul, perhaps, knew in one sense all the facts about Jesus *before* his conversion. He even knew, perhaps, that he cast out devils—but then non-Christian Jews had an explanation of this; he cast out devils, they said, by Beelzebub, the prince of the devils. Now what is the *factual* difference between casting out devils by Beelzebub, and casting them out by the finger of God? Or between either of these and curing mental disorders by suggestion (if that is the correct term)? The *fact* is that the symptoms of the disorder cease. It seems to me that one might, in one sense of the word 'fact', know all the facts about Jesus and still refuse to call him 'Lord' or 'Christ'.

'But', it might be said, 'this leaves out what from St Paul's point of view was the most important fact of all, namely what actually happened to him upon the road to Damascus. Surely here was a new fact, and one which made him ready to acknowledge that Jesus was the Christ.' Yet someone else might say 'What happened to St Paul was that he had a very powerful emotional experience, accompanied by an illusion of someone talking to him, which shook him a great deal, so that he couldn't even see for a bit, and after which he changed his pattern of behaviour.' The same objector would, no doubt, say the same sort of thing about the other appearances of Jesus after his death. What, then, when we are dealing with 'supernatural' facts, is the difference between facts and illusions?

There is another possibility which might be suggested at this point. It might be said: 'If one person says "Jesus is Christ" and another denies this, they may not be differing about the facts; it may be that they have different attitudes to the facts. St Paul, when this thing happened to him, changed his whole way of life; another person, if the same thing happened to him, might have said "Sign of overstrain! I've been driving myself too hard, persecuting these Christians; I must take a holiday and then I'll feel better".' According to this view St Peter, when he said 'Thou art the Christ', was not stating a fact; he was *doing* something, namely worshipping.

There is indeed such a thing as an attitude of worship; and it is plausible to say that to take up this attitude is part at any rate of what a person does when he is converted. It is therefore necessary to consider, in what can only be a superficial way, what is meant by 'worship'. The first thing to notice is that it is nearly always much easier to say of somebody *that* he is worshipping than to say *what* he is worshipping. 'The heathen in his blindness bows down to wood and stone'; but can we say that wood and stone, considered in themselves, are the real objects of his worship? We are not, for our present purposes, concerned with the answer to this old question, but with the logical character of the question itself. If we find a heathen bowing down to a piece of wood, and doing all the other things that would normally be called 'worshipping' it (suppose, for example, that he will not use the wood of that kind of tree for any profane purpose), then we can surely say that he is worshipping the piece of wood. If someone says 'He isn't really worshipping the piece of wood, but some invisible god whom he conceives of as resident in the piece of wood', then we may if we like agree with this; but I can think of cases in which this might well seem a distinction without a difference.

We are reminded here of Professor Ryle's views about the mind (1949). Suppose that we ask 'What is the difference between, on the one hand, doing all the things that I habitually do to my wife, and on the other, doing all the same things and in addition thinking of her as a person?' It is not at all clear to me how one would answer such a question. It may be said 'If you can love something in the way that you love your wife, you must be thinking of it (her) as a person.' But this remark is two-edged. For it is intended to be an analytic statement; and therefore it would seem that on this view thinking of something as a person is an analytically necessary condition for being said to love it (him, her). But if so, then loving it (him, her) is an analytically sufficient condition for being said to think of it (him, her) as a person. And if this is applicable to worship as well as to love, then we may say that worshipping something is an analytically sufficient condition for being said to think of it as a person. By this I mean not that if we find someone worshipping something we are entitled to say that thing *is* a person, but only that we are entitled in such a case to say that he *thinks* of it as a person. The further question remains, how we tell whether he is *right* to think of it as a person.

How then do I tell whether I am right to think of my wife as a person? I do not wish to answer this question at too great length. But if she does all the things which I expect persons to do, does not that show that I am right? And can we not say this of the piece of wood? Of course the piece of wood does not walk about or talk. But that is not what its worshipper expects. He expects only that worship of the piece of wood will be followed by a course of events favourable to him (rain at the right time, for example) whereas neglect of its worship will be followed by an opposite course of events.

If a person adopts an attitude of worship towards some object, and therefore thinks of it (or of something resident in it) as a person, and if everything which he expects to happen actually happens, shall we not say that he is right to worship it? Shall we not say that it is for him a proper object of worship? And if a proper object of worship, then a god; for only a god can be a proper object of worship (this statement is analytic). Moreover, on this interpretation the statement 'This piece of wood is a god' is falsifiable; for when the missionary comes and casts down the piece of wood, and the results which its worshippers expect do not follow, this is just the sort of thing that makes people say that it was false to call it a god, or, for short, that it was a false god. The more primitive a religion is, the more readily are its statements open to empirical falsification; religion has advanced from its more primitive to its less primitive forms partly by the empirical falsification of the claims of the more primitive forms, which then come to be known as superstitions. The less primitive a religion becomes, the less willing are its adherents to make predictions about what their god will do; in particular, they become less certain that he will act to what *they* conceive to be their advantage. Thus the prescriptive, attitudinal element in religious belief gains at the expense of the descriptive factual element.

If it be so, our God whom we serve is able to deliver us from the burning fiery furnace; and he will deliver us out of thine hand, O king. But if not, be it known unto thee, O king, that we will not serve thy gods, nor worship the golden image which thou hast set up. (Dan. 3: 17)

This process, as is well known, has caused certain empiricist philosophers to maintain that religious 'advances' have been made at the cost of making statements of religious faith less open to empirical falsification, and, therefore, by the empiricist criterion, less meaningful (see pp. 8 ff., 37 ff.). A possible answer to this attack is, first, that, as it is the purpose of this paper to show, the empirical component in the meaning of religious language is not the only one, nor even, perhaps, the most important; and secondly, that even advanced religions require of their adherents *some* empirical expectations.

Likewise, even in the most primitive forms of religion, what is being stated is not just empirical fact. For if, as I have implied, the meaning of the word 'god' (with a small 'g') is 'a proper object of worship', the word 'proper' in the *definiens* is a value-word. Here we come back to something rather like morals (for 'proper' as used here, though not a moral word, is, like moral words, prescriptive). According to this view, in calling something a god, we are saying, not merely that worshipping it will have certain results, but that it is *proper* to worship it; that is to say, we are at least in part prescribing the taking up of a certain attitude towards it. And whether we are to say that a person really believes in a certain god will depend on what attitude he takes up to the object which is said to be a god; that is, it will depend on what he *does*. Those who have followed recent discussions of the various elements of meaning possessed by value-words will recognize here familiar features. The word 'god' has both evaluative and descriptive meaning. In virtue of its descriptive meaning statements containing it may be said to be verifiable and falsifiable by those who accept the same standards of evaluation as the speaker (and this does not necessarily involve accepting the *whole* of his religious beliefs). In virtue of its evaluative meaning we say that a person who does not behave in a certain way towards a certain object is not treating it as a god.

I return now for the last time to St Paul. It seems fairly clear that it will not do to try to find some one thing about St Paul which changed when he became a Christian. If we ask 'Was it his beliefs about matters of fact which changed, or his moral principles, or some other kind of value-principles, or his attitude to something or other, or something else?' then we are asking for trouble. Surely we must say that almost everything about St Paul changed; he became 'a new creature'. If this is true, we shall not find a single simple analysis of religious statements which solves all philosophical problems concerning them; for not only are there many kinds of utterances which religious people make in the course of their religion (this would be difficult enough); but almost all these kinds of utterances are, so to speak, in circuit with all the rest. A religious person may make what is prima facie a statement of fact—perhaps even a statement of quite ordinary empirical fact like 'If I may but touch his garment I shall be whole' (Matt. 9: 21)—and yet perhaps she would not have made this statement at all unless it were bound up with all sorts of other beliefs, dispositions, attitudes, and so on. This is, to my mind, the chief reason why religious discourse has always baffled philosophers and, I am inclined to add, long may it continue to baffle them if they think that to understand it is a merely *philosophical* problem.

I wish, therefore, to conclude this paper by giving what is little more than a bare classification of some of the chief sorts of things that religious people say and do in the course of their religion, and which, taken together, constitute religious belief. I do not wish to claim that the list is either comprehensive or sufficiently finely distinguished. It will be noticed that the items group themselves into a triad rather like the thesis, antithesis, and synthesis of an earlier philosophy. I started, it will be remembered, by considering the suggestion that moral judgements are the distinctive constituents of religious discourse. This view I rejected, and then considered in turn the claim of statements of religious belief to be called statements of fact in the ordinary sense; and this, too, appeared unsatisfactory. If we take religious language as a whole, it is too factual to be called specifically moral, and yet too closely bound up with our conduct to be called in the ordinary sense factual.

I therefore came back to a position which has affinities with both the preceding ones. Taking up an attitude of worship to an object considered as a person is not quite like adopting a purely factual belief; nor is it simply subscribing to certain principles of conduct; but it involves both these things. The person who worships is bound to govern his conduct (or let it be governed) in a certain way; and he is also bound to believe in the truth of certain factual statements (empirical ones about what has actually happened in the world, and what is likely to happen). As a first sketch of a synthesis, it is plausible to say that in so far as religious discourse seems to refer to supernatural facts, this is the result of the superimposition of the attitude of worship upon factual beliefs which are themselves not other than empirical; that, in fact, we have here a case like that of 'non-natural qualities' in ethics. When we say that a strawberry is good because it is sweet, and yet by calling it good mean to say something else of it than simply that it is sweet, we are tempted to think that by calling it good we are attributing to it some *quality*, somehow like sweetness yet of a different, 'non-natural' kind—a quality which cannot be tasted but only grasped by thought, and which is the consequence of the natural quality of sweetness. In truth, however, what we are doing is not attributing to the strawberry any other quality at all besides sweetness; but we are, as well as attributing to it that perfectly ordinary quality, *commending* it for having the quality (*LM* 85). In the same way it might be that the *facts* that religious discourse deals with are perfectly ordinary empirical facts like what happens when you pray; but we are tempted to call them supernatural facts because our whole way of living is organized round them; they have for us value, relevance, importance, which they would not have if we were atheists. If this view were correct, then the belief that there are specifically religious, super-natural facts could be said to be the result of failing to distinguish in logic what cannot be distinguished in practice, namely facts and our attitudes to them.

Even this, however, will not do. For it implies that there *is* a clear distinction in logic between facts and our attitudes to them. But though it is most important to start by making this distinction, it is important to end not by blurring it, as is often done, but by articulating the relations between these two kinds of thing.

People sometimes talk as if facts were somehow given us entirely independently of any dispositions of our own with regard to them. Kant saw that this is not so; but I will not attempt to formulate what I wish to say in his language. I can put the point briefly (at the cost of obscurity) by saying that any statement of fact which claims *objectivity* will be found on analysis to contain an element which is ineradicably *modal* (a reference to causal necessity); and that such modal statements are not analysable in purely descriptive terms, but have a prescriptive element. This element is not the same as, but it presents certain analogies with, the prescriptive element in moral judgements. From this it follows that without principles of some sort we do not get any facts; there is no distinction between fact and illusion for a person who does not take up a certain attitude to the world.

This is obviously not the place to expand these somewhat pregnant remarks. But fortunately, in a subject the full logical discussion of which is too complicated to be attempted until logical studies have advanced further, a great deal of light has been shed by recent discoveries and probable conjectures of physiologists. That physiology should shed light on a logical problem may seem impossible to a philosophical purist; but if the thinking which is expressed in language is done by, or involves the use of, the brain, it is to be expected that there will be certain formal analogies between the features of language which logicians study and the processes which physiologists find going on in the brain. In the same way, if a computer does mathematics there will be formal analogies between the expression in mathematical language of the calculations which it does and the physical operations of the parts of the computer.

It is therefore extremely significant that, in his recent Reith Lectures (1951), Professor Young, speaking of the brain, said some things which must have a familiar ring to any philosopher who has read Kant. This is all the more paradoxical in that Kant himself would have considered it outrageous that empirical discoveries about the brain should have any relevance to his doctrines. But to us it may appear that, since to talk we have to use our brains, the fact that a student of the brain echoes what has been said several centuries before by a student of metaphysics shows that the latter's studies were very firmly based, as they should be, in the facts of our use of words. At any rate it seems to me that Professor Young has paid to Kant the same sort of back-handed compliment as Kant paid to Swedenborg; the dreams of the metaphysician have been considerably elucidated by the dreams of the neurophysiologist.

We cannot speak [says Professor Young] as if there is a world around us of which our senses give us true information. In trying to speak about what the world is like we must remember all the time that what we see and what we say depends on what we have learned; we ourselves come into the process. (1951: 108)

And elsewhere he says:

The brain of each one of us does literally create his or her own world.
To explain this we must answer the question: How does each brain
set up its own characteristic rules? How do those regular patterns of
activity in the cells of the brain . . . develop? This is the process that
I call the establishment of certainty, and it is a process that we may
consider as beginning in each human being at the moment when, as
a newly born baby, his eyes open on to the world. (1951: 61)

In his lectures Professor Young gives an account in some
detail of how these rules, as he calls them, are formed in the
brain (how, we might say, we learn to distinguish facts, or to
understand the concept 'fact'). It is to be hoped that these new
discoveries will finally and effectively remove from the
repertory of philosophical theories that one which Professor
Popper has called 'the bucket theory of the mind'—the theory
that facts drip into the mind like water into a bucket, where
they accumulate and are called 'knowledge' (1945: ii. 201 ff.).
The lesson that is to be learnt from Professor Young, as from
Kant (1781: A92 ff. = B125 ff.), is that (as Kant might put it)
nothing can become an object (or a fact) for us unless in our
thinking we follow certain rules or principles—that the mind
plays an active part in cognition, and that therefore the
principles which govern its action are part-determinants of
what we experience.

Considerations like these make one very chary of working
uncritically with a terminology which relies on an absolutely
hard-and-fast distinction between principles or rules or
dispositions on the one hand and facts on the other. For it
would appear that until we have accepted rules for discriminating between facts and illusions, we cannot talk of facts at all,
or for that matter of objects or entities in the sense of 'things
really existing'. Now Christians believe that God created the
world out of chaos, or out of nothing, in the sense of no *thing*.
What I am now going to say I say very tentatively. Is it
possible that this is our way of expressing the truth that
without belief in a divine order—a belief expressed in other
terms by means of worshipping assent to principles for
discriminating between fact and illusion—there could be no
belief in matters of fact or in real objects? Certainly it is
salutary to recognize that *even* our belief in so-called hard

facts rests in the end on a faith, a commitment, which is not in or to facts, but in that without which there would not be any facts. Plato, it will be remembered, said of the Idea of the Good, which was his name for God, that it was not itself a being, but the source or cause of being; the passage is worth quoting in full, and I will end with it:

In the case of those things which we see by the light of the sun, the sun is the source, not merely of the possibility of our seeing them, but also of their very coming to be, their growth and their sustenance. But it is not itself a coming to be. And in the same way in the case of those things which we know by the light of the Idea of the Good, it is the source, not merely of the possibility of our knowing them, but also of their very being—for from it their being comes. Yet the Good itself is not a being, but rather lies even further off, on the yonder side of being, excelling it in majesty and power. (*Rep.* 509b)

3

Are there Moral Authorities?

I have been struck, as many must have been, by the very small impact that philosophers have had on the current public debates in Britain on moral issues. This is partly because their help is not often sought; and partly because when it is sought the philosophers are not always helpful. There are now some good philosophers who work in applied philosophy. And there are also some philosophers who attempt this, but who, because of their faulty grasp of ethical theory, are not in a position to help very much. On the Continent the position is much worse. I have also been struck, on recent visits to Scandinavia and Germany, first by the great public interest there is in moral questions, especially in medicine, but secondly by how uncommon it is for philosophers to be asked to serve on committees and working parties that study such questions. It is much more usual for clergymen and lawyers to have a place on them. That perhaps shows that clergymen and lawyers are regarded as some sort of authorities on moral questions, but philosophers are not.

I do not want to claim that philosophers are authorities in the sense in which some people think that clergymen and lawyers are; I shall be arguing later that in that sense there are *no* authorities on these questions: we have to decide them for ourselves, though some people, through a combination of practical experience and clear thinking, may have become better able than others to handle them. But nevertheless it is striking how often, when these questions are discussed in Parliament or in the media, palpable confusions and fallacies are made in the arguments, and repeated again and again— confusions and fallacies which any competent philosopher

Previously unpublished. To appear also in *Ethics in Reproductive Medicine*, Proceedings of the Second International Conference on Philosophical Ethics in Reproductive Medicine, ed. D. Bromham *et al.* (Springer, forthcoming).

would at once spot. The role of the philosopher is not that of an authority, but of someone who is able to help avoid these blunders.

However, the position seems to be improving a little. I was much heartened to read my Oxford colleague Jonathan Glover's report to the European Commission, called *Fertility and the Family* (1989). This was prepared by a working party under his chairmanship, and deals with the same range of subjects, roughly, as the Warnock Report (1984). I find the Glover Report much more convincing. Lady Warnock came to some, on the whole, sensible conclusions; but, because the ethical theory she favours is of an intuitionist sort which is not strong on providing arguments, she did not afford much in the way of reasons for them which would stand up (H 1987). That is why the report did not do much to help Parliament when recently it debated the bill which deals with embryo experimentation. We are still not out of that wood, and will not be until we learn how to argue better. The members of Glover's working party were continentals from various related professions; I know only one of them, a very sensible and able German philosopher and medical doctor, Bettina Schöne-Seifert; but evidently Jonathan Glover, who wrote the Report, succeeded, in a way that philosophers ought to be able to, in getting his working party to be clear about the arguments and thus arrive at some helpful conclusions. It is a fine piece of work, and it is a great pity that it has not had in this country so much attention as the Warnock Report—partly, I think, because it was a report to the European Commission and not to HM Government, and partly because the publishers Glover went to are not at all enterprising and have not done much to help sell it.

There is also excellent work coming out from the Centre for Human Bioethics at Monash University in Australia, whose Director Peter Singer has with his colleagues produced some very well-argued books. Their conclusions may not please everybody, but the quality of their reasoning is a model of its kind. They also have some skill in public relations, and in Australia are attended to. Peter Singer himself had a rough passage in Germany two summers ago; he was demonstrated against, and some of his talks had to be cancelled; the

Germans have not yet, on the whole, caught up with ideas which are commonplace in countries like The Netherlands and Denmark, for example. But from a recent visit I think that things are going to alter once the supply of clear-headed philosophers increases in Germany, and once these philosophers devote more of their attention to practical issues. Both of these things are starting to happen.

Let me now address the question in my title, and say why I think there are no authorities, in the strong sense that some people think is the only sense, on moral questions, but that, nevertheless, thought about them can be done well or badly, and that philosophers can help us to do it better. Obviously the first thing I must do is to sort out the different senses of 'authority', and then examine the claims of various candidates to be authorities in these different senses. The first sense need not detain us, because it is really irrelevant to our concerns. This is the sense in which an authority is a person or body that *enforces* laws or moral requirements by imposing sanctions— in other words by punishing those who break them. I do not think that when people look for an authority on questions of morals, they are looking for someone who will punish offenders against, for example, the rules of medical ethics. It may be important to have authorities in this sense, but I shall treat as prior the question of who should decide what the rules are or ought to be. Till we can answer the latter question, it is too early to ask who should enforce the rules. (On the question of the justification of punishment, see H 1986.)

A sense of 'authority' that we do need to discuss is the one in which I said that some people think there are moral authorities, and that is the sense in which 'authority' means 'source of unchallengeable answers to questions'. In this sense we treat people as authorities on the content of their own experiences. Though some philosophers might dispute this, I think we can agree that if I say I am in pain, and mean it in the accepted sense of the words, nobody else can safely tell me that I am wrong, unless he can somehow show that I am speaking insincerely—that I do not really believe what I am saying. I shall not discuss in general what other questions can receive authoritative answers of this sort; that would be too big a topic. But we do need to ask whether moral questions can ever be answered authoritatively in this way. This would be the case if, sometimes, somebody could just pronounce that some act was wrong, and nobody could dispute this.

Let us then ask whether there is any person or body that can give answers to moral questions that simply cannot be disputed. Can judges, for example, fill this bill? If they are judges in the highest court in a jurisdiction, they can certainly give to *legal* questions answers that cannot be challenged. But one of the important distinctions between law and morality is that judges cannot do for moral questions what they can do for legal ones. The reason is that what judges decide is what the law is, and not what it ought to be, or in general what ought to be done. When the House of Lords has pronounced that the law is such and such, I cannot then turn round and say that it is not (though I can, if I am a rebel, challenge the legality of the entire jurisdiction—see H 1967). But if the House of Lords says that something is morally wrong and I do not think that it is, I am entitled to my opinion. Perhaps, though the law is as the House of Lords says it is, it ought to be changed.

If judges are not moral authorities in this sense, are legislators in any stronger position? Parliament can decide, not just what the law is, but what it is to be. In the United States the situation is not so clear, because they have a written constitution, and the Supreme Court, a judicial body, can say that laws passed by Congress are unconstitutional and therefore of no effect. And jurists dispute at length on the extent to which judges can be said themselves to legislate. Certainly it seems as if the Supreme Court in the United States, and even, though less commonly, the British House of Lords, do determine what the law is to be as well as determining what it is. But I shall not be expected to go into that tangled question here. It suffices to say that, when it comes to a question of morals, legislators are in no better position to decide than are judges. That something is morally wrong is never part of the content of a bill before Parliament; but if it were, and Parliament voted that it *was* morally wrong, it would still be open to any of us to disagree, and we should be entitled to our opinions. So we may conclude that legislators are not moral authorities any more than judges are. Members of Parliament, of course, have, and should have, moral reasons for voting as they do, but their votes, however unanimous, do not *make* something morally wrong, nor do laws enacted by the Queen in Parliament determine what is to be morally wrong, but only what is to be illegal.

At this point it may be suggested, as it is by some modern intuitionists like Ross (1930), that moral authority does not reside in any particular office or station, but in the generally accepted opinion of all morally educated people. It would not do to go further and say 'of all people'; for we cannot rely on a consensus for answers to questions on which obviously there *is* no consensus. But if we are to rely on the morally educated, how do we tell who is morally educated? On a question like abortion, for example, or embryo experimentation, or surrogate motherhood, or euthanasia, we find different people, all of whom can claim to be morally very well educated even by Ross's standards, saying opposite things. Unless we argue that the people on the other side must be morally uneducated because they disagree with us, how else are we to determine whether they are? I shall come back later to the question of how to decide what counts as good or as bad moral thinking; this is obviously going to be the crucial issue. Neither 'the many' nor 'the wise', as Aristotle (1095[a]18) might have put it, are to be relied on without our own independent scrutiny.

Having thus dismissed the State and other secular moral authorities, what about the Church? Here the matter is, initially, somewhat easier, because the Church does not ever claim to determine *by its own authority* what is morally wrong. In the eyes of most churchmen, God is the authority on moral questions, and the Church is at most passing on his commands to the laity. And not all Churches claim to do even this with authority. The same is true of the hierarchies of other religions. The Roman Church may be the only Church whose head claims to pronounce on moral questions *ex cathedra*; and even the Pope does not claim to *decide*, of himself, by his own authority, what is right or wrong. He claims only to be a mouthpiece for the divine commands.

So is God the ultimate moral authority? This question raises two further very difficult problems. The first is 'Even if we agreed that God is the ultimate determiner, by his commands, of what is right and wrong, how could we tell what in fact he does command?' The second is 'Even if we could determine this, would the fact that God forbade something necessarily, of itself, make it wrong?' I shall take these two questions in order.

There are various opinions on how God's will is to be known. The simplest one is the extreme Protestant doctrine, if I may call it that, that God, in the form of the Holy Spirit, speaks directly to the individual believer and tells him (or her) the answers to moral questions. To this Hobbes replied 'Though God Almighty can speak to a man, by Dreams, Visions, Voice and Inspiration, yet he obliges no man to believe he hath so done to him that pretends it; who (being a man) may erre, and (which is more) may lie' (1651, ch. 32; cf. H 1984: 118). Even if we allow that God speaks to men directly, the problem remains of when we can be sure that this has happened. The difficulty of 'discerning the spirits' already troubled the early Church, and St Paul's way out of it is not very helpful (1 Cor. 12: 3). It is significant that substantially the same difficulty arises, whether we ask who is an authority on moral questions, or who is a reliable mouthpiece of God's will. As we shall see, the only way out of the difficulty is to do some moral thinking ourselves.

It was, no doubt, in order to avoid the chaos that ensues if individuals claim direct access to God's will that the Church took on the office of declaring it. But the Church (even the Roman Church, whose head speaks *ex cathedra*) is in no better position than individuals are. After all, the Pope too is an individual; and he, also, 'may erre, and (which is more) may lie'. In order to decide whether a particular Pope has erred, or lied, we have to study the content of his pronouncements, and see whether it stands up.

Those Protestants (the great majority) who reject direct access to God by individuals, or at least desire some confirmation of what they claim God has said, are less likely to appeal to the Church as authority than to the Bible. Notoriously, different people seek support in the Bible for very diverse opinions, and find what they are looking for:

Hic liber est, in quo quaerit sua dogmata quisque,
Invenietque in eo dogmata quisque sua.

Nevertheless, nobody should deny that much wisdom is to be found in the Bible, and it is worth digressing a little to look for some of it on the question of morality. Morality is a very large part of religion, and Christian morality of the Christian religion; and since Popes and prelates are very apt to take for granted that Christian morality forbids this and that, without thinking that they need to substantiate their claims, it is worth while asking what is the central foundation of Christian and biblical teaching on moral questions. The answer, I am quite sure, lies in the doctrine of *agapē*, to which I shall be returning in greater detail on pp. 72 ff.

According to St Matthew 22: 39 we are commanded to love God, and this entails, according to St John 14: 15, keeping his commandments. Of the two commandments on which hang all the law and the prophets, the second is to love our neighbour as ourselves (Matt. 22: 39). This is put in other words in St Matthew 7: 12: 'All things whatsoever ye would that men should do to you, do ye even so to them; for this is the law and the prophets.' The law that we should love our neighbour as ourselves is found in the Old Testament too (Lev. 19: 18); it is Jewish as well as Christian, and is indeed a constituent of the moral teaching of all the great religions. Joseph Butler, the great eighteenth-century moral philosopher and theologian, writes:

From hence it is manifest that the common virtues, and the common vices of mankind, may be traced up to benevolence, or the want of it. And this entitles the precept, *Thou shalt love thy neighbour as thyself*, to the pre-eminence given to it; and is a justification of the Apostle's assertion, that all other commandments are comprehended in it; whatever cautions and restrictions there are, which might require to be considered, if we were to state particularly and at length, what is virtue and right behaviour in mankind.

And he later says forthrightly:

Thus morality and religion, virtue and piety, will at last necessarily coincide, run up into one and the same point, and *love* will be in all senses *the end of the commandment*. (1726, Sermon 12)

However, he heavily qualifies this claim in a footnote, and in the *Dissertation on Virtue*, admitting duties and virtues not based directly on benevolence, in opposition to the utilitarianism of Hutcheson. Both his main claim and the qualifications greatly influenced me when I was developing my two-level account of moral thinking (H 1976*a*, *MT*). In my view, we can at the critical level base morality on love or benevolence and hence on doing our best to satisfy the preferences of all impartially, but this very benevolence will make us cultivate virtues and acknowledge duties which on the face of it owe nothing to benevolence. To this problem we shall return.

I shall be claiming later that the same commandment of love, or a more general and clearer version of it, can be arrived at by reason, as Kant saw. If someone, using reason, concluded that this was the commandment that it was his duty to keep, he could go on to reason that since God is good, this must be what he commands. But this at once takes us on to the second, and more fundamental, difficulty in basing morality on the will of God. In a famous passage (1785: BA92 = 443), Kant repeats an idea which appeared in a more rudimentary form in Plato (*Euthyphro* 10a):

we cannot intuit God's perfection and can only derive it from our own concepts, among which that of morality is the most eminent: but . . . if we do not do this (and to do so would be to give a crudely circular explanation), the concept of God's will still remaining to us —one drawn from such characteristics as lust for glory and domination and bound up with frightful ideas of power and vengefulness—would inevitably form the basis for a moral system which would be in direct opposition to morality.

The argument is, in other words, that if we assume the premiss that God is good, we can infer that it is our duty to conform to his will; but that if we do not, there is no such implication; but in order to be assured that he is good, we have to make at least this one moral judgement on our own account; so although, once this judgement is made, we can make all the rest of our moral judgements on the basis of God's will, it would be arguing in a circle to base our belief in his goodness on the goodness of what he wills, and the goodness of what he wills on his goodness.

I think that Kant's argument is in substance correct. We have now come to the end of the list of possible moral authorities, in the sense of 'sources of unchallengeable answers to moral questions'; and none of them, whether human or divine, will do. In both cases, the trouble is the same; if the 'authority' is once assumed to be wise and good, then we can thereafter get all the rest of our moral judgements from the 'authority'; but we cannot assume this without making a moral judgement on our own part which is independent of the pronouncements of the 'authority'. It is easier to see this in the case of human authorities. For example, if we ask, concerning a supposed Platonic philosopher king, 'Is he really a philosopher king, or is he a tyrant masquerading as one?', we can only answer the question by ourselves assessing his moral worth and wisdom (on Plato, see Chapter 11 and H 1982, ch. 9). Kant argues that the same is true even of God.

If there are no moral authorities in the sense we have been using, how *are* we to settle moral questions? The answer is, By ourselves doing some moral thinking. But this raises a further question: 'Can this moral thinking be done well or badly? Can some do it better than others?' Plato certainly thought so, and so did Kant. Although the candidates we considered cannot, any of them, claim to be authorities in the sense discussed, they might claim to be authorities in a different sense: they might claim to be better at doing moral thinking, i.e. wiser, than the rest of us. But before we can assess these claims, we have to ask what it is to be good at moral thinking. And this in turn depends on what makes moral thinking good moral thinking.

Whether any kind of thinking is good thinking is in part, but only in part, a question of logic. We have to ask, therefore, whether there is a logic that applies to moral thinking. Let us assume that, at any rate, whatever additional logical restrictions there are on moral thinking, the same ordinary logic which governs thinking in general applies to moral thinking too; at least, in thinking morally, we have to avoid contradicting ourselves. But what is or is not a self-contradiction depends on what in particular we are saying. For example, it is self-contradictory to say 'It is red and it is not red' (in the same sense of 'red'). But it would not be self-contradictory to say 'It is red and it is not blue.' The alteration in the wording— the fact that we are saying something different—affects the logic. By substituting 'blue' for the second occurrence of 'red', we alter what is said, and this makes what is said no longer self-contradictory. Of course, if 'blue' and 'red' meant the same, the statement would still be self-contradictory; but they do not.

This illustrates the dependence of logic on language. There are a lot of complicated disputes among logicians about the nature of this dependence; but I hope that what I have said so far would meet with general agreement. We have seen that the meanings of the words 'red' and 'blue' can affect the logical restrictions on what is said. We have to ask, therefore, whether, and in what ways, the introduction of words like 'ought', 'right', and 'wrong', as they are used in making moral statements, affects the logic. In the example I have just given, the change from 'red' to 'blue' affected it. But it would have affected it just as much if we had changed 'and' to 'or'. 'It is red or it is not red' is not self-contradictory; indeed, it logically must be true. 'And' and 'or' are what are called logical words or logical constants; other logical words are the so-called modal operators like 'must'. They too affect the logic. If I say 'He is out, but it is not the case that he must be out', that is not self-contradictory; but if I say 'He must be out, but it is not the case that he is out', that *is* self-contradictory. I have argued elsewhere (*MT* 2, 10) that words like 'ought' resemble these modal operators, in particular in the fact that, unlike 'red' and 'blue', they owe their meanings entirely to their logical properties. And we determine what these logical properties are (what the rules are for their consistent use) by seeing what statements containing them correct speakers of the language treat as self-contradictory or inconsistent. This gives us a way of testing a piece of moral thinking to see whether it is logically in order.

What then are the logical restrictions on the use of these moral words, if we are to avoid self-contradiction? There are more than one; but the one that should interest us here is the so-called requirement of universalizability. This says that one contradicts oneself if one makes moral judgements about two situations which one agrees to be identical in their non-moral properties, and these judgements ascribe to one of the situations moral properties which they deny of the other. For example, if I say 'He did wrong, but there might be another situation just like this one, with people in it just like these, with the same characters, motivations, etc., but in that other situation the corresponding person would not be doing wrong', then I am contradicting myself. I think that most moral philosophers would agree that 'wrong' has this feature, though some hold that it is not logic alone that gives it the feature, but a substantial *moral* principle. I shall not argue about this here. Nor shall I argue with those few who claim that it is not a feature of moral words at all; they only claim this because they have not fully understood the thesis of universalizability. I have argued elsewhere that moral words do have this feature, and that it is a logical feature (*FR* 30). But I hope it will be agreed at least for the sake of argument that they do have the feature.

This feature is closely connected with the *agapē* doctrine that I mentioned earlier. Indeed, though I cannot substantiate this as a matter of history, I think it likely that the reason why we have in our language moral words with this feature is that the requirement to love our neighbour as ourselves has got built into the language as a result of the growth of Christian moral ideas and similar ideas in other religions. This often happens with words. For example, it was not until recently that scientists discovered that water is composed of two parts of hydrogen to one of oxygen; but now you may find in the dictionary that in one (but only one) of the senses of 'water' it is true *by definition* that water is H_2O. What has happened is that a thesis which was a substantial thesis about water has got written into the language as an analytic truth, true in virtue of the meanings of the words. I think the same has happened with 'ought' and universalizability. But this is not the place to argue that this is so.

If it is so, then we could free ourselves from this logical requirement just by stopping speaking in moral terms—that is, by giving up the moral language; but there would be a penalty for this: we should no longer be able to say the things, and in particular to ask the questions, that we now ask using the moral words. I shall assume that actually people will want to go on asking these questions and trying to find answers to them. And if we do go on asking them, we are bound, in thinking about possible answers, to follow the requirements of logic, and in particular the requirement of universalizability, which is the linguistic embodiment of the command to love our neighbour. We shall see later where this leads us.

So then, one necessary ingredient of good moral thinking is logic. But, as I said, it is not the only ingredient. Someone whose logic was faultless, but who paid absolutely no attention to the facts of the situations he was thinking about, could not be said to be doing his moral thinking well. These two ingredients, logic and the facts, are what determine the goodness of a piece of moral thinking. Richard Brandt has expressed this well: he says 'I shall pre-empt the term "rational" to refer to actions, desires or moral systems which survive maximal criticism by facts and logic' (1979: 10). But what facts do we have to attend to, if we are to do our moral thinking well?

What we have to attend to are facts about what we should be doing if we did one or other of the things open to us to do. But what we should be doing is affecting the course of events in some way. For example, if I give somebody a drug which kills him, what I am doing is (among other things) *bringing about* his death. It is the consequences of my action (for example, the action of administering the drug to him) that make it *that* action, the action of killing him. There are some confused philosophers who think that it is wrong to consider the consequences of actions when judging their rightness or wrongness; but if they were less confused they would see that the sense in which the consequences of actions determine what the actions are, and thus their morality, is a different sense from that in which they are using the word. Everybody must agree that, in the sense in which *I* have been using it, facts about consequences affect the morality of actions, because they determine what the actions are.

But what facts about what consequences do we have to consider? Some consequences, no doubt, are irrelevant to morality. For example, the fact that in giving a person a drug, which involves moving my hands in certain directions, I displace molecules of air which otherwise would have gone elsewhere, is almost always morally irrelevant. So we are unlikely to say that all the physical consequences of an action are relevant to the moral assessment of it. But some are, and we have to say which, and why. For example, many would say that if a drug would kill the patient if administered, that is a morally relevant consequence. About some consequences, though, people are likely to disagree. If what is killed is a one-week-old embryo, some would say that killing it just does not matter morally, but others would strongly dissent.

The consequences that we think morally relevant are going to be those which are mentioned in whatever moral principles we apply to the situation. For example, if we think that one ought not to kill any human being after conception, then we shall think it morally relevant that to administer a certain drug would kill an embryo. But if we do not accept such a principle, we shall not think it relevant. So the question of relevance boils down to the question of what moral principles we should accept.

If we take the command to love our neighbour as 'the law and the prophets', and accordingly accept the principle that we should do to others as we wish them to do to us, the question becomes a bit easier. We have to ask what in particular we wish should be done to us if we were in exactly the position of the person whom our action will affect. This means that what we have to consider is the effect on that person's preferences. If we were in exactly his (or her) position, we should have his preferences; for if the preferences were different the position would be different. If this is right, it is very important. It means, for example, that if, as is certainly the case, embryos have no preferences, we shall not mind what happens to us if we are embryos. But, I hasten to add, we shall mind what would happen to us if we were the person that an embryo would turn into if not killed. It matters very much to me that the embryo that turned into me was not killed. This is the basis of the so-called argument from potentiality that is much used by anti-abortionists. But we are not going in any case to bring to birth all the children that we in theory could bring to birth. The clearest example of this is where we have two IVF embryos but can only implant one of them; but the same applies where a family has, for good moral reasons, decided not to have more than one more child and to abstain thereafter; it will be this child now or another child later but not both. So the potentiality argument, as I have interpreted it, does not compel us to increase the population without limit, or indeed more than a justified population and family planning policy allows (H 1975, 1988, 1989*c*).

Normally, in doing something to one person, we are also doing things to a lot of others. For example, saving the life of one drowning person may mean leaving another to drown. To the question 'Who is my neighbour?' we might answer 'Whoever is affected by my actions'; but in most cases many people will be affected, and this raises the difficult question of how the interests of these various people (or what we wish should be done to us if we were each one of them) should be balanced. We wish that if we were either of the drowning people we should be saved; but how do we decide which we ought to save if we cannot save both. I can think of no better answer than that provided by a further application of the requirement to universalize (which, I said, was the embodiment of the *agapē* doctrine). We have got to find universal principles that we can accept for all situations, whatever role we ourselves occupy in them. I have to do what I wish should be done to me in each of these situations in which I occupy different roles; but when I have to balance the wishes I have for all these roles, I am likely to give greater weight to the stronger preferences. So, in our example, if I know that one of the drowning people is drowning because he was trying to commit suicide, and wants to die, and the other is a well-meaning person, but a poor swimmer, who is, perhaps mistakenly, trying to rescue him, but himself very much wants to live, then I shall think I ought to save the latter.

Such cases raise many problems which have been discussed, often helpfully, by philosophers; but there is no time to go into them now. Let us return to the main point, which is that good moral thinking demands attention to logic and to the facts. The logic of the moral words requires us to prescribe as if *we* might be any one of the people affected, that is, impartially, loving them all as ourselves. The facts of a situation determine what we should be doing to each of them if we acted in each of the alternative ways open to us. These two requirements will make us consider the interests, which are a function of the present and future preferences, of all the people affected, and to try to maximize the furtherance of these interests. This is substantially the view of a typical utilitarian. Kant would have put the same point in a different way; he would have said that we have to make the ends of the others our own ends (1785: BA69 = 430). Kant and the utilitarians, far from being diametrically opposed as most people think, have a great deal in common, and indeed almost everything in common when we are speaking of our duties to other people (H 1992*a*). And both, as J. S. Mill (1861, ch. 2) and Kant (1785: BA13 = 399) saw, have an affinity with the Christian doctrine of love.

So then, who are the authorities on moral questions? We saw that there are none, in the strong sense of 'authority' in which it means 'source of unchallengeable answers'. But in the weaker sense of 'people to whom we would be right to go for advice, because they are good at moral thinking', there are indeed authorities. I said that to do good moral thinking requires an understanding of the logic of the questions we are asking, and a knowledge of the facts. This neatly divides up the class of moral authorities in this weaker sense. For some people will be better at the logic, and others will be better at the facts. Philosophers *ought* to be better at the logic, though not all of them are. And practitioners of the disciplines concerned (doctors, for example) are likely to be better at the facts. To attend to the really important facts, however, they have to have more than medical knowledge, and more even than the knowledge that other disciplines could give of the consequences of actions; they have to have the sensitivity, the empathy, to know what it is like to be in the situation of the others affected, for example their patients.

Since these two kinds of authority, on the facts and on the logic, are not likely to be possessed to the same high degree by one person, there is everything to be said for teamwork. That is why I have got furthest towards an understanding of vexed questions like abortion and euthanasia when I have been in working parties and seminars which include both sorts of people. We help one another. What then about the lawyers and the clergymen? They can help too, and have done so on the working parties I have taken part in. But they have done so only in so far as they have been able to play one or both of the roles I have distinguished, either that of sorting out the arguments by a clear understanding of their logic, or that of making us acquainted with facts that we did not know about before, especially facts about the impact on people of what we do. So anybody can play a useful part who knows what he is up to, and does not claim to be any kind of pontiff.

4

Euthanasia: A Christian View

I have called this paper 'Euthanasia: A Christian View'. I almost decided to be provocative and call it 'Euthanasia: *The* Christian View', because, so far as I can see, it is the direct application of the only injunctions of Christ (discussed in the preceding paper) that bear immediately on the subject of euthanasia. But I have refrained, because these injunctions, if so applied, lead to a view of the matter which is so contrary to what is generally thought to be the Christian view, that I should be taken to be merely perverse if I advocated it as the Christian view. I will therefore call it *a* Christian view— thereby amicably leaving a place among Christian views, beside that which I say is immediately derivable from Christ's words, for the very different views which are commonly maintained by the representatives of the Christian Church. I shall, however, be bold enough to go on, in the latter part of the paper, to try to explain why the Church has, typically, advocated a view so much at variance with what I take to be the implication of Christ's own teaching. We shall see that it is readily explained by the exigencies of the human situation, and in particular the situation of any human institution which, like the Church, assumes the task of teaching people how they ought to behave.

The sayings of Christ to which I refer are the saying 'As ye would that men should do to you, do ye also to them likewise' (Luke 6: 31), and the command that we should love our neighbour as ourselves (Matt. 22: 39; see pp. 62 ff.). These are the most general summaries of Christ's teaching that survive; of the first he says, 'this is the law and the prophets' (Matt. 7: 12). I can think of no moral question on which they have a more direct bearing than the question of euthanasia. But

From *Philosophic Exchange* 2 (1975).

before I try to say what this bearing is, I want to make a few remarks about the sayings themselves. First I will take the Golden Rule. We must notice first of all that it is couched in the imperative 'Do ye also to them'. I hope I may be allowed, therefore, to bypass the controversy that has occupied perhaps too much of the attention of moral philosophers in recent years, that between descriptivists and prescriptivists. Here, at any rate, we have a piece of moral teaching cast in the form of a prescription, and I am going to examine it as such.

The injunction is also prescriptive in a second, indirect way. The first clause says 'As ye would that men should do'. If, that is to say, we want to know what we are to do to men, we are to ask ourselves what we ourselves will. We think at once of Kant's formulation 'Act only on that maxim through which you can at the same time will that it should become a universal law' (1785: BA52 = 421). Kant, indeed, calls the Golden Rule itself 'trivial' (1785: BA68 n. = 430 n.), and regarded it as a mere application of his more fundamental doctrine; but the two have in common their appeal to the will as the source of moral judgements; we are to ask ourselves what we can will or do will (i.e. what prescriptions we can or do accept to govern the actions of men), and found our morality upon a universalization of that. As Kant saw, once we are faced with the requirement that we universalize our prescriptions, the prescriptions themselves may change, because we shall not, and cannot, accept for universal application prescriptions which we should be very ready to act on ourselves, if nobody else did.

The Golden Rule is thus doubly prescriptive. It is a prescription of Christ's; and when we seek to know what in particular it prescribes that we do, we are referred to a prescription of our own, with the words 'As ye would'. These words themselves, however, in the Authorized Version, have been a source of confusion because of their apparently hypothetical form. The Greek has '*kathōs thelete*' (indicative); and the Vulgate has, correctly, '*prout vultis*'. The Authorized Version is not actually incorrect, but merely archaic: 'As you wish that men should do' in the Greek has been turned into 'As ye would that men should do', which is, I think, a mere attraction of the first auxiliary into a hypothetical form to match the second, 'should'. The New English Bible has, by the way, fallen straight into the trap and translated not from the Greek but from a misunderstanding of the Authorized Version: 'Treat others as you would like them to treat you.'

I am not indulging in pedantry for its own sake, because the difference between the conditional form of the verb and the indicative form is of crucial importance (see *MT* 95). We are being told not: Do to other men what you would like them to do to you (i.e. what would be to your liking) if you were in their situation; but rather: Do to other men what you do wish that they should do to you if you were in their situation. There are two mistakes to be avoided here. The first is that of taking the question as being a hypothetical one, 'What would you like?', instead of 'What do you wish (or prescribe)?' If this mistake is made, the rejoinder is open 'I know I would not like it; but nevertheless it is what I now prescribe (for universal application); it is what I think ought to be done.' The second mistake is that of failing to realize that the situations for which one is prescribing include the situation in which one is oneself in the victim's position with the victim's likes and dislikes.

The other saying of Christ to which I referred also needs a brief comment in order to forestall a possible misunderstanding (see pp. 62 ff. above). The command to love our neighbours as ourselves comes after another command to love God; and I suppose (though I hope that nobody would be so perverse) that somebody might object to the conclusions that I am going to draw from the second command to love our neighbour, that they run counter to the first command to love God. To this the simple answer is provided by another of Christ's sayings: 'If ye love me, keep my commandments'. If, that is to say, we love God in the person of Christ, we shall try to do what he tells us to—that is what loving God in such contexts amounts to, though of course there is more to it than that. And he has told us in the plainest terms to do to others what we wish that they should do to us. So if this last commandment leads to a certain particular conclusion, it would be absurd to reject that conclusion because of a supposed conflict between it and the command to love God.

I will now leave these exegetical points and come to the question of euthanasia. I am not going to take the usual hospital examples (though I have such examples in mind). I am going to take what is perhaps an unusual case, but one which did actually happen some time ago and was reported in the Press. The driver of a petrol lorry was in an accident in which his tanker overturned and immediately caught fire. He himself was trapped in the cab and could not be freed. He therefore besought the bystanders to kill him by hitting him on the head, so that he would not roast to death. I think that somebody did this, but I do not know what happened in court afterwards.

We have to ask ourselves, as I have many times asked myself, what we wish that men should do to us if we were in the situation of that driver. I cannot believe that anybody who considered the matter seriously, as if he himself were going to be in that situation and had now to give directions as to what principle the bystanders should follow, would say that the principle should be one ruling out euthanasia absolutely.

Please note that I am not drawing anything but a very limited and negative conclusion from this example. It does not follow, because anybody accepts the rightness of euthanasia in this case, that he is committed to acknowledging its rightness in all cases. That is just the sort of mistake which I shall be trying to guard against in the rest of this paper. All I am arguing for is the limited, negative point that, whatever principle we adopt about euthanasia, it is not going to be, if we consider this example seriously and apply Christ's words to it, the principle that euthanasia is always and absolutely wrong.

Why is it that although, as I have said with some confidence, nobody who applied Christ's words to this example and considered it seriously would accept the principle that euthanasia is always wrong, the Christian Church has, typically, maintained that it *is* always wrong? I must be careful here, because I have not done any historical research on what the view of the Church has been. Pope Pius XII (1957), addressing himself primarily to the question of how long and under what conditions it is obligatory to keep patients alive artificially, rightly distinguished this question from the question of euthanasia, which is rather the question of when and under what conditions it is legitimate to kill people in order to relieve their suffering. Killing is certainly to be distinguished from failing to keep alive, although I do not myself attach so much importance to the distinction, from the moral point of view, as some people have. However, the two questions are distinct. The Pope said that there were conditions under which it was, for example, legitimate to switch off an artificial lung with a living patient inside it. But in passing he made it clear that this pronouncement did not imply any sanction for euthanasia, which was still always wrong. The same seems to be the view expressed in the recent Vatican Council document (Congregation for the Doctrine of the Faith 1987). There have certainly been prominent Christians in other denominations who have argued in favour of euthanasia. But I think I am right in saying that it is orthodox to regard euthanasia as always and absolutely wrong; and I want to ask why Christians have taken this view.

The answer, as I have already suggested, lies in the function of the Church as a teaching institution. From its very beginning, the Church has, among other roles, assumed that of *custos morum*. In this the Christian religion is not peculiar. Whatever are the conceptual relations between religious and moral beliefs (discussed on pp. 16 ff. and 40 ff. above), it can hardly be doubted that, as a matter of historical fact, priesthoods of all religions have frequently been regarded as the repositories of moral tradition, and have been expected to play the chief part in preserving it.

For an institution which is cast in this role, it is almost essential to have simple moral principles. Given the extreme difficulty of teaching rules that are at all complicated, an institution like the Church is bound to look for moral rules that are as simple as possible. As regards killing other people, the simplest rule is never to kill them—that is, unless we go to an even greater length in our search for simplicity and say that we should never kill any animal (I do not think that anybody has ever advocated that we should never kill plants, because it happens to be a fact of life, failing a method of synthesizing foodstuffs from inanimate materials, that we should all perish unless we ate at least vegetables). The Jains and certain other Indian sects have, in their pursuit of simplicity, extended the ban on killing to include not only humans but all animals; but this has proved too difficult a doctrine for most religions to adopt, and so it has been rejected in favour of a rule which permits (with qualifications) the killing of brute animals but forbids the killing of humans at least under certain conditions.

As I said, the simplest rule about killing human beings would be an absolute ban. But this, the pacifist rule, has, for reasons which I will not go into, proved too onerous for most religions, although it has the great virtue of simplicity. The majority of Christians have therefore retreated one step further, and said merely that killing is wrong if it is *murder*; other sorts of killing are either permitted, or, if not permitted, at any rate a less serious offence than murder.

It might seem that simplicity is still preserved. But this is, unfortunately, an illusion. For with the introduction of the word 'murder', the problem becomes acute of deciding what is to count as 'murder'. We may note in passing that this sort of problem can arise even with the word 'killing', or with the word 'human'. We have only to think of the problem of abortion, which has been thought to turn on the question of whether the foetus is a human being; or of the problem about switching off the respirator to which I have already alluded, which some have thought to turn upon such questions as whether the patient in the respirator can be said to be still alive if his brain has deteriorated to such an extent that he will never recover consciousness. The trouble with these questions is that there are a whole lot of perfectly workable ways of defining 'human' and 'alive'; and there is no reason for choosing one of these ways rather than another (unless convenience is a reason), other than the fact that to adopt one of them will lead us to one moral conclusion about what we ought to do with the foetus or the patient in the respirator, whereas to adopt another of them will lead us to a quite different conclusion. Therefore, so far from the answer to the allegedly factual question of whether the foetus is a human being, or whether the patient is alive, helping us to solve the moral problem, it is likely, rather, that the answer we give to the allegedly factual question will depend on what moral conclusion we want to reach.

I think myself that it is a source of unnecessary mystery to put the problems in these terms. But for the moment let us concentrate on the word 'murder'. If we were to define this as 'wrongful killing of a human being', we should have made it clear that murder was always wrong, but at the cost of making it impossible to tell whether a particular act of killing was a murder without making the prior moral judgement whether it was wrongful.

To adopt such a definition would obviously not serve the purposes of the Church as a teaching institution; for then, by teaching that murder was always wrong, it would have taught a concealed tautology with no content. The purpose of the teaching was to teach people what things are right and wrong; but with this definition all that has been taught is that if an act of killing is wrongful, it is wrong. I do not say that the proposed definition is a bad one; it may even be a useful one for certain purposes. But if the Church wants to have a workable, simple rule governing homicide, and wants to use the word 'murder' to express this rule, it has to have a definition of 'murder' which gives more stuffing to the word. And, if the rule is to remain simple, the definition has to be a short one.

The most popular definition has been of the following kind: murder has been defined as the intentional killing of an innocent human being. So, cashing the definition, we have the rule that the intentional killing of an innocent human being is always wrong. But this is not so simple a rule as it looks. There are, first of all, the problems raised by the words 'human being' and 'killing' to which I have already referred, and additional problems of a similar sort about the word 'innocent'. There are problems about the word 'intentional' too; but I shall not go into them—I mean problems like that of the definition of *mens rea*, and problems about double effect. And if we are talking about euthanasia, which has obvious affinities with suicide, we shall have to make it clear whether our definition of murder is intended to include suicide or not; it is no doubt better to exclude it, by amending the definition of 'murder' to read 'the intentional killing of *another* innocent human being'. But even then the boundary between murder and assisted suicide is an obscure one.

We see, then, that the apparently simple rule about homicide which we have proposed (namely that murder is always wrong) in fact generates a very great number of problems—problems which have kept the casuists usefully employed for a long time. I am not going now to discuss these problems; for we are concerned with a further problem of the same sort—the problem of whether the definition of 'murder' should be restricted a little further, so as to read 'the intentional killing of another innocent human being, unless this is both in his interest and with his consent'. For the essence of the problem of euthanasia is whether the fact that it is in somebody's interest to die, and that he shows, by consenting, that he himself thinks this, makes a difference to the legitimacy of killing him. There are analogies which might lend support to such an extension of the definition. We think that interference with other people's bodies is in general wrong; but we make an exception of some kinds of interference on the ground that they are in the interest of, and with the consent of, the person interfered with—for example, in surgery. So there certainly are cases in which an act, which is generally agreed to be wrong when it is (as it normally is) against the interests and the will of the person to whom it is done, is thought not to be wrong when it is in accordance with his interests and his will. Voluntary euthanasia would fit this description.

I shall not, however, pursue this line of argument, because I want, instead, to make a much more general remark about the sort of approach to the question which I have been discussing. I started off by drawing an extremely simple inference from some words of Christ. I then asked why the Church has not been content with this conclusion, but has insisted on a stricter rule which would forbid us to save the lorry driver from roasting, even at his own entreaty. I now want to try to sum up more clearly my answer to this question (my explanation, that is to say, of the Church's attitude). I shall then try to say what I think is sound and what is unsound in this attitude.

The Church has insisted on a strict and simple rule about homicide because it has felt that, unless we have a strict and simple rule, it is going to be difficult to inculcate any rule at all. 'For if the trumpet give an uncertain sound, who shall prepare himself to the battle?' (1 Cor. 14: 8). In pulpits and in confessionals priests need to be able to tell people clearly and definitely that it is sinful to do certain simply described things. The Church has therefore adopted as simple rules as it has found it possible to do, not only about homicide, but about sex and about all the other important moral questions. Whenever hard cases have occurred or have been thought up, the Church has tried to allow for them by relatively simple modifications of the strict rule—but always such modifications as at any rate *seem* to leave its essential simplicity unimpaired. But such extensions are often resisted with the 'thin end of the wedge' argument: if you admit this qualification to the simple principle, where are you going to stop? The frequency with which this argument is used shows the attraction of simplicity. If abortion is in some cases allowed to be legitimate, why not in all cases? If abortion, then why not infanticide? If infanticide, why not the killing of adults? This argument is appealing above all to those who do not want to have to think about complex particularities, but rather to have a good simple rule and stick to it.

I think that this is a sound attitude. Just now I quoted St Paul's remark about battles. Soldiers (and officers) are trained in the simple rule, not to run away in battle. There are no doubt cases in which it would be perfectly all right, and even tactically useful, if they ran away; but if soldiers in the middle of battles allowed themselves to ask whether their own might not be one of these cases, they would all persuade themselves that it was, and run away. And that is why good soldiers will not run away even when it is tactically harmless or even useful; they just do not think of it; they wait for the order to withdraw given by somebody who, they hope, is not subject to the same stress as they are, and who can therefore weigh up what is tactically useful with less temptation to special pleading. I have used this military example; I could have given an equally good one from the field of sex, but I will forbear.

It is not just that these simple rules are useful to those in authority (though undoubtedly they are that). Even when a man has attained a high degree of moral autonomy, he had better have some fairly simple rules and stick to them if he does not want to be constantly at the mercy of the temptation to introduce exceptions to them when it suits his own interest. The upright man will quite often refrain from telling lies which it would be absolutely harmless or even beneficial to tell; because he is upright, it does not occur to him to tell them. And, because he is upright, he will in the course of his life approximate incomparably more often, in the matter of truth-telling, to the actions which would be prescribed by the ideally impartial and universally benevolent spectator (by God, we might say) than does a man who is prepared to ask on each occasion whether it would be right to tell a lie; because the latter, being human and far from an ideally impartial prescriber, will as often as not convince himself that it would be right to tell a lie when that would be in his own interest. This is the truth in the remark of St Ignatius (which Professor Anscombe is fond of quoting) that when the Devil wants to tempt us, the best means he has is to get us to consider peculiar cases in which it would be beneficial to depart from the simple general rules of morality (see H 1972*a*).

So I am on the side of the Church in liking to have these simple rules. But I think that the Church—at any rate to judge by the pronouncements of prominent members of it— has often gone wrong in two related ways. The first is that it gives to these simple rules an epistemological status to which they have no claim; the second is that it cuts morality off from its roots by producing these simple and admittedly useful rules without giving for them the only sort of reason which can really form the basis of an acceptable and stable morality, namely the words of Christ which I quoted at the beginning.

Let me start with the first point. I have implied that there is a sense in which we ought not to question the simple moral rules of the upright man. But it is easy to confuse this sense with another sense in which we certainly ought to question them, if we are ever to satisfy ourselves of the reasons for them. In the heat of battle, perhaps, soldiers ought not to question the rule about running away, or they will all run away. But if we ask, as we ought to ask, Why ought soldiers to have this rule, and is it the right rule, or should it be qualified in some particular respect to allow for an important class of cases in which it is not, as it stands, the best rule?—if we ask this, as Bishop Butler put it, in a cool hour (but remembering always the battles of which we have had experience, or the wisdom of those who have had experience of battles), then we are not displaying a corrupt mind (Anscombe 1958: 17), but rather doing something which has to be done if morality is to survive. We have seen plenty of examples in recent times of the breakdown of morality in families and in whole societies. If my experience is anything to go by, the cause is nearly always the same: that those who believed in these good simple rules failed to question them in the second of my two senses. The result was that their beliefs lost their roots, withered into mere conformism or lip-service, and could not reproduce themselves—or even produce moral beliefs of any kind—in a new generation. They were sterile.

There is no better way of remedying this evil than by seeking again the roots of morality in the duty to love our neighbour as ourselves. I shall not be able to do this for all our moral principles; I shall in what space remains apply this injunction of Christ's in what will have to be a very summary way to the problem of euthanasia. I have argued that a principle about euthanasia which was in accord with Christ's words could not possibly rule it out in all cases. I have also explained why the Church, on the other hand, has usually advocated just such a complete prohibition. Is any synthesis between these positions possible? I think that it is. Though I maintained that Christ's words, for anybody who takes them and the facts seriously, rule out a ban on euthanasia in the case of the lorry driver that I described, I said that my conclusion from this was limited and negative. It certainly does not follow from anything that I have said that euthanasia ought to be morally approved of, or legalized, indiscriminately. I would hope that the recognition by Christians of the inconsistency with Christ's words of a complete prohibition might lead them to address themselves to what is, I am convinced, the really important field of dispute—namely the question of how to formulate a moral principle governing this matter which is neither too restrictive nor too permissive. I see no reason why Christians and non-Christians should not co-operate in such an enquiry, once they have understood the points which I have been trying to make in this paper.

In that discussion, the argument on one side will lay stress on the duty to relieve the suffering of the patient and—far less importantly but not negligibly—that of other people. On the other side emphasis will be laid on the immense practical dangers that would attend any relaxation of an absolute prohibition. There is the danger, for example, that moral pressure would be put on people to allow their death to be hastened, when the real purpose of those exercising the pressure was their own convenience. I have heard of a doctor who said 'We shall start by administering euthanasia to put patients out of intolerable suffering; we shall end up doing it because we want to get away for the weekend.'

It is worth noticing that both these arguments, and not only the first, can claim to be based on the duty to love our neighbour. For, once we have abandoned the reliance on unreasoned traditional rules, we shall, in arguing the case against euthanasia, just as much as in arguing for it, have to rely on the need to avoid harming the interests of people unnecessarily. I am myself much more moved by this sort of argument than I am by the more traditional sort. I could even say that I do not know of any principle simple enough to be incorporated in legislation that seems to me preferable to the present practice of many doctors. This is based on an application of the principle of double effect (a principle which I gravely distrust, but which in this case seems to give the right answer); they give the patient enough drugs to relieve his pain, even when they know that this will also be enough to kill him, arguing that their intention is to relieve and not to kill.

However, it is one thing to ask what prohibitions and permissions ought to be written into the law, and another to ask what are the moral duties of individuals when faced with given situations. Suppose that a Euthanasia Bill similar to those which have recently been proposed were actually passed. What then would be the duties of doctors if patients requested euthanasia under the new Act? There would then be no arguing that euthanasia was morally wrong just because it was illegal (though I do think that if acts are illegal, that creates some presumption that they are immoral too; there is a *general* duty to obey the law, which, however, can have exceptions). But equally well the fact that euthanasia was legally permitted would not entail that it was morally permissible. Doctors would therefore have a moral problem on their hands. And I think myself that the only way that they could solve it would be by considering carefully the individual case and applying Christ's words to it. That is to say, they must think themselves into the position of the individual patient whom they are treating and do to him what they wish to be done to them if they were in a like position. No doubt, because of the difficulty of doing this in every individual case, and because of the dangers I have mentioned, wise doctors will make for themselves rules, in the light of their experience, which they do not easily depart from. But I do not think that these rules will amount to an absolute ban on complying with the wishes of patients for euthanasia as provided by the supposed Act.

Do I think that such an Act should be passed? I am ready to grant the absolute sincerity of people like Dr Cicely Saunders, who have made it their business to find out ways of making terminal patients happy and thus avoiding the necessity for euthanasia. I am prepared to believe that, if these methods are as devotedly used as they are by her, it really is unnecessary in most cases. But I also know, from my own personal experience and from that of close acquaintances, that the reality often does not correspond to her ideal. I know that aged people whose minds have gone present a particularly difficult problem.

However, this said, I might well be on the same side as her in opposing the sort of bill that is likely to be put forward, because of the immense practical difficulties and dangers. But I hope that those who feel as I do about this will not nail their flag to the very simple rule but will make a serious attempt to discuss and deal with this difficult and distressing problem, taking into account the economic impossibility of providing for everyone the sort of care for the dying that we should perhaps wish for ourselves, or indeed of providing all the medical help that could and ideally should be given even to those who are not dying and could be restored to health. As a last suggestion, which I have no time to develop, I am inclined to think that, if any legislation is desirable, it would better take the form, not of a Euthanasia Bill, but of a fairly small and fairly simple amendment to the law about suicide. For since the consent of the patient ought, in the view of most supporters of euthanasia, to be a necessary condition for it, it seems not unreasonable to suggest that the act should, in some sense, be that of the patient. This, at any rate, seems reasonable for the case of competent adults. For the cases of infants and incompetent adults this solution is not available; but these cases are outside the scope of my discussion in this paper.

5

How did Morality Get a Bad Name?

'I'm not making any moral judgements, of course' (sniff). How often have we not heard ordinary middle-class, moderately enlightened but not terribly sophisticated people say this sort of thing? I have read in the newspapers and elsewhere much to the same effect. This attitude to morality became popular a long time ago; even in 1971 it was not at all unexpected to see Paul Ferris, in the *Observer Review* (18 July), in a very good article called 'Teenage Sex: The New Dilemma', slipping into this way of speaking. He was discussing the problems of doctors at contraceptive clinics, and others who have to advise teenage girls about contraception and thus about sex generally: whether it is best to give them all the pills they ask for to prevent unwanted pregnancies, or to encourage them to keep off the pill *and* off extramarital sex in view of the dangers of venereal disease and the general undesirability of such behaviour. In the article the word 'moral' and its derivatives occur seven times only; nearly all these are heavily deprecatory; all represent morality as something extraneous and irrelevant to the real issue; and not one so much as suggests that the problem which is troubling these doctors is a moral question—though it *is* a moral question in what I think is the central sense of the word 'moral'. Here are some examples:

[a doctor speaking]: I've tried to dissuade girls, but . . . no amount of moralising on my part will stop them.

[with reference to a pamphlet of the Family Planning Association]: All it did, in fact, was to list the dismal alternatives [such as abortion and forced marriage], without any talk about 'immorality'. This absence of moralising gave considerable offence within the FPA.

[a pharmacist and chairman of the Birmingham Health Committee

Previously unpublished.

speaking, and justifying his authority's refusal to support the Brook Clinic]: It is a moral issue. A responsible public body doesn't want to condone things, to say 'Open the doors and let everyone have a good old time.'

[Paul Ferris himself]: From many quarters comes evidence of disquiet about sexual behaviour, especially the behaviour of the young. The moralists have no time for those who advocate cheap and easy contraception for teenagers either as their right, or as a lesser evil than unwanted pregnancy and abortion.... What complicates the picture is that contraception for teenagers is a special case, or seems to be. This is true not only for the moralists, but for many who would regard themselves as sexual liberals.

In the same way, Catherine Storr, in an article on marriage in the *Observer* supplement at about the same time, used the expression 'the morality brigade'.

Why is it that morality has come to stink in this way? I am going to answer that it is because many people have a quite misconceived idea of what morality is supposed to be. As it is not just one misconception that is current, but a whole complex of them that reinforce one another, most of what I say will be devoted to taking them one by one and explaining why they are misconceptions. Only then shall I be in a position to go on and say what *I* think morality is, and why we have such a thing, and what would be the disadvantages if we stopped having it. But in order to make clear what I am driving at when I speak about the misconceptions, I will start by just sketching what I think is the essential function of moral judgements. This is something so spare and formal that it may well be asked how they could have any application to our practical concerns; and many ordinary people (like many, perhaps most, of my philosophical colleagues) may think that I am just wrong in what I say morality is—that I have not put enough into it to make it of any use. I shall try later to show that my formal account of morality *is* enough to make it serve its purposes, and that to attempt to write any more into it actually defeats those purposes. But I am not yet in a position to do this.

The person who makes a moral judgement is offering guidance or advice about what somebody should do in some kind of situation. If the somebody is not somebody else, but himself (and this is really the central case), we do not speak of his *advising* himself, but what he is doing is similar: he is taking counsel with himself, and saying or thinking something that he can follow or act on in what he does. The advice may be about a particular situation; but it applies by implication to *any* situation which shares the features which made him make this judgement about this situation. And if he is uncertain just exactly what those features are (it is sometimes difficult to say just what it is about the situation that makes us say that *this* is what one should do) then he can always get out of the difficulty by saying 'at any rate my advice would apply to any situation that was *just* like this one'. This requirement to universalize our moral judgements is, as we shall see, one of their most important features.

Sometimes the guidance that is given by a moral judgement is not directed to any actual situation in particular, but to all situations which share a certain feature. This happens when we say things like 'One should never treat people as if they existed simply for one's own convenience.' The guidance here is quite universal; it is meant to apply to *any* situation in which somebody is tempted to do this. That is why we can make moral judgements about past or imaginary situations; we cannot act in these situations; but situations *like* them may occur, and, if we have accepted the guidance in principle, this will help us when they do.

Not all guidance-giving is moral. We also give prudential advice, which is about how best to advance the interests of the person advised, without thought for anybody else's interests; and technical advice, which is about how best to realize some particular end, which may or may not be a morally desirable one. The task of distinguishing moral advice from these other kinds is a difficult one, which I shall not embark on now. I shall touch on it later.

The first thing that many people hold against those who make moral judgements (sometimes they say 'who *pass* moral judgements') is that they are being *censorious*. 'Who are you to pass moral judgements on me?', they say. This association of the phrase 'moral judgement' is due more to the word 'judgement' than to the word 'moral', as the existence of the phrase 'pass judgement' (without the word 'moral' at all) shows. Passing judgement is something that judges do; and judges are people to whom society has given a special position (an especially elevated position, not shared by the rest of us), from which they can look down on the prisoners in the dock and pass judgement on them for their misdemeanours. So, it is thought, if we pass moral judgements on other people, we are not merely being censorious; we are claiming an *authority* to be censorious. We are, by implication, claiming that we are the embodiment of the moral law, which *other people* have broken. It would not be surprising if such a posture made us unpopular.

Since this false association of the phrase 'moral judgement' will go on confusing us unless I get rid of it now, I must explain that it is due to a quite irrelevant historical accident that philosophers use the expression 'moral judgement' in the technical sense in which I am using it. In the generation of philosophers of whom Bradley and Bosanquet and, a good deal later, their disciple Joachim were typical representatives (i.e. from about 1880 to about 1930), the word 'judgement' was used as the most general word for *any* act or product of thinking. It took the place of the word 'proposition', which had been used for this purpose by many earlier thinkers, emphasizing, more than 'proposition' did, the *act* of thinking as opposed to the *product* or the *content* of thought, but comprehending all of these. There were, just before my time as an undergraduate at Oxford, some famous lectures called 'Joachim on the Judgement', which were not, as might be thought, about the last trump or anything like that, but were a very difficult and profound account of what it is to think, involving a lot about the logical relations between universal judgements, particular judgements, hypothetical judgements, categorical judgements, and so on—in fact all the stuff that one has to go into if one engages in the study called, according to fashion, either metaphysics, or conceptual analysis, or just logic, which will always be the kernel of any genuine philosopher's work, as it has been from Socrates onwards.

The word 'judgement', then, had, as it was used by philosophers, absolutely no association with the special position of judges. The person who makes a moral judgement is, in this sense, simply someone who does a piece of moral thinking, forms a moral opinion, and perhaps, if he is sufficiently bold to give somebody else the product of his thought, makes a moral statement, or, more grandly, propounds a moral proposition. He is not offending against the precept 'Judge not, that ye be not judged', any more than is the person who, in Joachim's terminology, makes a hypothetical judgement (for example, the judgement that if it rains tomorrow the roads will be slippery).

I have myself found 'judgement' a useful word to use in talking about the products of moral thought, for reasons which I will now briefly explain. When it was generally realized (during the period that began in about 1910) that not all the things that we say or think are about matters of fact, and that this is of importance for philosophy, one of the first applications of this doctrine was to moral philosophy. It was suggested that perhaps moral judgements were not statements of fact in the narrow sense; and the first attempt to say what they might be, if not statements of fact, was the so-called 'emotive theory of ethics'. This held that in making a moral judgement what we are doing is expressing a feeling or an attitude (for example, of approval), or seeking to arouse it in other people. Not many people hold this theory now; but in trying to find out what was right or wrong with it, it was most important to have a terminology which did not beg questions against the theory. If one said 'moral statement', for example, one would be loading the scales against a theory which held that moral utterances do not express statements at all. So the word 'judgement' found favour, as sufficiently neutral between the emotive theory and its opponents. And it seems to have stuck, although 'moral statement' is now often used, now that the controversies started by the emotivists have to some extent subsided.

The purpose of this historical digression has been to warn us not to read more into the technical expression 'moral judgement', as used by philosophers, than it really contains. I will now go on with my list of misconceptions of what morality is. I have said, so far, that the person who makes a moral judgement (or expresses a moral opinion) is not necessarily being censorious, nor is he arrogating to himself an authority over those about whom he is making the judgement, or claiming to be in any way superior to them. I do not want to deny that there are censorious people, or people who like to assume a superior attitude to others. All I am saying is that one can express a moral opinion without doing this.

There are, however, other misconceptions about morality which are less easily dispelled. These form, with those that I have already mentioned, an amalgam which is hard to divide into its constituents, because they are easily mixed with one another, and thus, as I have said, reinforce one another. I will just run through them, and it will be clear why this is so. Morality is thought of as something handed down by tradition and known by everyone to be true—an institution that we had nothing to do with setting up, imposed on us by those unpleasant people that I mentioned earlier. They can give no reasons why they try to impose it on us—indeed, it sometimes seems to be implied that it is presumptuous to ask for reasons. It is also thought that, because there is sometimes a conflict between duty and interest (as indeed there is), morality is something that has nothing to do with human interests, and can even be antagonistic to them. It is something which exists to prevent us from enjoying ourselves. Even if we do not go as far as that, it is easy to think that morality is something that disregards people and their interests and even their ideals. This conception of morality is often quite wrongly fathered on Kant, although he lays enormous emphasis on the duty to promote the ends and the happiness of other people (e.g. 1797: A34 = 398). This would be most unfortunate if it led us to think that personal interests and ideals are not relevant to moral questions in the ordinary sense of the word.

We may perhaps sum up what is thought objectionable in all these supposed features of morality by saying that, if morality is as these people conceive it to be, *we* have no say in deciding what we ought to or ought not to do; we just ought or ought not, irrespective of our or other people's interests and ideals, and no reason can be given why we ought, other than just that we ought. All this is of course a caricature; but it is worth while sketching it in, because it is a caricature which lies in the background of many people's thinking about, and perhaps rejection of, morality; this bogy can be exorcized only by bringing it out into the open.

If we are to exorcize it, there is one basic source of confusion that must be exposed, because it underlies many of these misconceptions. It is connected with the word 'objectivity'—a word which, with its opposite, 'subjectivity', has caused more confusions in ethics than perhaps any other, and indeed might best be abandoned altogether from the subject, since there is not much practical hope of ever securing for it an unmuddled use (see H 1976*b*). It is crucial to be clear about the distinction between subjectivism (the view that moral judgements state facts about the subjective states of the speaker or of people generally—for example, approval and disapproval) and non-descriptivism (the view that their central function is different from that of stating facts). The former view is open to many serious objections, but some form of the latter is probably correct. Both views, however, are opposed to objectivism— the view that moral judgements do nothing but state facts about the world independent of people's subjective states.

The harm of objectivism, and the reason why it gives rise to many of the misconceptions I have mentioned, is that it represents moral thought as a process of discovering facts with whose origin we have had nothing to do, and which we just have to accept. It is indeed true that in moral thinking there are facts that we have to face—things are as they are. About these facts we have to be objective. We have to accept that the situation in which we find ourselves is as it is. But the question of what we ought to do in such a situation is not a question of fact, but a question of a very different sort—a question demanding a decision on our part; and any theory which robs us of this decision will be rejected by anybody who understands what moral thinking is and is trying to do it. So he will not be content to be told that such and such is what is traditionally believed or accepted by common consensus or that it just is the case that we ought to do so and so, and no reasons can be given.

If anyone *is* content to be told this, there is a still greater danger, namely that he will recognize that he 'ought' to do this or that, but will not regard that as, in the least, a reason for doing it. On such 'So what?' moralities see pp. 159 f. They are the almost inevitable result of a thoroughgoing objectivism. If we are faced with the choice of retaining either the certitude as to what we ought to do, or the certitude that what we think we ought to do is what we are going to do if we can, it is always the latter that we should retain.

At this point we have emerged from theory into practice; I hope that it will not be hard to recognize examples of what I am speaking about. It is no use saying to people who are thinking seriously about morality that extra-marital sex is just wrong, or that it is just wrong to appear naked on the stage. They will want to be let in on the processes of thought or reasoning that could lead to such conclusions; and if there is no reasoning, they will not accept the conclusions. If we want to take people with us, especially the young, we shall have to do some moral thinking and let them share in it; we shall have to ask the moral questions that they are asking, and join in finding answers to them. What makes it necessary, and more than an academic exercise, to find answers is that we and they have to act in the world, and how we act is going to depend on the answers we give to the questions.

This is especially important in a pluralist society, which is what ours is (see pp. 137 ff.). A pluralist society is one in which people who accept very different moral viewpoints are trying to live together in amity. If there are all these different viewpoints accepted by different sections of society, and somebody stands up in the pulpit and says that one of these viewpoints is the right one and all the others are wrong, the congregation, if it has not gone to sleep, will want to know *why* he thinks this. They get all the other viewpoints put before them in the newspapers and on television, and they know a great many people who are trying to live according to them. It is no use just *proclaiming* Christian morality. What we have to do is to start with the questions which people are asking: 'Ought I to give my daughter a latchkey at her age?' and the like, and try to *understand the questions*, and, as a result of this understanding, to answer them and give reasons for the answers. Only then shall we be able to make any contribution to the discussion when we meet our friends who do not accept the Christian viewpoint.

The trouble with 'objectivity' is that it tends to occupy the stage in these discussions about morality to the exclusion of the subject that really ought to be occupying it, namely *rationality*. People tend to confuse these two notions (see *MT*, ch. 12). The really important thing to get hold of is that it is possible to *reason* about what one ought to do. To show this is a prime task for moral philosophy. But people keep on urging moral philosophers to undertake another task, which is not important in the least, even if a sense can be given to it: the task of showing that moral judgements are 'objective'. Of course there is a sense in which they are objective—the sense in which it means the same as 'rational'. In this sense moral judgements are objective if any rational thinker must agree to them; and this perhaps *can* be shown. But to show it does not demand showing that they are objective in the sense of being descriptive or factual.

The best way of showing that it is possible to reason about morality is to do it; and that is what I recommend. But in this paper all I aim to do is to say how I think the possibility of moral reasoning comes from the nature of the moral concepts themselves. Morality is most essentially a kind of language. I anticipate here what I shall be saying at greater length on pp. 154 ff. and 188 ff. It is a kind of language of relatively recent origin, having grown up within historical times in the same way as the language of mathematics has, the Christian contribution to its growth being very great. Its two central features are those I have mentioned already. First, a moral judgement is something that, if you agree with it, you act on; this feature is known by philosophers as *prescriptivity*. Secondly, one is not allowed to make different moral judgements about two situations which one agrees to be identical; this feature is what philosophers call *universalizability*. These two formal features of moral judgements are the basis of all moral reasoning. Both of them are implicit in the injunction 'As you wish people to do to you, do the same to them' (see pp. 62, 72).

I suggest in all seriousness that, when we are faced with moral problems, and when we are discussing these problems with other people, who may not share our detailed moral opinions, these formal features are what we should start from. I am firmly convinced that anybody who is talking about morality at all, and understands what it is, will accept these two formal features of the language he is using, and that, if he accepts them, argument can get going. I am convinced of this because in a number of studies of practical moral problems such as those concerning war, revolution, medical ethics, etc. I have always found that these two features could serve as a basis for a treatment of the problems which ought to satisfy people starting from quite diverse initial standpoints. This is common ground on which they can meet and discuss the questions which concern them all.

The answer, then, to the problem of how to live in a pluralist society is to use the language of morality, relying on its formal features alone, and not trying to presuppose any particular content to our morality before the argument begins (that would merely scare off those who do not share our presuppositions). The beauty of the Christian approach to morality, as expressed in the words I have quoted, is that it is completely formal, yet at the same time immensely powerful as a weapon in moral argument.

Suppose that we are engaged in an argument about sex. If we start with all kinds of presuppositions about chastity as a divine command and that kind of thing, we shall lose the non-Christian parties to the argument right at the beginning. They will simply stop listening, because they do not accept that kind of authority. But if, instead, we ask them what they are ready to prescribe universally for anybody in a situation of a given sort, no matter at which end of the situation they may find themselves, then at least they have to start thinking what it is like for the other parties in the situation. They have, in fact, to start trying to love the other parties as themselves, which means, at least, considering their interests on a level with their own (or, as Kant put it, making others' ends their own ends (1785: BA 66 f. = 429 f.)). And this is the basis of sexual morality, as of all morality. If we could follow this method to the full, nothing could go wrong with our sexual morality. That is, if everyone showed as much consideration for the interests of the other parties to their love affairs (not just their partners, but all those affected, including the actual or possible, existing or future, children of all of them), and were therefore concerned to provide a stable framework in which those interests could be looked after, then nothing could go wrong; what we should have, in fact, would be Christian marriage, in more than a conventional sense. But that is the conclusion of the reasoning; and I hope that, if we started with the formal features of morality, and were careful to take our non-Christian through the details and keep him with us all the time, he would follow us that far. And I would hope that the same would be true if we were talking about revolution, for example.

My advice, then, to those living in a pluralist society, is not to go to rallies in Trafalgar Square with the 'morality brigade' to protest against pornography and the like, but to preach the Christian doctrine of love, interpreted in the way I have tried to interpret it, that is to say in an entirely formal way. If we follow this advice, we may find that we get people to think morally with us, instead of parting company just because we are talking about morality, and because they think that morality is something that no enlightened person will have anything to do with. That, at least, is my experience.

All I have to add is a horror story about what is likely to happen if morality in *my* sense gets lost (as I suppose it might, just as we might forget how to do mathematics). After what I have said, I hope I shall not be misunderstood; it would not be too tragic if morality in the style of Malcolm Muggeridge, Mary Whitehouse, and Victoria Gillick got lost—that is to say, a morality that has nothing to do with love but only with repression. I do not deny that these people do some good, if only by castigating the opposite party (Richard Neville and all those), who are just as bad. But what I want to urge above all is that if we stop asking moral questions in *my* sense (the formal one), and acting as best we can on the answers to them, then not only in matters of sex but in all other moral issues (and of course, in spite of the people that Paul Ferris quoted, sexual morality is only a very small part of morality)—if we stop asking moral questions and trying to act on the answers to them, the world will become a much nastier place even than it is.

The reason why I say this is that moral thought is an essential factor in the functioning of any society in which people try to live together—and especially, as I said, if it is a pluralist society. For the interests of the different individuals in that society, and perhaps their ideals too, are bound to conflict. If they stop asking moral questions, in answering which they would have, for the reasons I have given (connected with universalizability), to give equal weight to the interests of other people, then presumably the questions they will ask will be prudential questions about *their own* interests or those of a highly selective list of people for whom they feel some kind of concern. The result will be a pursuit of self-interest ending up in a war of every man against every man. That is what life would be like in the absence of morality.

Those who attack morality conceal this from themselves by the kind of language that they use. They seem to imply that if we could all get rid of our moral inhibitions and give free rein to our impulses (especially in sexual matters) then the world would be all love, and a heaven on earth could begin. But many of people's interests (though not of course all) are selfish ones; and it is very easy to persuade oneself that one is being sincere and open and uninhibited and all kinds of other good things, when what one is really doing is seeking what will satisfy one's own lusts. I return to this topic on pp. 107 f. below.

Morality, in sex as in other matters, is a wonderful and indeed indispensable invention for enabling people to love one another without hurting one another. If clergymen and others could preach *this* gospel whole-heartedly, we might not be so troubled by amoralism. I am not saying that it is easy to think morally and live accordingly. On the contrary, it is very difficult. But have we ever supposed otherwise? We can at least remove some of the obstacles by getting rid of false ideas of what morality is; and that is what I have been trying to do.

6

Satanism and Nihilism

In this paper I wish to discuss two sorts of things that can easily go wrong in the transition from intuitive to critical thinking—that is, from the everyday moral thinking that suffices, and should suffice, for most of our moral thought, to the higher-level thinking that we have to do if we need to scrutinize the principles we are using at the intuitive level. This is a transition which in the course of our moral education we all have to learn to make if we are ever to get beyond intuitive moral thinking. I shall give to these two pitfalls in moral education the perhaps rather too dramatic names 'Satanism' and 'Nihilism'. They both have some kinship with the amoralism that I discussed in *MT*, chs. 10 and 11; but they are different from it and from each other, though all three can be combined in various more or less confused mixtures. The discussion of these pitfalls will enable me both to clear up a theoretical difficulty which has often been raised against my views, and to shed some light on a pressing social problem.

The theoretical difficulty is this. How, on the view of a prescriptivist like myself, is it possible for somebody deliberately to do wrong just because it is wrong? Once, when I was young and inexperienced, I thought this so easy a problem that in *LM* 175 I left it as an exercise for the reader, in the unfounded hope that I would not be troubled with it further. But many people think that it is possible to pursue evil just because it is evil. It is well known that various colourful figures, from Satan in *Paradise Lost* (*PL*) to Eartha Kitt in one of her songs, have claimed to do just this. A former pupil of mine once presented me with a gramophone record of Miss Kitt singing her song 'I Want to Be Evil'; and he wrote on the sleeve:

Previously unpublished.

For your rogues' gallery, dear Mr Hare,
To set beside the Devil and Baudelaire.

Actually, I do not think that Baudelaire himself was like the Devil, and so perhaps he should be left out of this discussion— though I shall be alluding to one of his characters. But the names of Casanova, de Sade, Théophile Gautier, Huysmans, Oscar Wilde (not for his own performances but for those of his character Dorian Gray), and Aleister Crowley are often mentioned in this connection (for examples, see Gaunt 1945). My favourite, though, is not any of these, but another instance with whom I happen to be more familiar, namely Miles in Britten's opera *The Turn of the Screw*— partly because I find this incipient boy Satanist a more attractive subject than the middle-aged variety. He eagerly assents as Quint, representing the Devil, sings to him:

> I'm all things strange and bold,
> The riderless horse
> Snorting, stamping on the hard sea sand,
> The hero highwayman plundering the land.
> I am King Midas with gold in his hand.
> I am the smooth world's double face.
> Mercury's heels
> Feathered with mischief and a god's deceit.
> The brittle blandishments of counterfeit.
> In me secrets, half-formed desires meet . . .

(1. 7)

The libretto was based by Myfanwy Piper (1955) on Henry James's short novel with the same title.

It is important not to confuse the Satanist with the weak-willed person or backslider, although both have been thought to create trouble for me. Satan is not *weak*—far from it. He is as tenacious of his purpose as the just man in Horace (*Odes*, 3. 3). The backslider does what is evil, not because he wants, or purposes, to do evil for its own sake, but because he wants something else which he cannot have without doing evil. The Satanist, by contrast, is alleged to want to do evil just because it is evil. I am not now going to say any more about the backslider, about whom I have already written a lot (*FR*, ch. 5; *MT* 57–60; H 1992c). The Satanist, however, is thought to give me trouble for a rather similar reason: if moral judgements were prescriptive as I say, it is hard to see how someone could want to do evil just because it was evil; for this would seem to be to accept simultaneously a prescription and a prohibition with the same content. I know that it is commonly and perhaps rightly said that a sufficiently irrational person can think contradictory things; but one should hesitate to take this way out if there is a better one.

Does Satan have any practical importance? Aleister Crowley and the others are an eccentric lot, and it might be argued that such people are never likely to be numerous, and that the world would be less interesting without a few of them. Besides, some of them wrote very well. But the reason why the question has practical importance is that a large—perhaps increasing—number of people behave in ways resembling these cases. Perhaps something important is to be learnt about the motivations of some quite unpoetical people by studying these peculiar cases. We must not jump to conclusions about any individual case; but every time I read in the papers about some boys who have, for example, unscrewed a section of railway line, or about some young men who have battered an old lady to death, not from any financial or political motive, but just 'for kicks', I am set thinking what could make them do it; and then I think that perhaps a clearer understanding of these extreme cases, leading to a clearer understanding of morality itself, would put us into a better position to deal with this difficult social problem.

The first thesis that I want to maintain about the Satanist is that he could not exist unless moral judgements were thought to be purely descriptive statements of fact. I deliberately said 'thought to be'. The thought that the circle could be squared would do as well to set people trying to square the circle as its actually being squarable. If this thesis were true, it would explain why descriptivists have seized so eagerly upon the existence of Satanism as evidence that moral judgements *are* purely descriptive; but, as we shall see, it only shows that the Satanists themselves, and no doubt a sizeable and influential part of their society, *use* them in a purely descriptive way. It remains perfectly possible that they are misunderstanding their use. But this I shall amplify later. I must make it clear that in what follows, as usual, I shall use 'descriptive' for short to mean 'purely descriptive'; prescriptivists can well grant, and I do grant, that moral judgements have a descriptive *element* in their meaning. We must also be clear that in my terminology, which I think corresponds to normal usage, *some* moral judgements are purely descriptive; it is the prescriptive or evaluative moral judgements which cause the trouble. For these distinctions see *FR* 26 ff.

We can see that Satanism requires a descriptivist background if we take the case of Satan himself as Milton portrays him. He says:

> but of this be sure,
> To do aught good never will be our task,
> But ever to do ill our sole delight,
> As being the contrary to his high will
> Whom we resist.
>
> (*PL* 1. 158)

Suppose we ask 'How does Satan know what in particular to do?' To be a Satanist one has first to find out what is the good or right thing to do, and then deliberately do the opposite just because it is wrong or evil. So it would seem that the Satanist at any rate must rely on moral words having a descriptive meaning. This, however, does not necessarily make him a descriptivist; for even prescriptivists, as I have just said, can allow that they have. But, further, he cannot himself determine the descriptive meaning he is going to give to moral words by accepting a general prescriptive principle; for that would bring with it a prohibition on *doing* the acts stigmatized in the principle as evil, and such a prohibition he rejects. So he has to rely on some external source (some authority) to determine the descriptive meanings of the moral principles against which he is going to rebel. God was such a source of authority for Satan. If moral judgements were purely descriptive in their meaning, then the thought which led to their adoption would be confined to the intuitive level. We could never criticize, ourselves, the moral principles which our intuitions (if we are intuitionists) or the descriptive meanings of the moral words (if we are naturalists) deliver. We see here the connection between prescriptivity and what

is called moral autonomy. Satan achieves a perverse autonomy by retaining the delivered descriptive meaning and the
intuitions, affirming the moral judgements which they require, but then adopting *his own* prescription to do the
opposite of what is demanded by them. He could not do this
without self-contradiction if the judgements he was making
were prescriptive. Whether Satan's rebel prescriptions are
moral prescriptions depends on how we understand that
slippery word. They may well be overriding and prescriptive
and universalizable, and therefore moral in that sense; but
they are not moral, if the word is defined in terms of content as
Sir Geoffrey Warnock would wish (1967: 55 ff.). Satan
represents all those who, in order not to be trapped in the
intuitive level, think it necessary to throw over morality
altogether, because they have not realized that there is a
critical level.

Satan, then, in order to know what to rebel against, has to
have an external source of moral principles. It might be
objected that even someone who wants to do what is good,
instead of what is evil, needs such a source. But this would be
a mistake. To argue thus is to beg the question in favour of
descriptivism. For non-descriptivists can follow Socrates in
thinking that to pursue something *is* to think of it as good. The
good is what everything pursues or desires, as Aristotle says
(1094^{a}2). *Quicquid appetitur, appetitur sub specie boni.* There
are not, therefore, two stages in the procedure, one consisting
in finding out what is good and the other in deciding whether
or not to pursue it (nor, I must add, as the subjectivists think,
one consisting in pursuing it and the other in calling it good
because that is what we are pursuing). A non-descriptivist is
not faced with the problem of how, *before* we start pursuing
something, we find out what is good. By pursuing some end,
we already show that we think it good (though not, of course,
that it *is* good—that would be subjectivism —see H 1976*b*,
MT 206 ff.). But this will not do for the Satanist. For in his
case, it is said, he pursues the evil because it is evil; so he must
be able to find out what is good and evil antecedently to
eschewing the former and doing the latter. And that, indeed,
is why descriptivists appeal to the example of Satan in order to
support their case against non-descriptivism.

But it does not support it unless Satan is shown to be correct in his descriptivism. What if Satan were shown to be the victim of muddle and misunderstanding about the use of the moral words? That is what I am going to try to show—not because I hope by clarification to help Satan out of his troubles (he, presumably, is irredeemable), but because there is some hope that we can in this way do something for the proliferating brood of modern Satanists.

Satan thought he could find out what was good and evil by finding out what God commanded or forbade. This, in the situation of *Paradise Lost*, would be the easiest possible way, because in that picture God is portrayed as accessible and his commands knowable, as they notoriously are not in the real world. But it is easy to understand how, even without direct access to the voice of God, human Satanists—or the rest of us for that matter—manage to build up for ourselves a solid, objective-seeming idea of what is evil or wrong. They find the established authorities—the Church, the powers that be, parents, teachers, and the rest—all condemning certain kinds of actions; they have themselves from their earliest years been subject to influences—not all of the same sort—whose effect on them has been that, when they think of certain kinds of actions, they get unmistakable feelings of horror and revulsion —feelings which can easily come to have an attraction because they are exciting. In short, that part of their moral education which consists in the inculcation of prima facie principles and their associated intuitions and feelings has been only too well done. So wrong and evil are solid enough things for the Satanist rebel to identify; he has no difficulty in finding out what they are, and doing them.

If all users of moral language were, as Mackie thought, descriptivists (1977: 35), and were simply in error in thinking that there exist real objects or properties corresponding to the moral words, then Satan would find it even easier, in a way. For he could determine what the *putative* evil things are by observing what people apply the word 'evil' to. Mackie could, I grant, dispose of Satanism, as I wish to do, but by a different method: he could simply point out the error. He seems to have thought that it is a question of fact whether these objects and properties exist, and that therefore, by simply saying to people

'Look, there is no such thing', he could dispel Satanism and many other errors. But what is wrong with this remedy is that people are genuinely confused about their use of the moral words, and it is this confusion and not any factual error that leads to trouble. Mackie has no *empirical* means of showing people that there are no such things—for we have known for a long time that (*pace* the naturalists) they are not *supposed* to be empirically observable. The way to dispel the error (which is not open to Mackie) is to show by conceptual analysis that that is not how the words function. In so far as there are any good arguments for the error theory, they are conceptual ones. But in that case it must be a conceptual error and not a factual one, and its exposure demands conceptual analysis and not, as Mackie seems to think, empirical observation (see *MT* 82 f.).

However, there may be a lot of people who think they are using the words purely descriptively, and therefore can be plausibly thought to be making a factual error—just as there are a great many people who think causes are like wires and pulleys and therefore can plausibly be thought to be making a factual error when they talk as if causes were like this—as if there were real connecting strands between causes and their effects. I do not think that Mackie wants to take the same line with them; he is more likely to say that they are conceptually confused. I therefore do not see why he does not say the same about 'ethical realists'. Either factual error or conceptual confusion could engender Satanism—but the second is much the most plausible explanation.

Descriptivist confusions, and Satanism their consequence, are likely to be most prevalent during the period of decadence of an authoritarian, paternalistic morality. The breakup of Victorian morality in England, and even more the corresponding phenomenon on the Continent, provide examples; and, though I do not think that Baudelaire himself was a Satanist, he certainly expresses this kind of feeling very well when he makes his character in 'Le Vin de l'Assassin' (1857), who is celebrating his murder of his nagging wife, say:

> *Me voilà libre et solitaire!*
> *Je serai ce soir ivre mort;*
> *Alors, sans peur et sans remord,*
> *Je me coucherai sur la terre,*

Et je dormirai comme un chien!
Le chariot aux lourdes roues
Chargé de pierres et de boues,
Le wagon enragé peut bien

Écraser ma tête coupable,
Ou me couper par le milieu,
Je m'en moque comme de Dieu,
Du Diable ou de la Sainte Table! (1857)

There I am, free and alone!
Tonight I shall be dead drunk;
And then, without fear or remorse,
I shall lie down on the ground,

And sleep like a dog!
The cart with its heavy wheels,
Full of stones and mud,
The indignant wagon can, for all I care,

Crush my guilty head,
Or cut me in two pieces,
I laugh at it, as I do at God,
At the Devil and the twelve apostles!

An ecclesiastical hierarchy is always a good backcloth for
Satanism, just because it assumes objective authority, which,
however, is contained in the earthen vessels of a human
priesthood.

Having got thus far, it is easy also to see the attractions of
Satanism. First, it is a blow for liberty. '*Me voilà libre!*' says
Baudelaire's murderer; 'I sdeind subjection' says Satan (*PL* 4.
50). Newman makes much of this aspect of the matter when in
The Dream of Gerontius he makes the devils say:

> The mind bold
> And independent,
> The purpose free,
> So we are told,
> Must not think
> To have the ascendant.
>
> (1865, l. 440)

Newman was condemning as sinful an attitude which he owns
to having had in his youth, in the famous hymn:

I was not ever thus, nor prayed that thou
Shouldst lead me on;
I loved to choose and see my path; but now
Lead thou me on.

(1834)

Newman was an apostate, therefore, from the kind of liberty
we are considering: 'Pride ruled my will', he says; and pride
has always been considered the fundamental sin of Satan.
Newman was no doubt seeking another kind of freedom,
whether, like the second collect in Morning Prayer, we call it
the 'perfect freedom' of God's service, or, without committing
ourselves to such theological terms, we borrow Sir Isaiah
Berlin's allusion (1958) to *The Magic Flute* and call it the
freedom of the temple of Sarastro.

Both kinds of freedom are illusory. That of Satan is illusory
because he has not reckoned with the reactions of God, or
Nature. He says 'Better to reign in Hell than serve in Heaven'
(*PL* 1. 261); but this is bombast, because the mind is *not* its
own place, and cannot 'in it self . . . make a Heav'n of Hell, a
Hell of Heav'n' (*PL* 1. 254). In more philosophical terms: our
actions, and the evaluations which prompt them, take place in
a given situation, which is as it is. We may *wish* that it were
otherwise; but if we want to have any control over our actions
and their consequences, our value-judgements must be about
the situation as it is, and about the alternative courses of
actions, with their alternative consequences, which are
actually available to us. The situation includes other people.
If the consequences of our actions and the reactions of other
people are not at all what we would choose, then it is no use
pretending that what we have obtained is freedom.
Baudelaire's drunkard, who lay on the road, may have said
before he lay down '*Me voilà libre!*'; but was he free when he
was squashed by the wheels of the cart?

But Newman is not free either. It is possible to envisage his
being free in the Sarastran sense if, as he seems to have
supposed, there really was a light giving *particular* guidance,
step by step ('One step enough for me'!). For then he would
just have to go where the light indicated, and, since that
would be where he wanted to go, simply because the light
indicated it, he would have brought his desires and the actual

situation into harmony in one of the two ways that are in theory possible. But it is not particularly unorthodox theology to say that there is no such light—no such step-by-step guidance. An intuitionist account of conscience may pretend so, and those who have never seen the need for critical moral thinking may suppose so; but in fact God, if there be one, has put us into a world in which, if we do not merely drift, some of us at least (and a democrat or a liberal would say as many as can do it) have to 'choose and see our path'; and the unfortunate others, if there are any, will have to take it from them. Newman, when he wrote this hymn, was ill and depressed; I hope it does not represent his considered thought. If it did, we might be tempted to think that he mistook for a divine light the promptings of his own psyche, conditioned by his early upbringing and his later religious struggles. I have said that the early stage of moral education, in which we acquire a conscience, is important; but if we get stuck in it, we are likely to become either Sarastrans or Satanists.

These are two possible reactions to the incipient breakup of a too rigidly established morality, whether we look at it in its social aspect (the Church and society, with their demands for conformity) or in its psychological (the irrational feelings of guilt which anybody who has had a rigid upbringing will experience). They are essentially adolescent reactions, both due to the failure to make the transition from intuitive to critical thinking, i.e. to grow up. The biggest service that philosophy can perform at the present time for moral education is to point out the difference between these two levels of thinking, and thus help people over the divide between them. This was what Socrates was trying to do when in the *Meno*, for example, he laid such stress on the difference between knowledge, or understanding, and right opinion (98b, cited *MT* 1); for, given his account of the relation between knowledge and virtue (a prescriptivist account in some ways) he could be taken as making the same sort of distinction of levels as I have been, and representing the problem of moral education, as I have been representing it, as one about the transition between them.

Before I end I must say a word about what I shall call *nihilism*. To be accurate, I should call it *moral* nihilism—for it is not the rejection of all values whatever, such as I spoke of in H 1960. Moral nihilism is the rejection of all moral values, but is consistent with the retention of other values and of desires, likings, purposes, etc. In its most persuasive form, the argument for nihilism goes something like this. Morality is a set of rules which claim objectivity but have none. These general rules are in any case quite inadequate to cope with particular cases of even ordinary complexity. But, more important, they are a denial of liberty: why should society impose its moral principles on me? I have my own desires to guide me; and so have other people. By being frank about these and dispensing with any external guidance we can surely manage to arrive at an accommodation, a *modus vivendi*, which will satisfy these desires so far as is possible. Why bring in moral rules (see p. 91 above)?

The position of the nihilist is in some ways similar to that of the amoralist, discussed in *MT*, chs. 10 and 11. But his motives are different. Whereas the amoralist is out for himself—he rejects moral rules because they interfere with his pursuit of his own interests—the nihilist sometimes puts on an appearance of almost saintly universal love. He thinks that we can get on without morality because he thinks that we could all share this attitude.

The nihilist's case receives a good deal of support from the fact that the moral rules which are commonly discussed are a rather dubious collection. Certain of them do seem to have some basis in the interests of people; others none. It therefore looks plausible for the nihilist to claim that if moral rules were abandoned altogether, we could still look after our own and other people's interests by other means, and thus we could get rid of the pointless rules without any loss of ability to lead happy and useful lives. Intuitionists are largely responsible for the growth of this attitude, as of Satanism; indeed, whether one becomes a Satanist or a nihilist when one rebels against intuitionism may be partly a matter of temperament. The intuitionists and other 'objectivists' tend to wrap up all our moral rules into a single package; they cannot give reasons for keeping any of them, so there is a great temptation to throw away the lot. The Roman Church has been the worst offender. It thinks it knows the truth about contraception. It is against

God's laws to use contraceptives, and to commit adultery, and to commit murder. Since few even of the faithful see anything wrong in contraception, it would be hard to think of a better way of bringing the moral law into disrepute.

I have the greatest sympathy with the nihilist; but he is nevertheless making a bad mistake—or rather several mistakes. First of all, he is almost certainly making the common confusion between universality and generality (see *MT* 41 and H 1972*a*). Moral principles do not as such have to be highly general; at the critical level they can be as specific as need be, and even at the intuitive level they can be a good deal more specific than is sometimes supposed, although in order to apply to a useful range of cases they have to be to some degree general. Secondly, the nihilist is almost certain to be failing to distinguish between the two levels, just as are the intuitionist moralists against whom he is rebelling. When he rightly finds the intuitive level inadequate, instead of ascending to the critical level he abandons morality altogether. Thirdly, he thinks of morality as something external imposed on people by authority of some sort, whereas at the critical level at least we have to do our own moral thinking. And fourthly, he may not understand the prescriptivity of moral judgements; they may seem to him to have no bearing on what we are to do, and therefore their utterance may seem to him at best a waste of breath.

If the nihilist could be got to understand that critical moral thinking is possible, and that he can do it for himself, and that its function is to guide his and other people's actions, morality might come to life again for him. He might even come to see how hard it would be to do without it. He says that he has his own desires to guide him, and so have other people, and that, by being frank about these and dispensing with external moral constraints, he and they can arrive at an accommodation or *modus vivendi* which will satisfy these desires as much as possible. What he does not see is that any such *modus vivendi* has to be a morality, in the essential sense; otherwise it is unlikely to work.

We all have our desires, and they cannot all be realized, because, as the world is, they conflict. These desires, if expressed, would take the form of *singular* prescriptions: let me do *a*, or let me get *b*. But if these are all we have, we shall end up fighting one another to realize our own desires at the expense of other people. Of course, in theory, we could arrive at an accommodation in a non-violent way by examining all the individual singular desires, and seeing how their realization could be maximized. But this problem in computation is beyond our practical capacity, even if, as is not the case, we had the necessary information about the future results of various courses of conduct. What we actually do is to adopt *principles* of conduct such that we can prescribe their observance by ourselves and other people (by *anybody*) in the specified circumstances—i.e. we universalize our prescriptions. This involves the abnegation of some of our desires in return for securing a principle which requires that others abnegate their similar desires—e.g. the desire to take the food off other people's plates. And this is morality, in its essential character of a set of overriding universal prescriptions. It is the only practicable, and certainly the most convenient, way of achieving the *modus vivendi* that the nihilist says he seeks.

So far as what I have just said goes, the universalization of our prescriptions could be done in highly specific terms, so that we had a multitude of moral principles, each fitting a particular highly specified situation. This would reconcile the desires of different people and establish the *modus vivendi*, if it were possible to carry it out. But it is not in practice possible, for the same sort of reason as it is not possible to carry out the exercise of reconciling people's desires without having a morality at all, as the nihilist proposes. It would be just too complicated. Therefore in practice we adopt for ourselves much more general (but still perhaps not *very* general) prima facie principles and use them in our everyday moral thinking, though keeping them subject to critical appraisal. This, I think, is what we actually do, and it works; I am not making a new proposal, but trying to describe, in a schematic way, the moral thinking that we have found to be apt for our purposes. If morality were better understood, it would not be so much under attack.

I have in this paper considered various types of reaction to the decay of an over-rigid morality: Satanism; Sarastranism; amoralism and nihilism. The cause of them all is that kind of

misunderstanding of the nature of morality which I have
called descriptivism, and in particular the intuitionist variety.
If this bad kind of moral philosophy gets a grip of popular
thinking about morality (and it has done this to too great an
extent) we are likely to see these reactions. Satanism is
perhaps the most important socially, not only because its
results are the most damaging, but because in default of an
understanding of what morality is, it is the most likely to
spread. The evils that I have briefly mentioned can only be
cured by a more effective moral education; and we shall not
have this until we have understood what the problem is.

For this purpose it is quite indispensable to distinguish
between different types of attitude to morality which can lead
to undesirable conduct. To take an example: it is no use
treating a Satanist as if he were a backslider, or vice versa.
The backslider—the person who is too morally weak to do
what he acknowledges he ought to do—needs help to
overcome his weakness. Alcoholism is an obvious example;
irresponsible driving is a less obvious one which needs to be
more studied. If any type of backsliding is serious enough in
its consequences, the person who is liable to it has a duty to
get what help he can in overcoming his weakness; and, if he
does not, and the social effects of it are serious for other
people, society ought to constrain him to.

Satanism is quite different. The Satanist, as I said, is not
weak. He is following, sometimes with tenacity, his own
prescriptions—which is not to deny that others who join his
gang may follow his prescriptions through weakness. The
successful moral re-education of the Satanist involves getting
him to rethink his prescriptions. The first step in this is the
abandonment of all forms of descriptivism. This, indeed, is the
most important thing I have to say in this paper, and it cannot
be said too often to parents and other authorities who are
troubled by Satanism in the young. We have, when children
reach a certain age, to stop trying to impose morality on them
from without. We have, rather, to help them find their own
morality (see pp. 113 ff., 131 ff.). One of the best ways of doing
this is to put them into situations in which they have to do
some moral thinking. It may be said 'We don't have to *put*
people into such situations; they can't avoid being in them

often.' This is true, though there are still too many schools and families in which the reasons for moral and other rules are never explained, and morality is made to appear something external, so that no thinking on one's own part is called for. And so, even if *occasions* for moral thinking present themselves, the need to think is not suggested by anything in the child's environment.

If the values of one's peer group take over from those of one's parents, this does not make things any better; the only good to come of it may be if the contrast between the two stimulates thought. It has often been suggested in recent years that schools could do more to help in the process of moral education, and there are a number of systems and books beginning to be used, the more promising among which lay stress on the need to stimulate critical thinking rather than on the imprinting of the accepted mores (see pp. 137 ff.).

Parents too have to realize that, in a period of rapid social change like the present, their children are more likely to come to have firm moral principles if they have themselves played a part in the critical thinking which is necessary for their selection. And if neither the parents nor the children are doing any critical thinking, it is highly likely that a proportion of the children will never realize its necessity, and that therefore they will achieve only a truncated understanding of what morality is. Of these, some are likely to become Satanists or amoralists or nihilists; and even those who do not will be likely to become Sarastrans, and so do nothing to strengthen morality, although they themselves may observe its requirements.

I do not wish to deny that life in families and elsewhere has to be ruled by external prescriptions in the early stages. But we have to get our children, by the time they reach their teens, accustomed to thinking about moral questions for themselves. Then they will be able to sort out the moral principles which they are going to live by from the irrational prejudices and taboos which they are going to discard—a thing that nobody can do for them. We shall then not be faced so often with people who just discard the lot.

7

Adolescents into Adults

Since I am going to criticize Mr Wilson (1964) in some respects, I must start by saying that I am, in all essentials, on the same side as he is. I believe in a distinction between education and indoctrination; and I believe that indoctrination is a bad thing. But I also believe that he stated his case somewhat too extremely; and I think that by so doing he exposed himself to some possible attacks from the propagandists of indoctrination. It is of the highest importance to safeguard Wilson's liberal views against such attacks; for otherwise advocates of the closed mind and the closed society may find it easier to enlist the support of moderates against Wilson; and that would be a pity. I need to make clear, therefore, that my criticisms of Wilson will bulk large in this paper only because, to avoid repetition, I have left out all those many points on which I should agree with him.

Wilson thinks that education is a good thing, and indoctrination a bad thing; and it is therefore very important for him to state clearly wherein lies the difference. He considers two possibilities: a distinction on the basis of *method*, and a distinction on the basis of *content*. According to the first distinction, education differs from indoctrination because there is a difference in *how* we teach; according to the second, the difference is a difference in *what* we teach. Wilson plumps for the second sort of distinction. He rejects a distinction on the basis of method on the following ground. 'Since young children and infants', he says, 'cannot discuss, the methods we use to educate them are bound to resemble hypnosis and brain-washing more than they resemble a democratic exchange of views' (1964: 34). So if indoctrination is a kind of

From *Aims in Education*, ed. T. C. B. Hollins (Manchester, 1964), in a lecture series with G. A. Beck, A. MacIntyre, J. Wilson, and others.

method, we shall have to admit that this method has a place in the teaching of young children. But Wilson does not want to admit this, because he wants to use the word 'indoctrination' for something that is always bad, on whomsoever it is used. So he cannot admit that non-rational methods of teaching, such as we have to use with young children, are indoctrination. So it cannot be the *method* that makes a kind of teaching into indoctrination. So, he thinks, it must be the content—what is taught. We shall avoid indoctrinating our children if we only educate them 'to adopt behaviour-patterns and to have feelings which are seen by every sane and sensible person to be agreeable and necessary. These behaviour-patterns will be rational in the sense that they derive from reality rather than from the values, fears, desires or prejudices of individual people' (ibid.).

This, it seems to me, will not do at all. For who are to count as sane and sensible people? Most people think that they themselves and the majority of their friends are sane and sensible people. So if that is what Wilson says, he will not succeed in barring the way to a great many educational practices that I am sure he would want to call indoctrination. Take, for example, those Roman Catholics who, as the Archbishop of Liverpool so disarmingly says, 'insist that their children should be entrusted in school to Catholic teachers [because] the teacher's causality'—sinister word—'in the educational process has results in terms of the appreciation of truth, natural and supernatural, standards of values, moral, aesthetic and literary which depend ultimately on the personality of the teacher himself' (Beck 1964: 128). These Roman Catholics and the teachers to whom they entrust their children will no doubt all think that they are sane and sensible, and that they are in touch with reality (perhaps they will add 'natural and supernatural reality'). So when these children have been duly indoctrinated and turned into good Roman Catholics, the parents and teachers will claim not to have offended against Mr Wilson's canon. And the same can be said if we substitute for 'Roman Catholics', 'Communists', 'Victorians', 'ancient Spartans', 'Trobriand Islanders', or, for that matter 'Anglicans'. Yet surely Mr Wilson will want to say, with Dryden, of such a case:

By education most have been misled
So they believe, because they were so bred.
The priest continues what the nurse began,
And thus the child imposes on the man.

(1637, pt. 3, p. 389)

Dryden, it will be remembered, was speaking of Anglican indoctrination.

If we distinguish indoctrination from education in terms of their content, we are bound to reach this *impasse*. For to make the distinction in this way is to say that there is a *right* content —a *right* doctrine—and, furthermore, that the teacher is the person who knows what it is. It is to say that, provided that this right doctrine is adhered to, it is not indoctrination that is being done, but education. I know very well that Wilson does not want to say this, and that it is inconsistent with other things that he says; but I wanted to show just how easily a clever propagandist could twist his words into something that he and any liberal would abhor.

Why has Wilson fallen into this trap of saying that indoctrination is distinguished from education by its content? I think it is because he does not consider a third possibility, besides saying that the distinction is one of content, and saying that it is one of method. This third possibility is that it is one of *purpose*, or *aim*. The volume in which both our papers first appeared is called *Aims in Education*, so I am surprised that he did not see this third possibility. Perhaps we can discover why he missed it if we consider in more detail what he said about methods. We have to admit, as he does, that, in the early stages of the education of young children, some non-rational methods of teaching, especially in matters of moral behaviour, have to be used. But, he seems to argue, if we have to use these methods, it is pointless to condemn them; but we should be condemning them if we called them 'indoctrination'; therefore we must not call them indoctrination. But since the *methods* do not differ fundamentally from some things that we *should* call indoctrination, the difference between indoctrination and other kinds of teaching cannot be one of method. And with all this I agree. If one wants to keep 'indoctrination' as a bad word, one cannot start using it of methods which everyone thinks legitimate, because inevitable.

But it does not follow that the difference is one of content.

Suppose, for example, that one of my children is going through a phase of telling a lot of lies. It may be that his (or her) age is such that no rational discussion of the evil consequences of lying is much good; I may engage in such discussion as a kind of lip-service to my liberal principles, but I may know that what will really influence the child to stop lying is not the discussion, but the tone in which it is conducted. Psychologists can perhaps advise on the best method of getting young children out of the habit of lying; but we can be sure that the method will not be, in Wilson's sense, a rational one. Let us suppose that what happens is that the child senses that I disapprove very strongly of lying, and therefore stops doing it—let us ignore the question of whether this is a psychologically desirable method or not. Have I, by using this non-rational method of affecting the child's behaviour, been *indoctrinating* the child? I do not think so. For I do not *want* the child to remain such that non-rational persuasion or influence is the only kind of moral communication I can have with him. The difference lies in the aim.

There is a German rhyme that I was once taught which goes:

> *Was der Vater will,*
> *Was die Mutter spricht,*
> *Das befolge still.*
> *Warum? Frage nicht.*
>
> What your father wishes,
> What your mother says,
> Do it in silence.
> Why? Don't ask questions.

If I wanted my children to *keep* this sort of attitude to me, or to what I was teaching them, then I should be indoctrinating. But I do not want this. I may have *now* to use non-rational methods of teaching, but my wish is that they may as soon as possible become unnecessary. So, though on occasion I may use the very same methods of teaching as the German who wrote this rhyme, and though my teaching may have exactly the same content, that it is wrong to lie, he is indoctrinating and I am not, because he wants the child always to go on taking his morality from his elders, even after they are dead, whereas I want the child as soon as possible to learn to think morally for himself.

I hope that this example will show what I think is wrong with what some enlightened people say about the moral education of children. One sometimes comes across extreme examples. I know a man who has a child of 1 year old, and he keeps on saying that he is absolutely determined not to influence his child's moral growth in any way; the child must find his own morality; to try to influence him would be to 'diminish [his] human personality' as Wilson put it (1964: 33); and my friend thinks that there is only a difference in degree between such attempts to influence the morality of one's children and the grossest forms of parental violence.

This is obviously absurd, and I do not suggest that Wilson would go as far as this. To begin with, we cannot help influencing our children; the only question is how, and in what direction. This, I think, Wilson realizes. And, if we are going to influence them anyway, what can we do but try to influence them in the best direction we can think of? But indoctrination only begins when we are trying to stop the growth in our children of the capacity to think for themselves about moral questions. If all the time that we are influencing them, we are saying to ourselves 'Perhaps in the end they will decide that the best way to live is quite different from what I'm teaching them; and they will have a perfect right to decide that', then we are not to be accused of indoctrinating. We deserve this name only if we say 'I'll try to make this child such a good Communist, or Roman Catholic, or teach him the American way of life so successfully, that he'll never even be able to ask the question whether, or why, one ought to be like that.'

What I have said about the *aim* which distinguishes education from indoctrination has a profound bearing upon both the method and the content of education—only these other things are not fundamental; they come from the aim, not it from them. If you are wanting your child in the end to become an adult and think for himself about moral questions, you will try, all the time that you are influencing him by non-rational methods (as you have to), to interest him in rational thinking about morality (this, I know, is a rather solemn expression, but I will try to explain what I mean by it later). That is why I said that I might talk to my child about the evil consequences of lying even though I knew that that was not what would really stop him lying. You can tell what are the aims of a teacher, and whether they are indoctrinatory or not, by studying his methods. Suppose that he carefully arranges for there not to be any free and open discussion of questions of morality until he is absolutely certain that his pupils have, by non-rational methods, been got into a state where they are bound all to give the 'right' answers. Or suppose that he takes enormous care that, though his pupils are encouraged to read books, the books are all ones which say the same thing. Then we shall know what his object is; it is to prevent them asking the questions that might cause them in the end to come to a different moral attitude from his own. Suppose that, on the other hand, he really senses that his pupils are perplexed about some moral question—about sex, for example, or pacifism—and, seeing this, is prepared to discuss it with them, with no holds barred and no questions banned, and is himself prepared to ask the questions again—really ask them— and is prepared to answer them in a different way from the way he has up till now, if that is the way the argument goes. Then we know that he is concerned to get his pupils to think for themselves (see Chapters 10, 11).

This matter of the teacher himself really treating the questions as open ones is crucial. There is no possibility of pretence here; one cannot act this sort of thing, though we all know parsons and teachers who try. Wilson said something that may mislead when he said that 'questions of moral integrity, honesty, or overt truthfulness do not arise. We live in a mad world; what counts is not preserving our own integrity, but making the world saner' (1964: 41). I understand what he meant; he meant that we all sometimes have to temporize with the powers that be. But in our dealings with the young, nothing short of absolute integrity will do.

Yet it is not easy really to give one's own deepest moral opinions a turning over. This, however, is what we have to do if we are going to have honest discussions with younger people about the moral problems that perplex them. Because it is a painful process, various ways have been devised of making it less painful. But they are only pretences. There is the expedient of discussing questions which do not really hurt— academic questions which might have troubled people once but are not the ones that trouble us now. There is the even worse expedient of taking questions that really do trouble us, but discussing them in a superficial debating style without really becoming involved in them. This is a thing that the young will often do when they have not yet got personally involved in some moral question. It is a thing that they should never be encouraged to do, about serious questions.

If a teacher is willing to engage in serious and honest discussion with his pupils about moral questions, to the extent that they are able, then he is not an indoctrinator, even though he may also, because of their age, be using non-rational methods of persuasion. These methods are not, as is commonly supposed, bad in themselves; they are bad only if they are used to produce attitudes that are not open to argument. The fact that a teacher does not himself have such attitudes is the guarantee that he is not an indoctrinator.

I said that the difference in aim between education and indoctrination will result in a difference in content. This is because of the methods which, as we have seen, are appropriate to these two aims. The method appropriate to indoctrination shelters both teacher and pupil from the fresh winds of argument, and this is bound to have the result that things will get taught which would not get taught if the whole process were exposed to these breezes. If the teacher speaks with the voice of authority, however cunningly disguised, and is prepared to use every persuasive device to close the minds of his pupils, there is almost no limit to the irrational taboos and myths that he can successfully inculcate. If, on the other hand, the pupils are not protected against other influences, and the only pressure on them is to consider seriously and rationally what is said and come to their own decisions about it, then it will be less possible to put over these received opinions, and what can be put over will to a certain extent have its content circumscribed. Irrational attitudes cannot flourish when rational methods of argument are seriously practised.

I must say a word here about the attitude a teacher ought to take to the various outside influences, most of them non-rational, which all the time surround his pupils in the Press, television, etc. Mr MacIntyre (1964: 7) has said something about these; and I do not dissent from the value-judgements he made about the need for encouraging a critical spirit. But why did he have to be so *gloomy*? Knowing him, I was sorry to see him assuming—I hope only temporarily—the mantle of the professional literary pessimist. I was even sorrier to see Wilson, briefly, joining in this familiar chorus; for I myself am much more inclined to sympathize with the attitude of Professor Medawar:

The Predicament of Man is all the rage now that people have sufficient leisure and are sufficiently well fed to contemplate it, and many a tidy little literary reputation has been built on exploiting it; anybody nowadays who dared to suggest that the plight of man might not be wholly desperate would get a sharp rap over the knuckles in any literary weekly. (1961: 105)

The state of the world is bad enough in all conscience without adding a dose of quite factitious depression. We might even get so engrossed in moaning about the mess we are in that we became unable to do any constructive thinking about how to improve matters. Indeed, if we do not look out, MacIntyre will label us 'improvers' (happy term!) if we so much as suggest that there *is* any way in which the world could be made better (cf. 1964: 13).

But I hope that teachers, when they rightly take Mac-Intyre's advice and teach their pupils to criticize what they see around them, will make it clear that 'criticize' is being used in the sense of 'appraise' and not of 'find fault with'. Otherwise they will only be producing a brood of grumblers who have closed their minds to hope. Rather, I would say, teach them to look up out of their books sometimes—even if the books are novels by the most favoured authors; teach them to look out of the window; teach them sometimes, even, to go out of the door —and *look*. If the view that they see is good, or has good in it (as it always will have if they look), teach them to enjoy it and help others enjoy it. If it is bad, or has something bad in it (as it always will), teach them to *think*: What can I do to make it better? How can I get other people to help me make it better

—even if MacIntyre calls us 'improvers' for our pains. This, surely, is better than breaking out into barren and futile jeremiads. But I must not digress.

I was speaking about the influences of the Press and television. Surely the harm that these do has been somewhat exaggerated, and the good correspondingly underrated. Take advertisements, for example. If all the advertisements were advertising the same brand of soap, as might be the case in a Communist country, then it would be time to get worried— though even in that case good would come of encouraging people to wash. But since they are all advertising different brands, the consumer very soon realizes that there is not much difference between the brands, and, though of course he will probably go on buying some heavily advertised brand, will not very much care which. The same applies to more important things than soap. Advertisements keep branded goods before our attention; and if this is not done, we shall probably stop buying them and buy some other brand. But in choosing between the brands which are competing in this way, does not the multiplicity of the advertisements make us stop caring which we buy, unless, indeed, we think there is a real difference between the brands? If we do, and if we think it is important to have the best one, do we not then make some effort to find out which the best one is? This, at any rate, is what the schools ought to be teaching their pupils to do; and I do not think it is so difficult. Listen to any two young men discussing the merits of two kinds of motor car. Which influences them the most—the blurbs in the advertisements or the reports of performance in the technical Press, which they read avidly? I must admit that they are also influenced by the appearance of the cars; but ought they not to be? Are we not continually told by the supporters of good industrial design, of whom I am one, to *look* at what we are buying?

The same applies, with very few changes, to politics, morals, and religion. If there is plenty of variety in the market place, discernment and discrimination will be fostered. That is one reason why I have the deepest misgivings about what is euphemistically called 'Church Unity'. It is true that all Christians ought to be allowed to worship at the same table, and to live and pray together without acrimony. And I am convinced that nothing now prevents their doing this but the purely political rivalries between the various ecclesiastical machines. But in order to bring about unity of worship, is it necessary to have a single 'Church' in the organizational sense? It seems to me that to do this would be to create a religious monopoly of the most pernicious kind, a sort of totalitarian Church, whose main function would be to perpetuate the power of its leaders to indoctrinate and thereby control. So I hope I shall not be misunderstood when I say that more good than harm comes from competition, both in commerce and in politics and in religion.

So, by and large, I think that teachers have little to fear from the Press and television, provided that there is diversity, and provided that the teachers are themselves trying to educate and not to indoctrinate. Nor, I should like to add, subject to the same proviso, have they anything to fear from philosophers.

There was one more gap in Wilson's exposition that I should like to fill, if I can. Having distinguished between education and indoctrination in terms of their contents, it was important for him to state clearly the distinction between the contents of these two things. This he did not do, though he gave examples; and I have already said that it is no use saying that we can avoid indoctrination if we teach only those moral opinions that sane and sensible people would agree with—for who are the sane and sensible people? I have maintained, for this very reason, that a distinction in terms of content will not do; but that if we have the aim of educating people, this aim will determine the method, and the method will to a certain extent determine the content. But this is not nearly specific enough; I am sure that it will be asked what, in more detail, is this method of rational discussion that I have been advocating, and why I think that it will be inimical to what I have called myths and taboos and will let in only rational opinions.

To ask this is to ask me to launch out into a treatise on moral philosophy. I could not possibly say anything at all profound in the space remaining. But I will try to give an outline of what I have said elsewhere (*FR*, ch. 6, *MT*, chs. 5, 6). The two essential features of moral opinions are that they are not primarily about matters of fact, but about how one ought to behave (this is what is meant by calling moral judgements 'prescriptive'); and secondly, that if I hold a certain moral opinion about an act done by one person, I must hold the same moral opinion about a similar act done by a similar person in similar circumstances. This is often referred to by moral philosophers as the principle of the 'universaliz-ability' of moral judgements. Both of these are *logical* features of moral judgements; if we do not understand either of them, we do not understand the uses of the moral words. Roughly speaking, a moral opinion is *rational* if it is not taken on authority as a matter of fact but freely accepted as a prescription for living, and if it is recognized as holding good irrespective of whether it is I that am the subject of it or someone else. The reason why, if someone transgresses either of these two requirements, he is not being rational, is that they are requirements of logic, having their basis in the meanings of the moral words; therefore someone who transgresses them is being as illogical as someone who says 'All the books are red but there is one which is not' (*MT* 8).

The consequences of the first of these features of moral judgements for moral discussion have been adequately dealt with by Wilson. Briefly, since moral judgements are not statements of fact or pieces of information, they cannot be taught out of a textbook like the names of the capitals of European countries. It is not a question of *informing* those whom we are teaching, but of their coming to accept a certain opinion for their own.

But Wilson does not say anything about the second feature. Now, as I could show if I had time, it is this feature, in conjunction with the first, which really limits the moral opinions that we can hold. It is by applying these two characteristics of moral judgements together that argument really gets a grip on moral questions. What we have to teach people, if we are educating them morally, is to ask themselves the question 'What kind of behaviour am I ready to prescribe for myself, given that, in prescribing it for myself, I am prescribing it also for anybody in a like situation?' I could, but I will not, go on to show how this question, if we can get people to ask it, circumscribes their moral choices in a rational way, so that the abandonment of taboos and irrational prejudices which Wilson recommends does not, as has sometimes been feared, open the way to unbridled licence.

I said 'if we can get people to ask it'. But one of the most important things for educators to remember is that morality, as governed by this question, is a very *difficult* thing to accept. Because it is a difficult and sophisticated thing, it does not come naturally to children. It is no use, as Wilson sometimes seems to imply, merely leaving children as free as possible from external moral influences, and hoping that the thing will just grow. It *will* grow in most cases, but only because the seed is there in our own way of thinking, from which it is well-nigh impossible to isolate a child. It is not, however, something innate; it is a question of tradition; morality is something that has to be handed down; if it were not—if the process were interrupted—our children really would grow up as savages.

What has to be passed on is not any *specific* moral principle, but an understanding of what morality is and a readiness to think in a moral way and act accordingly. This could be put in other words by saying that children have to learn to use the moral words such as 'right' and 'wrong' and to understand their meaning. That is why it is so very important for philosophers to study what their meaning is—how silly it is to say that philosophers ought not to occupy themselves with matters of words! It must be emphasized that it is not the content of any particular morality that is being handed down— that would be indoctrination, if the aim was, at all costs, to implant *these* particular moral principles. It is not a particular morality, but morality itself that we are teaching: not to think this or that (because we say so or because the good and great have said so) but to think morally for oneself. And to learn this is to learn how to *speak* morally, understanding what one says (see pp. 154 ff.).

Doubtless it is not possible in practice to pass on the mere form of morality without embodying it in some content; we cannot teach children the abstract idea of a moral principle as such without teaching them some concrete moral principles. And naturally we shall choose for this purpose those principles which we think in themselves desirable. This, as I said, is not indoctrination provided that our aim is that the children should in the end come to appraise these principles for themselves. Just so, one cannot teach the scientific outlook without teaching some science; but the science that is taught could be radically altered in the light of later researches, and yet the scientific outlook remain. The good science teacher will teach what he thinks to be the truth, but his teaching will not have proved vain if what has been taught is later rejected as false; and similarly, if we can teach children what morality is, using our own moral thinking as an example, we shall have done our job, even if the moral thinking which they later do leads them to different conclusions. Fortunately there is a close connection between the form of morality and its content. As I could show if there were room, and have attempted to show in my books which I have already referred to, once the form of morality is accepted in our thinking, it quite narrowly circumscribes the substance of the moral principles that we shall adopt. We can therefore happily start by securing the adherence of our children—if necessary by non-rational methods—to the moral principles which we think best, provided that these are consistent with the form of morality; but we must leave them at liberty later to think out for themselves different principles, subject to the same proviso.

In conveying to children what morality is, our method is governed by what it is that we are trying to convey. Because moral judgements are things that one has to make for oneself, we have to get children to understand, in the end, that 'wrong' does *not* mean 'what the parent or the schoolteacher forbids'; the schoolteacher might forbid it, and the child might still think it right, and the child might have a right to his opinion. On this aspect of the matter Wilson has laid enough stress. But secondly, and arising out of the universalizability of moral judgements, the child has to realize that what is wrong for another to do to him is wrong for him to do to another. This is the foundation of all that part of morality which concerns our dealings with other people. And this gives us an important clue about method. Children must learn to think about what it is like to be the other person. They must cultivate their sympathetic imaginations. And this is not easy. It will not be brought about without effort on the part of parents and schoolteachers. And it will not be brought about by rational discussion alone.

Suppose that somebody who took Wilson too literally, and did not realize the importance of this feature of morality which he left out, resolved to confine himself, in his dealings with the young, in the early stages to plain imperatives like 'Go to bed', which make no pretence to be moral and therefore can do no harm, and in the later stages to rational discussion. His charges really would, if he could observe this principle in isolation from other influences, grow up without an understanding of morality. Of course, this is unlikely to happen in practice, because there are, fortunately, other influences on children than their parents and schoolteachers, and many of them are media for the handing on of an understanding of moral thinking. The mere use of moral words by a child's contemporaries does a great deal. So nobody is going to be able to carry out this too literal interpretation of Wilson's prescription; and we are in no real danger of relapsing into a Hobbesian state of nature, in which every man's hand is against every man. But unless *some* non-rational methods are used, it is unlikely that all our children will come to absorb this principle as deeply as we could wish; and to that extent less of their thinking about action will be moral thinking, and their actions will show this.

The non-rational influences I have in mind are chiefly two; environment, and example. The examples that one has set before one are *part* of one's environment, so this division is not a neat one; but it will do for what I want to say. The first important thing, if we want our children to learn morality, is that they should be put into an environment in which the unpleasant effects of other people's lapses on them are as obvious as possible. This means that they must have plenty of opportunity of rubbing up against other people in some sort of more or less constant group—more or less constant, because they have to have time to get to think of the other people in the group as people (i.e. as like themselves), or the treatment will not work. In such an environment, children can easily absorb the lesson that they ought to do unto others as they would that others should do unto them. The family is such a group; but families are not enough, because some families fall down on the job, and delinquency is sometimes the result. Schools, therefore, have a lot to contribute, as have clubs; and they have one very important advantage over the family, that in them the child rubs up against a large number of people of his (or her) own age, whom, therefore, it is easy for him to think of as like himself, sharing his likes and dislikes, and therefore hurt by the things that hurt him and pleased by the things that please him. It will be easier in such a group for the child to learn to universalize his moral judgements.

Secondly, the group must have a good tradition. If it is a St Trinian's, the child will indeed suffer from the misdeeds of other children, but its reaction will be one of self-defence merely, and we shall have a reign of blackboard jungle law. There has to be a tradition of kindness to, and co-operation with, other people. I am sorry to repeat these platitudes; but I want to show how they are the consequences of the nature of morality; *that* they are true is obvious, but we need to understand *why* they are true.

But, thirdly, how do we start these good traditions? This seems to me to be the most important, perhaps the only essential, function of the adult in moral education. After a certain age, children and young people will get their moral ideas and ideals and attitudes for the most part from each other; either from their schoolfellows or from the rest of the gang. So the most important point at which the adult can intervene, *if* he can intervene, is by influencing the morality of the group; and this is done by example.

We must at this point avoid what is a very easy mistake to make. 'Setting a good example' by itself is no use at all. The people to whom it is being set must want to follow it. We need to know what can make them want to follow it. All good teachers know the answer to this question. Children desire to imitate particular traits of a person whom they desire to imitate as a whole. If an adult is *merely* an example of desirable moral attitudes, they will not take much notice. But if there are a great many other things about him (or her) that they admire—usually things that have nothing to do with morals—then they will swallow the moral attitudes too.

There are a lot of things that children and young people will willingly learn from their elders. Sometimes, if they are intellectually gifted, they will even willingly learn from them Latin and French; but this is unfortunately not common.

They will, however, very often be anxious to learn to play football, or sail boats, or play the violin in the orchestra; and if there is an adult whom they trust to teach them these things, they will pick up from him much besides. That is why those who are employing schoolteachers look, not merely for good teachers of Latin or French or football or music—they look for people who, in teaching these things, will hand on something that is of much more importance.

This is one of the sources of the value of so-called out-of-school activities like games and music, as well as the more wide-ranging ones like sailing and mountaineering, which are now becoming so popular. They are vehicles for the transmission of an understanding of morality from one generation to another. But they also have another importance from the moral point of view: all of them, to a greater or less extent, are co-operative activities; they therefore require, in all who participate in them, a standard of behaviour. On a small scale, but intensely, they reproduce those very factors which, I suppose, have led to the development of morality in civilized communities at large. One learns, in such teams or groups, to submit oneself to a rule—a rule not dictated by some particular person, but freely accepted by all the participants, either because, like the rule about not passing forward, or like watching the conductor, it is a necessary condition for the doing of *this* particular activity called orchestral playing or rugby football; or else because it is dictated by the realities of the situation, like not sailing by the lee, or not getting lost in the mountains and causing other people to organize search parties to rescue one.

The second of these two kinds of rules is the more important; and therefore the second of the two kinds of activity—that which includes sailing and fell-walking—deserves the increasing attention that it is getting from teachers. Perhaps music should be after all included with these; for music also is in touch with reality: if one plays a wrong note it is not just that one has broken the rule of a game. But games, in the narrow sense, will always have a certain artificiality. And of course compulsory games, whose rules are not freely accepted by the participants, do no good at all from the point of view that we are considering, though they may have some of the other virtues that used to be claimed for them.

The point that I wish to emphasize by saying these familiar things is that these practices, which teachers have found useful, owe their usefulness to the nature of what they are trying to hand on, namely morality. Morality has, of its nature, to be freely accepted; therefore in this respect the rules of seamanship are a better analogue of it—and their strict observance actually a better example of it—than the rules in the school rule-book. And secondly, morality is impartial as between persons; therefore, to learn to accept rules applicable impartially within a group is a good schooling in morality. There is, of course, a danger in this; we all know the kind of team spirit which counts anything as fair against the other side, or against those outside the team. To become a loyal member of a group is an important step on the way from egoism to altruism; but it is a step at which it is all too easy to get stuck.

I must add here that, important as membership of groups is in the formation of moral ideas, it is important also for the development of the individual's personality that he should be able sometimes to break away from the group and pursue his own ideals, if necessary entirely by himself, if he is that sort of person. For all morality is not social morality—to think that it is, is a mistake that has often been made by moral philosophers and by educationists. There are moral ideals, some of them very fine ones, which have nothing to do with our fellow men; and although it is necessary to learn to live with our fellow men, it is restricting to the personality to be unable to get away from them. This educational requirement has, like the others, a theoretical basis in moral philosophy (see *FR*, ch. 8).

I have mentioned two ways in which adults can help to pass on the idea of morality to another generation. But the power of adults to do this is severely limited by what adolescents will accept from adults. They want to imitate adults; but they want to imitate them in one thing above all—*in being adult*. They want, that is to say, to be their own masters. They will only feel that they have really succeeded in imitating the adult when they have got the adult out of the way.

It is by the readiness to retire gracefully, indeed, that we can most easily tell the educator from the indoctrinator. I said earlier that I agreed with Wilson that education might sometimes have to use the same methods as indoctrination, and that therefore the two cannot be distinguished by their methods. I said that they were distinguished by their aims; the educator is trying to turn children into adults; the indoctrinator is trying to make them into perpetual children. But I said that the aim would all the same make a difference to the method; and this becomes evident, if we watch the process over a period. Many of the methods I have alluded to can be used for indoctrination in the most deplorable doctrines; the Nazi youth organizations used them, fortunately without lasting success, to pervert a whole generation of German youth while they thought they were just youth-hostelling or playing games or whatever it might be. But if one watches carefully one will notice a difference. The educator is waiting and hoping all the time for those whom he is educating to start *thinking*; and none of the thoughts that may occur to them are labelled 'dangerous' a priori. The indoctrinator, on the other hand, is watching for signs of trouble, and ready to intervene to suppress it when it appears, however oblique and smooth his methods may be. The difference between these two is like the difference between the colonial administrator who knows, and is pleased, that he is working himself out of a job, and the one who is determined that the job shall still be there even when he himself retires.

So there is, in the end, a very great difference between the two methods. At the end of it all, the educator will insensibly stop being an educator, and find that he is talking to an equal, to an educated person like himself—a person who may disagree with everything he has ever said; and, unlike the indoctrinator, he will be pleased. So, when this happens, you can tell from the expression on his face which he is.

8

Autonomy as an Educational Ideal

It must have occurred to many people to ask what the connection is between the psychological state, state of mind, state of character, or whatever, which is called 'autonomy', and what others call 'the *logical* autonomy of *moral* discourse'. We are accustomed in philosophy to slip back and forth between logical and psychological ways of speaking; but all the same the transitions need to be explained. I am going to try to do this, and shall maintain in the course of my explanation that at least one of the issues about autonomy is an issue in philosophical logic.

Autonomy, as an educational ideal, seems most often to mean a disposition to think in a certain way. Even when it is action that is called autonomous, it is called that because of the nature of the thinking which has led up to it. By 'thinking in a certain way', I mean, of course, not 'thinking certain things' but 'doing one's thinking in a certain manner'. The manner is characterized, as Mr Dearden (1975: 3 ff.) has brought out, by two features corresponding to the two parts of the word 'autonomy': the thinking has to be done by a man for himself (*autos*); and he has to do it in accordance with some regular procedure (*nomos*). I should not be thinking auto-nomously *as a mathematician* if I either, instead of calculating for myself, looked up the answer at the end of the book, or, instead of employing arithmetical procedures, picked the answer by jabbing a pin into the table of logarithms. However, we must not exaggerate the second point into requirements which are *not* part of autonomy. As Miss Telfer rightly says (1975: 24) it is not a necessary part of autonomy that the thinking should be done correctly. A man may be thinking autonomously (for himself and applying a regular

From *Philosophers Discuss Education*, ed. S. C. Brown (Macmillan, 1975), in a conference with R. F. Dearden, R. K. Elliott, E. Telfer, M. Warnock, and others.

procedure), but he may not have mastered the procedure, and so may get the answer wrong. Nor do I like Mr Dearden's use (which Miss Telfer takes over) of the word 'criterion'; regular procedures do not involve the matching of results against criteria; in mathematics, again, we do not tell whether someone is really doing the sums for himself autonomously by seeing whether he checks his results against criteria, but by seeing whether he arrives at them by certain procedures which he himself follows.

Next (and this is important when considering Mary Warnock's paper, 1975: 159 ff.) the procedures will differ with the subject-matter. I was therefore a bit suspicious of the slide which she seemed to be trying to institute from Latin, French, and mathematics via science and history to morals. If the procedures of these kinds of thinking are all different, it may be that some of them do, and some of them do not, require submission to the discipline of (for example) empirical facts. Empirical science does require this—and in empirical science we must perhaps include linguistics and therefore Latin and French; so if the teacher knows that this is not the way native speakers of French would express a certain thought, of course he can tell his pupils so, and invite them if they disbelieve him to ask a Frenchman. All of these procedures are subject to the discipline of logic—and mathematics to that alone. Art, which is also taught in schools, is not subject even to logic, but perhaps has its own disciplines. We have therefore to ask separately in each case in what autonomy, and therefore in what neutrality, will consist.

Professor Elliott (1975: 45 ff.) may disagree with this; for he thinks that the same 'powers of the mind' fit us for engaging in *all* disciplines, and therefore, presumably, for engaging autonomously in them all; and so differences in subject-matter will not make the sort of difference that I am going to claim. But since he does not mention the empirical work that has been done on the particularity or generality of mental powers, and does not produce any at all solid conceptual arguments either, I do not know what his grounds are for being so sure of what he says.

In any case, the procedures of the different disciplines are different in fundamental respects. The problem therefore arises of how the procedures are to be determined in each case. Mr Dearden rightly says of his 'criteria', and I would say the same of the 'procedures' I have been speaking of, that the autonomous thinker has to be able to review or even reject them in favour of others (1975: 9). But within what limits? I think that this is the basic issue. We have to determine, in the case of each discipline separately, the ways in which the liberties of the thinker are restricted by the nature of the subject. Of course, as we shall see, even though there are these restrictions, the thinker can escape them by no longer studying *that* subject—for example, the historical novelist or playwright can take liberties with the facts; but then he is not doing history, and it is part of the education of a historian to learn to tell the difference between this sort of thing and genuine history, and also between the latter and political propaganda.

However, having said this, we must admit that the autonomous thinker cannot be confined within the strait-jackets of subjects as currently delimited, nor even of education as currently understood. That is what is wrong with what might otherwise seem a short way of solving our problem about how the procedures are determined—that of saying that they are determined, of conceptual necessity, by the subject, whatever it is, that is being studied. For example, if one claims to be doing *mathematics*, one is not allowed to make logically invalid inferences, just as, if one is learning to *ride* a bicycle, one cannot claim success if one falls off. If one does not know this (we are tempted to say) one does not know what mathematics or bicycle-riding is, or what the words mean.

The problem remains, however, even on this view, of how to extend this idea to the more difficult cases. There are two opposite dangers to be avoided here. Take history, for example. If someone occupying a position in a department of history gave lectures which were more like historical novels or like political pamphlets than like attempts to determine the facts most relevant to his topic, however repugnant to his own views, then I should think him worthy of censure and even, in extreme cases, of expulsion, irrespective of the complexion of the politics or novel-writing in which he was indulging; and bogus appeals to academic freedom would not move me. I am not saying that historians are not allowed to make political or moral judgements about the facts, once established; it is a good thing if they sometimes do. But the two activities can be kept distinct, and so can that of selecting the field of enquiry; and we should not allow ourselves to be persuaded of the opposite view just because it is repeated so often—if there are solid arguments for it, I do not know what they are. It seems to me that the same principle should be applied here as lay behind the Trade Descriptions Act and the prohibition on people practising as doctors when what they are doing is not medicine as usually understood.

On the other hand, we do not want professors to be able to say to junior colleagues 'What you are doing in your lectures is not history as I understand the word, so I shall see to it that your appointment is not renewed.' Is there any middle ground between these two objectionable positions, one of which would allow anything whatever to be taught under the name of history, and the other of which would allow various 'authorities' to impose their definition of what history is on unwilling colleagues? If there is, it can best be found by means of democratic decisions (for *somebody* has to do the deciding) between clearly understood alternatives. The clarity is at least as important as the democracy. We shall achieve it only if we distinguish carefully between two questions, the confusion between which can easily lead to acrimonious muddle. The first is 'What are the limits of what is to be described as, for example, history?' The second is 'How much of the academic cake ought each of the subjects, as so delimited, to be given?' I offer this as an example of the utility of separating questions of definition from normative questions.

The utility is doubly apparent in cases like psychology and, I regret to say, philosophy, in which agreement is lacking as to the limits of the subject. Even there, by separating the questions, we can *first* allow that there are different and mutually compossible answers to the first one—that there are, for example, different things that are called psychology or called philosophy, one of which demands, as the case may be, controlled experiment or logical rigour in argument, and the other of which does not, but is perhaps more exciting to immature minds (which is undoubtedly a virtue)—and only then go on to the inevitable political infighting about the extent to which these various sorts of philosophy or of psychology are to be studied in a given place, or how much money they are to get. If these decisions are made by reasonably democratic procedures and accepted, by and large, within a given institution, then we shall have a regime in which those of us who are seriously interested in our subjects (which does not include all academics) can get on with our work and teaching, and so exert whatever good influence on the world is made possible by the nature of our subjects and our own abilities.

But the main point for my argument is that subjects are different, and therefore what constitutes thinking auto-nomously or teaching neutrally in them will be different too. When we come to moral and other evaluative questions we have to ask afresh whether, here too, there is a subject called, say, 'art' and another called 'morals', which, of conceptual necessity, impose certain disciplines that the teacher can know just as he knows Latin or mathematics. Geoffrey Warnock thinks, if I am not getting him wrong, that in the case of morals there is (1967: 52 ff.), and so do I (see also pp. 174 ff.); but I think we differ about what restrictions the discipline imposes upon autonomous thinking. Obviously on this will depend what a teacher can legitimately do when professing to discuss a *moral* question (as classes should certainly be encouraged to do).

And this is where the issue in philosophical logic emerges which I mentioned at the beginning. Those who believe, as I do, in a viable distinction between analytic and synthetic propositions will be able to state this issue clearly; those who reject the distinction will not (see pp. 203 f.). However, for those who understand what a conceptually valid argument is, and what is the difference between things which we cannot deny without self-contradiction and things which we can, the issue can be stated as follows: When children are learning the moral language from their parents, teachers, and others (and the best way of doing this is by hearing the language *used* in discussing questions they think important), does the learning of the language, by itself, (for example, the learning of the use of the word 'ought' as it is used in moral discourse) entail the adoption of certain moral opinions? Or can children learn the language *without* thereby being committed, on pain of self-contradiction, to embracing certain moral opinions (those of the people from whom they are learning it)? If they can, then the teacher can be neutral about moral questions, though he can, and ought to, be *not* neutral about the language itself and its logic—which means that he ought not to be easygoing about sloppy thinking in morals any more than he ought to be in mathematics. Miss Telfer is right when she says (1975: 33) that intellectual autonomy requires moral virtues—honesty, courage, patience, and thoroughness, and I would add clarity and rigour, which, though not themselves moral virtues, are such that the failure to strive for them is a sign of moral defect.

It is the teacher's task, in morals as in mathematics, to help the children to learn the language so that *they* can do the sums; his job is not to teach them answers but to raise questions, and at the same time to initiate them into the logic, which is an inherent property of the language, in accordance with whose rules those questions have to be discussed. So the question arises crucially: '*What are* the logical properties of the moral words, and what restrictions do they place on what we can or cannot consistently say?' I hope that we philosophers, when we discuss moral education, will not allow ourselves, in the pursuit of relevance, to be diverted from this, the most relevant question of all.

9

Value Education in a Pluralist Society: A Philosophical Glance at the Humanities Curriculum Project

I start by explaining the scope of this paper. I am going to discuss the problem of how educators in our society (which makes it so difficult for them and their charges) are to help people to face, in as rational a way as possible, the bewildering choices of values, principles, ideologies, ways of life, etc. with which they are confronted. I chose the Humanities Curriculum Project as an example of a kind of approach to this problem which I wish to defend, because it is well known and has attracted much criticism. But, since there are many who would subscribe to the general approach which I shall be defending, but would criticize the Project's particular way of following this approach, I must explain that in this paper I shall be defending the approach in general against those who criticize it in general. There may well be criticisms of the practical execution of the Project with which I should agree, if I knew enough about educational practice to venture an opinion. But I shall leave these practical questions to others more qualified than myself.

Let me start by describing the problem. Perhaps there are some who need convincing that there is a problem, or who think that, if there is one, it is created by schoolteachers and education authorities. On this view there is, or was, a set of values (the *right* or *best* values) in which people used to be brought up, so that, as is said, they 'knew the difference between right and wrong', and lived accordingly. If, it is said, this happy state of affairs no longer obtains, it is only because of the malign influence of a few people in our own and preceding generations, who have, acting partly through the

From *Proc. of Ph. of Ed. Soc. of GB*, ed. R. Peters (1976).

colleges of education, won the ears of a very large number of schoolteachers, who as a result are now systematically corrupting the youth, and producing an ever increasing number of criminals, vandals, hooligans, drifters, and drop-outs.

According to this view the problem, if there is one, is a relatively simple one, to be solved by a return to the good old methods of education, which, if single-mindedly pursued by parents and teachers, will restore order and tone to our society. At this point I cannot forbear to quote an extract from Samuel Butler's *The Way of All Flesh* (1903: 36 f.). What Butler says about parents could no doubt be said equally well, with but small changes, about schoolmasters of the same and earlier generations.

To parents who wish to lead a quiet life I would say: Tell your children that they are very naughty—much naughtier than most children: point to the young people of some acquaintances as models of perfection, and impress your own children with a deep sense of their own inferiority. You carry so many more guns than they do that they cannot fight you. This is called moral influence and it will enable you to bounce them as much as you please; they think you know, and they will not have yet caught you lying often enough to suspect that you are not the unworldly, and scrupulously truthful person which you represent yourself to be; nor yet will they know how great a coward you are, nor how soon you will run away, if they fight you with persistency and judgement. You keep the dice, and throw them, both for your children and yourself; load them, then, for you can easily manage to stop your children from examining them. . . . Feed them spiritually upon such brimstone and treacle as the late Bishop of Winchester's Sunday stories. You hold all the trump cards, or if not you can filch them; if you play them with anything like judgement you will find yourselves heads of happy united God-fearing families even as did my old friend Mr Pontifex. True your children will probably find out all about it some day, but not until too late to be of much service to them or inconvenience to yourself.

Mr Pontifex, it will be remembered, 'thrashed his boys two or three times a week and some weeks a good deal oftener, but in those days fathers were always thrashing their boys' (ibid.: 31). Liberals are still busily reacting against the wickednesses of those bad old days; but those parents and schoolteachers who are in contact with the real situation must give a wry smile when they read that 'You carry so many more guns than they do that they cannot fight you.'

We do, indeed, find Mr Stenhouse repeatedly saying things rather like this, when he speaks of 'the inescapable authority position of the teacher' (1971: 155). But I do not think that he really means to endorse Samuel Butler's remark. He means by 'authority' something much more limited, namely the ability of the teacher to prevent the expression of views contrary to his own *in the classroom*. This a teacher who knows his job may well possess. But I am talking about what the children will think when they are a few years older. 'We asked a teacher', Stenhouse reports, ' "Do you meet the problem of pregnancy often with your pupils?" Her reply was: "Almost never, and you'd be surprised the number who get pregnant in the year after they leave school." She said this with satisfaction.' A teacher who, in our present society, wished to use his position of authority in order to determine what his pupils would think about sex, or about anything else, *in five or ten years' time*, would be taking on an impossible task. I know this, because I see in the universities the results of unsuccessful indoctrination in the schools.

Perhaps there was a time when the methods of Mr Pontifex really did work. But it is indeed laughable to compare his happy situation with that of most modern parents. Why was it so easy for him, and so difficult for us now, to bring up our children in the way we think that they should go? The answer lies in the completely different social situation. There may be, even now, parts of the world in which methods like those of Mr Pontifex are possible. I should guess that there are still very many places where the young have access to only one set of values, those of their elders. In such places somebody (and who it is differs in different places) is in a position to dictate the set of values that are to be inculcated in the young, and the inculcation is on the whole fairly successful. We have psychologists who claim that this situation might be restored in our own society by humaner and more effective methods (see pp. 183 f.).

But actually we have opted for a wholly different, pluralist, liberal society; and it would be impossible, short of some kind of totalitarian revolution of the right or the left, to alter this.

One would have to ban, not just *Lady Chatterley*, but all the works of D. H. Lawrence and most of the other writers that the young read. In practice it is not possible to insulate them from the voices, some wise and some quite crazy, according to one's point of view, which compete for their attention. I do not, therefore, feel called upon to answer the question of whether it would be a good thing to put the clock back; we cannot. For as long ahead as it is possible to foresee, there will be no chance, even if it were a good thing, of seeing to it that only one set of values is available to the children in our society. We have got to try to fit them to make, *for themselves*, the choices with which they will inevitably be faced. And these will be choices, not just of hair-styles, but of some of the most fundamental elements in their ways of life. The choices may be made explicitly and with an understanding of what is happening, or they may be made by going with the crowd, which nowadays means the crowd of their own age-group; but they will be made. It is this situation to which, as I understand it, the Humanities Project is addressed.

The Project is ambitious but in essence simple. Its aim is to facilitate discussion of important current issues in the class-room—issues like, for example, race, or living in cities. To this end 'packs' of material on each of the issues can be bought, with one copy of each of the items for each pupil. These are distributed for the children to read in advance. The teacher has a larger handbook explaining in more detail what is in the pack and what questions arise from it. The material in the pack consists of newspaper cuttings, cartoons, extracts from literature, and the like. The children then discuss the issue under the chairmanship of the teacher. Thus the children, it is hoped, become more conversant with the issue, and also better able to handle controversial issues in general. The aim is to provide a technique for teaching this.

I should like at this point to rub in the fact that there is a problem to be addressed (whether or not the Project is successful in addressing it) by giving some figures which, although I am only an amateur in statistics, I am sure are extremely reliable. Let us suppose that someone got married, or started on a career as a teacher, at the age of 24. And suppose that by the time she (or he) is 30 she has a 5-year-old child in her care—either her own or somebody else's—and is worried about how to bring him up. The statistics establish that by the time that child is 15, the parent or teacher, if she survives that long, will have (believe it or not) a 100 per cent chance of being 40; and by the time he is 25, she will have, if she is still here, a 100 per cent chance of being 50. We should have to ask the actuaries what her chances are of *being* still here. Anyway, by the time her child is 45, and making some of the most crucial decisions in his career, she, if she is still alive, will be 70. And by that time the child will not be paying all that much attention to what she says. Parents and teachers are all on the way out.

It follows from these statistics that one is not going to be able to do the child's thinking for him for ever. He will in the end have to do it for himself. All one can do is prepare him for the task. But it does *not* follow that the policy of the Humanities Project is the only possible one. One might admit all that I have said so far, and still claim that the best policy, since complete thought-control is impossible, is to do what one can; that is to say, one should, while recognizing that the child will have to make his own decisions in later life, go as far as the situation permits in determining what those decisions will be. On this view we ought (to adapt Charles Lamb's phrase to a new use) to 'seize every occasion . . . to inculcate something useful' (1818: 72). By this means we can, it might be hoped, make it at least probable that the reactions of the child to new situations when he is grown up will be such as we would ourselves approve of. Granted, he will have to confront a lot of extremely diverse opinions about questions of value in a lot of extremely diverse situations, and we do not even know what these will be; but the grounding which we shall have given him will prepare him to sort out the wheat from the tares.

This policy has been called indoctrination; but I have no wish to condemn it simply by name-calling. We want to know why such a policy is a bad one, if it is (see pp. 113 ff.). But is it? I have no doubt that this policy is used even today with success in many places on many children, and that in most cases the children turn out well. So what is wrong with adopting this as our universal method of education in values?

It may well be that it is a good thing for all of us, however intellectually sophisticated we later become, to have been brought up in sound general principles selected for us by our elders, as Plato brought up the subordinate classes in his Republic, and indeed the highest class too until they reached very mature years (see pp. 178 ff.). But our environment is neither simple nor static (especially nowadays) and what were sound principles may be so no longer. Moreover, if somebody claims that he can tell us better principles, and attracts a following, we need to be able to argue with him and decide whether to accept his opinions. As Plato well realized, it is necessary, if our 'sound principles' are to survive, or even be changed for the better, that *somebody* in society (and, whatever Plato may have thought, I would say for as many people as possible in society) should be able to ask and answer deeper questions about values than 'Is this in accord with the way of life which we have absorbed from our elders?' In a pluralist society like our own, in which nobody has the power to indoctrinate everybody, the only solution is to teach as many people as possible to think as well as possible. And this means, inescapably, leading a double intellectual life. On the one hand we have to absorb and try to propagate what we think are sound values; but on the other we have to be ready to ask whether they really are sound, and answer the questions and criticisms of those who say that they are not (see H 1972a and *MT*, chs. 2 and 3 for these different levels of moral thinking).

It seems to me that the approach to this problem of Stenhouse and other advocates of discussion in the classroom (and I am sure that he would not wish to claim that his Project is the only source of this doctrine) is a fruitful one. I now wish to point out that its success depends absolutely on understanding a distinction which has its roots deep in moral philosophy. The Project has been criticized for asking the teacher to remain neutral on questions about which nobody ought to be neutral. If we look carefully at what Stenhouse and others have said, we shall find that they are more aware of the distinction than are many of their critics. It is the distinction between what I will call substantial values and methodological values. Stenhouse is advocating 'a pattern of discussion teaching in which students review evidence under the chairmanship of a teacher who represents educational values and critical standards, but maintains neutrality on the controversial issues under discussion' (1970).

If we are discussing, say, race relations, we have before us questions about how members of one race ought to treat members of another, and of what controls legislators ought to impose on their behaviour. Stenhouse is telling us that when we are discussing these substantive questions in the classroom, nobody ought to set himself up as an authority on the right answers to them. In saying this, he is only saying something with which anybody must agree who wishes these moral questions to be discussed as moral questions; for there are no authorities in that sense on moral questions (see pp.56 ff.). That is to say, the question of whether it is right to keep Blacks in a position of inferiority is not to be decided by asking what X thinks about the question, whoever X is. This is one of the most important things that children have to learn about the nature of morality; and the classroom is one place in which they can learn it.

But Stenhouse is not necessarily confusing the many different senses of the word 'authority' that there are. Nor, even if we stick to one sense at a time, is he confusing two different fields over which authority can be exercised, as my last quotation shows—the field of substantial questions and the field of the procedure used in discussing them. He is not saying that classroom or any other discussion of such questions ought to be a free-for-all without any intellectual discipline whatever. He is saying, rather, that if the right intellectual discipline, embodied in sound rules of procedure, is imposed, we shall have done the best we can to fit the children, now and later, to answer such questions for themselves. It is a presumption of this method that a distinction can be drawn between the methodological principles or values (the logic of the argument) and the substantial views or values that the participants may come to hold about the questions at issue. People who disagree about these substantive questions may yet agree about the methodology and the logic, and the best way to help children to answer the substantive questions is to teach them a method of arguing fairly and clearly and logically about them.

There are two classes of people (both of which include, I am sorry to say, a great many philosophers) who with the best of intentions attempt to break down this distinction and others (as we shall see more than one distinction is involved), a grasp of which is essential to the rational discussion of questions of value. The first class says that, because questions of value are all subjective, argument about them cannot be governed by any rules or any methodological discipline. I will not now go into the meaning of that terrible word 'subjective' or its near neighbour 'relative'. Actually, if anybody says that values are subjective *or* that they are objective there is a very high probability that he is deeply confused about the whole matter. What most people who say either of these things think they mean is false. But that question must be left for another occasion (see H 1976*b*; *MT*, ch. 12). All I will say here is that to think that, because value-judgements are not statements of fact in the ordinary sense, we therefore can have no rules for argument about them is like thinking that, because the laws passed by Parliament are not statements of fact, there is no point in having rules of Parliamentary procedure to make as sure as we can that laws are made only after careful and thorough deliberation in the light of the facts; or that because the sentence of a court is not a statement of fact, there is nothing to choose between different rules of procedure, or no rules at all, for the trial of cases in court.

It may be true (I believe it *is* true) that on questions of value we have ultimately to make up our own minds. But it does not follow that in arguing with one another there is nothing to learn about what makes an argument a good one. Is there no difference between two arguments, in one of which the disputants are careful to understand the question that they are disputing about, and especially what the terms in which it is posed *mean*, and to understand fully each other's point of view, and to look carefully at the facts which the other side adduces as relevant, and in the other of which they just go at each other without any regard for such niceties? Not from the way some people talk. But it seems to me that, although we have to reach our own decisions about values, the methods for reaching and discussing them are determined by the natures of the values in question (for example, morality), i.e. by the meanings of the value-words; and these can be taught.

The second class of people who blur the important distinction I am speaking of are those who deny that factual questions can be distinguished from evaluative ones. This second class is divisible into two subclasses. We have, first of all, those who do not think that it is possible to make value-free or evaluatively neutral statements about social and other human concerns. This has become the orthodox opinion among sociologists, at least among left-wing sociologists (and I think a great many right-wingers too). I have never seen any attempt to argue for this opinion that was not riddled with confusions (that may only be because I am not well read enough). It must at once be granted that social scientists write about what they think important, and select the things to say about it that they think relevant. This must be so in any piece of writing of finite length. Therefore certain judgements of value are involved in the selection of their topics, and in the selection of facts to adduce. That a sociologist chooses to talk about the effects of horror comics on the attitudes of children to the use of firearms tells us something about his values; he thinks it important to know what effects they have. If he tells us that, of children who have read a certain serial, *n* per cent buy toy guns, compared with *m* per cent of a control group, that shows that he thinks facts about the buying of toy guns relevant to the questions in which he is interested. This does not stop the facts that the children read the comics and buy the guns being 'value-neutral' facts. They may of course reveal the *children's* values; but that has nothing to do with the question of whether the statements of the *sociologist* are value-free. The statement, by *X*, that *Y*'s values are of a certain description, may be itself a descriptive statement of fact.

It may also be granted that sociologists often do have certain values of their own which they wish to propagate, and that they may seek to do this by emphasizing certain facts and neglecting others, if not by other purely rhetorical devices. They may also use, in 'describing' what goes on, words which are overtly or covertly evaluative. However, the fact that it is possible for social scientists to do this does not show that it is inevitable—only that they and their readers ought to be on their guard against it. Nor is it a sin for the social scientist to have values of his own; if he is concerned about the state of affairs in his society, he will. But when he is doing social science he is under an obligation (another value!) to be critically aware of them and keep them scrupulously distinct from the statements of fact that he makes. If he does not do this, his scientific statements will be of little help, in their thinking, to those who do not share his values.

I do not need to rub in the relevance of what I have said to the discussion of values in the classroom. Even if children are set a bad example by some philosophers and sociologists, it is possible, if they are clear-headed and have clear-headed teachers, for them to learn to distinguish the facts of the situation they are discussing from the value-judgements which they may come to make in the light of those facts. In other words, the situation, what courses of policy are possible, and the results of those policies, are all factual questions, ascertainable with greater or less probability from the evidence; but what policies they are to choose when they have surveyed these facts is not a factual question. They have to choose. It is no help towards an education in rational thinking to suggest that this distinction cannot be made. Nor is it a help to suggest, as do the people I discussed earlier, that, the distinction once made, we should stop arguing about values altogether. Both of these views might be covered by a phrase which Collingwood (1940: 133) used of the positivists, but which can with justice be used more generally: 'the propaganda of irrationalism'. The facts determine *between what* we have to choose; but we still have to argue about what we should choose in the light of these facts.

However, it will be said at this point that we cannot separate questions of fact from questions of value because they just are not distinct. This brings me to the second subclass of my second class of Aunt Sallies. It consists of those moral philosophers (usually belonging loosely to the school known as the Naturalists) who say that no distinction can be drawn, because questions of value just are a species of factual questions. *What* species will of course vary from philosopher to philosopher. A popular view is that at any rate moral value-judgements are really factual statements about what will or will not conduce to good or harm to human beings. I hope no one will ask me how these latter are to be interpreted as factual statements (what evidence, for example, would count for or against them); that is a task for the proponents of such views. I wish merely to point out that if such a view were accepted, it would strike at the root of the Humanities Project.

If questions of value are just one kind of questions of fact, then there is a right answer to them, and a teacher can say authoritatively, sometimes, what it is. He can, that is to say, not merely teach authoritatively the method to be used in discussing them (for I agree that he can and should do that), but teach authoritatively the right answers to the questions (see pp. 131 ff.). We are here up against one of the deepest disputes in moral philosophy. On one side of it are those who say that if we understand what morality is and what the moral words mean, we can derive from this knowledge, in conjunction with factual data about particular situations, answers to every moral question. On the other side are those like me who think that, although the nature of morality and the meanings of the moral words establish the canons of moral argument, they do not by themselves uniquely determine its conclusions, given the objective facts.

At this point, however, we must be careful to avoid confusing two different distinctions; otherwise we shall be overstating the case. There is first of all the distinction between the teacher who expects the children to take his word for it that the facts are as they are, on his authority, and the teacher who wishes the children to believe what they come to believe for the reasons which really make it rational to believe that. This distinction is implicit in the title of one of Stenhouse's articles: 'Pupils into Students' (1970). University students of mathematics, we hope, do not believe that seven eights are fifty-six because that is how the seven-times table goes, which they learnt by rote from their schoolteachers, but because it can be shown to be a theorem provable in arithmetic. And students of history ought to require better assurance that George I succeeded Anne than the fact that their teachers all said so. It is an empirical matter, on which I am not competent to pronounce, to what extent a style of teaching which is general in universities can be introduced with the same sort of results in schools. But this is not the most important distinction for our purposes, if only because its importance is generally recognized and therefore needs no emphasis. It is a distinction which separates, not one subject from another, but one method of teaching from another. It will therefore not serve to distinguish subjects for which the methods of the Humanities Project should be used from those where they would be inappropriate. In spite of the existence of this distinction of method, it might be possible and desirable, in handling the subject of race in the classroom—and for that matter in handling subjects like mathematics—for the teacher to remain neutral for reasons of pedagogical tactics, and let the children discover as much as they can for themselves, given certain materials and evidence. I think that this *is* a good method in mathematics.

The more important, because frequently neglected, distinction is that between different kinds of subjects, which vary in the reliance they place, not on mere authority, but on the ability by established methods, which are themselves determined by the nature and definition of the subject in question, to arrive at determinate answers to questions within the subject. In mathematics and French and physics and (in spite of what some have said) history, if you are doing *those* subjects, you must apply *those* methods, and will get *those* answers (see pp. 131 ff.). For example, if you are studying French, and want to know how '*avoir*' is conjugated, you have to study the speech of Frenchmen by the methods of the linguists. It follows from this (though this is not really the important point) that teachers who have access to these methods or their results can speak with authority to their pupils who have not; but all the same it might be the aim of a good teacher to *give* the pupil access to the methods, thereby renouncing his own authority and turning the pupil into a student.

But are all subjects governed by methods of this sort, which yield determinate answers? What about subjects which contain ineliminable questions of value (for example, moral questions)? These are the questions with which the Humanities Project deals, and so we have now come to the really crucial point in appraising it. And it is crucial also to keep clear my earlier distinction between a determinate *method* and determinate *conclusions*. I agree that there is a determinate method which has to be used in discussing and arguing about moral questions, such that, if you understand what a moral question is, you must know which arguments are legitimate, in the same way in which, in mathematics, if you know what mathematics is, you know that certain arguments in that field are legitimate and certain arguments not. But does this method by itself, or in conjunction with factual data, lead inevitably to a determinate set of evaluative conclusions?

It can at any rate be said in passing that the method in question is one which itself requires the participation of the pupils. This participation, which in other subjects may be only desirable or perhaps not even that, in moral issues is essential and indispensable. But I do not wish to exaggerate. In other subjects, too, if what you want to teach *are* their methods, you will have to get your pupils to participate in applying them, otherwise they will not learn. That is why we have laboratories for science teaching. And in morality, you could teach what *you thought* were the right answers some- what as one teaches the seven-times table. I say 'what *you thought* were the right answers' because what is at issue is whether there are determinate unique right answers, as there are in science or mathematics. But at least there is this difference, that in morality it is much more important that the children should get hold of the method, because they will have to decide moral questions in later life, whereas, since they are not going, most of them, to be advanced mathematicians, the seven-times table will perhaps do. Be that as it may, if you are going to teach children *how* to think, and not merely *what* to think, about moral and other evaluative questions, you will have to get them to participate in discussing them, and familiarize them with the rules of reasoning in this field. I think that that is the aim of the Humanities Project.

The question remains, however, of whether the method will yield unique and determinate answers. This divides into two questions. The first is, Will it yield determinate answers if we go on discussing long enough and familiarize ourselves with all the relevant evidence? I am inclined to say that that depends on whether one is seeking practical agreement or theoretical irrefutability. There are theoretical difficulties, connected with the possible existence of amoralists and fanatics, which I have discussed in my philosophical writings

(*MT*, ch. 10), and which prevent us from speaking of a derivation of moral conclusions from factual data by means of the logic of the moral concepts. But in practice, if we explore the possible answers in the light of the facts and of an understanding of the questions, we are likely to reach agreement in any careful and fair and clear discussion between people that we are likely to meet. So the answer to this first question is, for practical purposes, 'Yes', but with the proviso that in practice we shall never have gone on discussing long enough, or familiarized ourselves with all the relevant evidence. So, paradoxically, the conditions that would in practice yield a determinate answer will never in practice be realized. But this should not alarm us too much; it is true in history too, and even in certain branches of science, for example cosmology. The children when they grow up will have to reach the answers that they think best, and these may differ, not because of ineliminable disagreements about value, but because of the finitude of our grasp of the facts. That is why our society is likely to remain a pluralist one, and why it is so important that the children should absorb at school the canons of moral argument, so that the views which hold the field at any one time will at least be reasonably tenable.

The second question is, Will the method yield determinate answers within the confines of forty-minute discussions in the classroom? To this the answer is obviously 'No'. But this does not terribly matter if our aim is to teach the children how to think and not what to think. If in later life they think more rationally about moral questions, we shall have succeeded, whatever they think now.

I wish now to revert to the position of the teacher in all this, and to the question of his authority. I think I agree substantially with Stenhouse, but with a marked difference of emphasis. Stenhouse is (surprisingly to me) so impressed with the power of teachers to impose their authority in the classroom that he counsels them to abdicate from this authority without, perhaps, making it clear enough (or at any rate without getting the message over) that there are certain questions on which authority is still in place. These are the questions of method and procedure and logic. Now that class teachers are not normally allowed to thrash their pupils physically, I see no reason why they should not thrash them verbally if they are guilty of rambling off the point, or going on too long when others are wanting to speak, or appealing to prejudices, or using rhetoric when argument is required. It may be that if these disciplines were practised more in schools, we should have better students in the universities. But I do not wish to imply that a good teacher cannot impart them by gentler methods.

In practice, though, it is difficult to be a disciplinarian about method and procedure without creating the impression that one is forcing one's own substantive opinions down one's pupils' throats. No doubt that is one reason why Stenhouse is cautious. But, that said, I am for more discipline in discussion rather than less; I am old-fashioned enough to believe that people *can* be got to speak and write and think coherently and logically, and that one good ingredient in the recipe for this is to insist on them speaking and writing the English language correctly. It is this power of coherent thought, rather than explosions of sentiments, arising from prejudices, that teachers ought to be trying to bring about. But that is another topic.

I have been discussing the Project, as befits a philosopher, from a rather exalted level, and have said little about practical difficulties that have arisen. I will end with a few more down-to-earth comments. First, there are two things about which I have been agreeably surprised (Elliott and Macdonald 1975). The first is that by all accounts discussions in classes doing the Project have not, in general, polarized into a state in which the pupils all take one view (a left-wing one, perhaps) and the teacher has either to let the opposite position go by default or, in order to get it a hearing, put it himself, contrary to the rules of the Project and contrary perhaps even to his own views. I say that I am surprised, because this is what often happens in discussions with university students.

The second agreeably surprising thing is that the Project seems to have had some success with classes of quite limited or even low ability, and with quite young children. If you had asked me before the Project was tried out, I would have said that these methods were fine with university students or older schoolchildren, but might be too advanced for the younger or less able ones. But there is some evidence that they work lower down the school and in places like approved schools (ibid.: 129). The work of Matthew Lipman and his colleagues at his Institute for the Advancement of Philosophy for Children, who have used a very different method, seems to confirm that quite young children can handle philosophical ideas.

Next, there is a real danger in the method which needs to be watched. The compilation of, or the selection from, the 'packs' of evidence may be consciously or unconsciously biased in one direction. There have already been complaints of this—I do not know how well justified (see *Daily Telegraph*, 3 July 1969). Obviously this could be used as a subtle means of indoctrination. There is the same danger, even, if the more palatable and easy items in the pack are mostly from one side. I should like in this connection to voice a warning about the use of fictional materials, valuable as these may be for stimulating interest. It is easy for a fictional writer to distort (perhaps for good artistic reasons) the picture of life that he gives. Classes which use fictional materials should be constantly invited to ask whether real life is like it is in the novels they are reading, and *how often* it is like that. In this, the Project has an advantage over other uses of fiction, in that the factual evidence is there in the pack too.

Lastly, if children learn the virtues needed for rational discussion of values, it will be above all by example. Rules of procedure and well-balanced and informative packs of evidence are no substitute for fair-mindedness and clear-headedness in the individual teacher, any more than the best rules of court procedure are a substitute for these same qualities in a judge. And there is something else of which a teacher has to set an example: the strenuous desire to find the answers. It would be a pity if teachers created the impression that it does not matter what you say about these questions. Neutrality, or even impartiality, ought not to be interpreted to mean *that*. It is part of the example which the teacher has to set that he has views, or at least is trying to reach them, on the questions at issue. Admitting, therefore, the initial merits of the 'neutral' approach, I should like to add, *pace* Stenhouse, that, if the class progresses, and if it becomes accepted that the teacher is not trying to put over a doctrine by means of his authority or by other irrational means, but that he is in the discussion as an equal, then he ought to give his own substantive opinion and his reasons for it.

It may be objected that this is an impossible ideal in schools (it is certainly realized at universities). It may also be objected that participation in the discussion is incompatible with the position of chairman. But perhaps, when the children have internalized the rules of procedure (the respect for each others' opinions and for the evidence, and for clear and logical thinking), they will be to some extent able to do the chairman's job for themselves and for each other; and then the teacher may, without incurring the dangers which Stenhouse foresees, be able actually to join in the discussion. I hope so.

10

Language and Moral Education

In this paper I am going to try to bring philosophy to bear on a practical problem. What then is philosophy, as I am using the term? It is the art or science which does for words what mathematics does for numbers. We all spend quite a lot of time talking; and some of this we spend arguing with one another, using words for this purpose. It is no accident that philosophy started in Greece, because the ancient Greeks were perhaps the most argumentative people the world has ever known. It was one of them, Socrates, who made for the first time the move which started philosophy in the sense in which I am using the word. He found some people arguing about some substantial question; and instead of joining in the argument on one side or the other, he insisted on having some key term in it explained to him. He did not put his questions as questions about the meanings of words; but they *were* that. To know what rightness is, is to know what we mean by 'right' (see H 1982: 27 and p. 178). In the same sort of way, a father and his son might be having an argument today about whether something is right or wrong (it could be about something important or about something unimportant— about whether it is right to fight for one's country, or about whether it is right to grow one's hair long); and one could imagine some modern Socrates coming along and saying to them 'How can you possibly settle your argument if you don't know what you mean by "right"?' And this advice would be sound. For until we understand the questions we are asking, how can we possibly set about answering them?

Although this kind of demand for the explanation of the meaning of a word could come up in many fields (and there are, correspondingly, many branches of philosophy), moral

From *New Essays in the Philosophy of Education*, ed. G. Langford and D. J. O'Connor (Routledge, 1973).

philosophy, which tries to elucidate the meanings of the moral words like 'right' and 'wrong', has always been one of the most important branches, simply because questions about right and wrong are both very important and, often, very baffling. Certainly, if philosophers could help us to answer questions about what is right and wrong by explaining the meanings of these words, they would be doing us all a service.

Can they help? It might be thought, and has been thought by many people, that mere verbal elucidations can never help us decide substantial questions. These are the people who urge philosophers not to waste their time—or at any rate not to waste other people's time—by engaging in these 'verbal trivialities'. Socrates in his day was subject to the same sort of attack. However, I do not think that anybody will join in this attack who has spent much time discussing serious and difficult moral problems. For one does not need to be a philosopher to see that what often leads to a complete impasse in such discussions is that the disputants are utterly at a loss to know what would settle the argument; and this, if one looks a little deeper, turns out to be because they do not fully understand the meaning of the moral question they are asking. The rules of valid argument about any question are determined by the meanings of the words used in discussing the question; if one does not know these meanings and these rules, one cannot distinguish for sure between valid and invalid reasoning.

There is certainly one way in which we might hope quite easily to settle moral arguments by establishing the meanings of the moral words. Unfortunately the hope turns out to be illusory; it is too short a cut, and it was, historically, the realization that it was too short a cut that led people to say, as so many people have said recently, that philosophy can do nothing for moral argument. This is the way advocated by the kind of moral philosophers I am going to call descriptivists— of whom the largest party are those called naturalists (see p. 206). It was the rejection of this short cut that led people to think that there was no way at all, even a longer way, of bringing philosophy to bear on practical moral problems. This has led in recent times into a division of moral philosophers, in many people's minds, into the good guys and the bad guys. The good guys are the ones who think that the short cut I have mentioned really after all exists; the bad guys are those who think that it does not. I am one of the bad guys. But, unlike the rest of the bad guys, I do think that there is another way of reaching the same objective—that is, of making philosophy relevant to practical questions.

Let me try to explain how I think this can be done. I said earlier that philosophy is the art or science which does for words what mathematics does for numbers. What then is this? What mathematics does for numbers is to reveal the logical properties which are implicit in the very meanings of the number-words, and the other words that we use in mathematics like 'plus' and 'equals', and thus show us that we cannot consistently say certain things, for example 'Two plus two equals five'. In short, it establishes the *logical properties* of numbers. Ethics or moral philosophy does the same for words like 'right' and 'wrong'. It thus shows us that there are certain things that we cannot consistently say, using these words. What both mathematics and ethics do is something absolutely and purely formal. They explain to us the logical properties of the words in question, which are implicit in their meanings, and thus show us how to avoid inconsistencies in their use. And the way this helps to settle arguments in both fields is the same. Just as, once you know the formal properties of the numbers, you know that there are certain things you cannot consistently say, so, once you know the formal properties of the words 'ought', 'right', 'wrong', and the like, you know that there are certain things in morals that you cannot say.

I shall be explaining and illustrating later what I think are the two main formal properties of moral language. These are what we have to understand, if we are to make anything of the moral education of our successors. They have to be taught this language, because knowing and using it is an essential condition for taking one's part in a civilized and peaceful or even a viable society. The language of morality is as essential a requirement for the building of societies as is the language of mathematics for the building of spacecraft. Both are relatively recent inventions (one can trace the development of our moral language in recorded history, just as one can trace the development of mathematics and its language; the ancient

Greeks did not have either mathematical or moral languages which were as developed as ours). And both could get forgotten. The effect of failing to pass on the language of morality would be as disastrous in its own way (indeed more disastrous) as it would be if we never taught our children to count.

Having said how, in theory, moral philosophy can be relevant to the problems of moral education, I am now going to be much more rash, and give my opinions about some practical problems in moral education, on which I can make no claim to be an expert. These are problems on which empirical work is needed, and is being done, by psychologists and sociologists in particular. Philosophy can do nothing to render superfluous, or anticipate the results of, such empirical work. I am not trying to do any armchair psychology or sociology. But all the same, I have been struck, during the time my own children have been growing up, and in the course of many conversations with other parents and children, by how often what was happening seemed to illustrate particular points in moral philosophy.

This was no accident. For moral education is, at least in part, education in the use of a language—that is to say, in the use of the moral language. Thinking morally—which is one of the things that a morally educated man has to do—is only the mental correlate of speaking morally. Indeed, for obvious reasons, the speaking has to come first. We are taught to speak morally by hearing other people do it (for example, our parents). When we have learnt to use the moral words out loud, we must have learnt also to use these concepts in our thought. If we had not, we should not be using the words in our speech to others with an understanding of their meaning. Learning to use a word for communication with others, and learning to employ the same concept in one's thought, cannot be two separate and independent processes. Therefore, what we are learning when we learn to think morally (and this, as I say, is involved in becoming a morally educated person) is determined by the nature of the moral language in which we do our thinking. And this is the province of the conceptual study called moral philosophy.

The moral philosopher, therefore, has some right to give his opinions about the practical problems of moral education, because he has studied the nature and structure of the language, and learning this is part of getting morally educated. Just as a person who was going to do research into mathematical education would do well to study the logical character of the mathematical concepts, so a moral educator would be well advised to know something about the logical character of the moral concepts. For if he does not, he may not really be educating people in the right subject at all. And this is what has actually happened in some cases—indeed, I think, in a great many. Some parents and schoolteachers and other moral educators are like people who try to teach mathematics without knowing the difference between, say, mathematics and an empirical science. And the relation between language and education is much more general than this; it is now realized that if a child has a family background which hampers the acquisition of a rich and articulate language, his whole education will be handicapped, because he will simply lack the linguistic vehicle for the thoughts which otherwise he might have had.

I want to take each of the two main features of moral language in turn and ask what practical implications for moral education there are in the fact that moral language has those features. First I shall have to explain, in a crude way, what each of these features is. I am not going to try to justify my assertion that moral language possesses these features; I have done this to the best of my ability in my other writings. The first of these features is what has been called 'prescriptivity'; this is the one that is most neglected by moral educators. It can be described roughly by saying that moral judgements are things that you are supposed to act on. To see this, just consider how strange we should think it if somebody came to us and said 'I'm very bothered about what I ought to do; can you advise me?' and then it turned out that he did not think that whatever answer he gave to the question had the slightest bearing upon his actions—on what he actually decided to do. We ask what we ought to do because we have to decide what to do, and think that the two questions, though not identical, are connected. Exactly what the connection is I am not going to discuss; it is a difficult matter. For my argument it will suffice to say that it is a very intimate one.

One of the practical consequences of this feature of moral judgements will be immediately obvious. This is that nobody is likely to be much of a success as a moral educator if he is not himself trying sincerely to live up to the principles which he is advocating. If he is not trying to live by them himself, this at once gives rise to the suspicion that he does not really and sincerely hold them. This has always been realized by anybody who thinks about moral education; but the reason for it has not always been understood. The reason is that since the *raison d'être* of moral principles is to guide our actions, the person whose actions are not guided by his (alleged) moral principles may well be only paying lip-service to them (*LM* 124). I am of course excluding the case of the man who succumbs to temptation, as we all frequently do. The man who succumbs to temptation and breaks one of the moral principles which he says he holds may not incur the charge of insincerity if he is obviously upset about what he has done. But if he plainly regards his own transgression with equanimity, he is not likely to be very successful in teaching that principle to either his own children or anybody else.

But there is another consequence of the prescriptivity of moral judgements which is even more important. This is that if moral judgements are prescriptive, it is no use treating them as if they were just like ordinary statements of fact. Teaching children morality is not going to be like teaching them the names of the Great Lakes or the properties of the potassium salts. For if they adopt a certain set of moral principles as a result of the moral education they get, this will be the adoption of a way of living; and one is not going to get them to adopt an entire way of living just by *informing* them that that is, as a matter of fact, how they ought to live. Adopting a set of moral principles—which is what, at the end of the process of moral education (if it ever ends), they will have done—is (however inarticulate or even unconscious it may be) a *choice* of a way of life; and choosing a way of life is obviously a very different thing from learning the names and dates of the Roman emperors. The better educated they are in general— the more they have learnt to be alive to, and to enquire into, what is going on around them—the less likely they are to accept what you tell them about morality as if it were a piece of information. And even if they did do that—even if they did take your word for it that those were the facts about morals, namely that they ought to do such and such and refrain from such and such, the result would not be a moral education. For if that were the sort of thing they had learnt, they would be unlikely to think of it as something that had a bearing on their actions. They would be more likely to turn into what may be called 'So what?' moralists. These are the people who say 'Yes, I know I ought—so what?' (see pp. 92, 175, 210).

There is another even more insidious danger in thinking that moral education is the teaching of a lot of moral facts. One sees it happen so often. Children are brought up by their families or their schools with the idea that moral principles are matters of objective fact. Then, later, they get wise to the impossibility of ever establishing what these alleged moral facts are. Some people say you ought not to practise birth control; other people say it is quite all right and even in some circumstances laudable. There is no way of telling which of these parties is right. So, after engaging in these discussions for a bit, they come to the conclusion that there are no moral facts to be ascertained. And since they have been brought up to believe that morality, if there is such a thing, is a body of objective facts, they at once, having decided that there are no moral facts, come to the conclusion that there are no such things as moral principles—that it is just not the case that one ought to do or to refrain from anything in particular. So, as I said, the effect of a descriptivist moral education is often complete moral nihilism (see pp. 107 ff.).

If only these people had had it explained to them, much earlier on, that that is not the sort of thing that morality is! If only somebody had said to them 'You have got to live some way or other—you can't get out of that; so you had better start thinking before you get much older what way it ought to be. We older people can perhaps help you by suggesting possible ways of living which we have found satisfactory; you may decide in the end to live a different way, and that's up to you; but perhaps if you look at how other people live and what they say about it and what results it has, it may help you to reach a firm conclusion about how you ought to live yourself!' Of course we may not actually say this to our children; but if it is clear to them that this is our attitude to their moral education, one of the essential conditions of moral education may be achieved, namely communication. Our children will go on talking to us about their problems. Even when they are away from home, they will write us letters raising questions that have struck them; we shall learn from the way they put these questions, and they may learn from the way we answer them, if we can answer them. If, on the other hand, they think that we have a ready-made set of answers which is not open to discussion, they probably will not write or talk to us at all.

At this point I want to say something about two catchwords that are all too current in discussions of this subject, and are often used as a substitute for thought. One is 'permissiveness' and the other is 'rebellion'. People talk nowadays about 'the permissive society'. The use of expressions like this has done enormous harm by giving the impression that the choice that faces us in moral education is one between prohibiting things and permitting them. The 'permissive society' is, presumably, one in which a great many things which used to be prohibited are now permitted. But it cannot be emphasized too often that morality is not primarily a matter of prohibiting or permitting things; it is a matter of deciding what one ought to make of one's life in society and one's relations with other people. The principles one adopts for determining this life and these relations will, of course, prohibit some things (for example, killing people just for kicks) and permit other things. But the picture evoked in my mind when people talk about 'the permissive society' is one of some curious creature called 'society' which used to go about prohibiting things but now goes about permitting the same things, with the suggestion that this creature (whatever it is) had no reasons for prohibiting the things it prohibited, and has no reasons now for permitting the things it permits. In the mouth of somebody like Malcolm Muggeridge, the phrase 'the permissive society' makes me think that its user considers it a good thing, for its own sake, to prohibit things, and a bad thing to permit things. In the mouths of people on the other side, it gives me the impression that they think that to permit *anything* is to strike a blow for liberty. But is it not really more important, not to have arguments about whether it is a good thing to prohibit or a good thing to permit, but to discuss, as we try to form for ourselves and help our children form for themselves a viable morality—to discuss *what* things, in this morality, ought to be permitted and *what* things ought to be prohibited? If we had that sort of discussion with our children, we might get somewhere.

The same sort of thing happens with the word 'rebellion'. One lot of people goes round shaking its heads about the rebelliousness of the young; and another lot of people goes round talking as if rebellion were in itself a good thing. You even hear parents saying something which I think they must have got from popular psychologists who write in the newspapers—for they would never have thought up anything so silly for themselves; they say that their object in bringing up their children is to give them something to rebel against. But surely the point is that rebellion is in itself neither a good thing nor a bad thing. It depends on *what* you are rebelling against, and *what* you are trying to put in its place. If parents are trying to force on their children moral rules which have no basis in rational thought, then it is perhaps a good thing for the children to rebel. If, on the other hand, the rebellion is just the result of impatience or of a desire to have a good time regardless of the sufferings imposed on others, then it is a bad thing. Perhaps in general it is more likely to be a bad thing than a good thing, because it is, after all, one of the most wonderful things in family life if parents and children can, after the children have grown up, go on loving and respecting one another, and rebellion often puts an end to this. But as a parent I neither want my children to rebel against me nor want to crush the rebellion if it occurs; what I want is that we should be able to go on talking to one another about moral questions—because I know that I shall learn a lot from these discussions, and I hope that my children will.

I must say something now to correct a false impression which may have been received from what I have said so far. I have been talking as if it were all a matter of rational discussion with one's children about the moral principles which they are adopting. But of course neither parents nor children are entirely rational; and children start off by being almost completely irrational. You can hardly have rational discussions with a 2-year-old about whether he ought to pour his food on the dining-room carpet. Children are bound to go through what Piaget called the heteronomous stage in the development of their moral ideas—the stage in which they take them as given, or as a question of what their parents and schoolteachers as a matter of fact permit or prohibit. What I am saying is: Try to help them to pass on from this to the autonomous stage, in which they do their own moral thinking. For this is what they have in the end to do if they are going to be morally educated. The most common cause of failure in moral education is that children get stuck in the heteronomous stage. Parents sometimes behave as if this were what they wanted; but the results are usually disastrous. Either the children never learn to think for themselves or they learn to think, but not morally.

What I have been calling the heteronomous stage in moral education is not merely a regrettable necessity. It is also a useful part of the preparation for moral autonomy. For what has to be learnt is moral thought; and this means thought directed towards the formation and adoption of moral principles. Nobody can learn to do this kind of thinking unless he knows what sort of thing a moral principle is. So it is a real advantage to be brought up, even heteronomously, in a system of moral principles which is a working example of the sort of thing that morality is. The child may later reject some of these moral principles and adopt others with a different content; but at least he will have learnt the form of a moral principle (see p. 87). If the child has been brought up to think that one ought to fight for one's country and kill its enemies, but then becomes a pacifist and thinks that one ought not to kill people in wars, at least he will still be meaning the same thing by 'ought'; he will still be using the same moral language that he learnt earlier. And it would be difficult to learn this moral language without learning it in the context of *some* given set of moral principles, even if those principles are going later to be abandoned or modified. So it is no help to one's children to keep them insulated from one's own moral principles, such as they are. The child may later reject these principles; but he may at least have learnt what a moral principle is. Perhaps, even, the principles of the parent will be a useful foundation for building on; the child may modify a lot, but he will not be in the bewildering position of having to start from nothing.

What I have said is actually not quite right. If the child had learnt the moral language in a merely heteronomous way, and meant by 'wrong', for example, no more than 'forbidden by my parents', he would not have learnt even the form of a moral principle. He would have learnt the wrong language altogether. But what I mean is this: If the child can see that the *parent* is using the word in an autonomous way, and understand what this involves, in terms of the content which the parent gives to his moral principles, the child may learn, through observing and copying his parent, what it is to think morally. Then, even if the child later, in thinking morally himself, comes to reject the *content* of the parent's moral principles, he will still retain a knowledge of their form; he will still be thinking morally, which is the essential thing that moral education has to achieve. For this process to be successful, it is necessary that the parent should himself be thinking morally, and thus autonomously, and should make it plainer than some parents do just what this involves. We have to start sharing with our children, quite early on, the secrets of our moral thought. This means letting them know about the processes of thought that we are going through, as well as about their conclusions. If parents could become more articulate and clear-headed and honest in their own moral thinking, their children would pick up the art a lot more easily.

I now want to try to sum up the lessons that are to be drawn from the fact that moral principles are prescriptive. The first is that parents and other older people are trying, if they are setting about the moral education of their children in the right way, to help them choose for themselves a morality or way of life. They will do this most successfully if they are facing the same way as their children, towards the future, difficult and uncertain as it is. They are then doing the same kind of moral thinking about the same kind of problems—problems which the parents may, but very likely may not, have themselves faced in the past. For though some of the problems are old, some of them are new. Nuclear weapons have been invented, and so have more or less reliable methods of contraception;

boys and girls behave quite differently from the way they used to, and expect others to behave differently. Parents and children face the same future, though they will play different roles in it, and the children probably have more of it to face than the parents have. The parents have, correspondingly, more past, and in it have played roles not altogether unlike those which the children are playing now—they have faced if not the same, at least similar, questions. If, when facing these questions, or even in retrospect, they have thought coherently and sincerely about them, they can help their children—but on one condition, that the relation between them is such that the children are interested in what the parents have to say. Their past is not going to help the parents if all it has given them is a morality of 'What will the neighbours think?' Only in so far as their children believe that the parents are themselves thinking sincerely and prescriptively about what people ought to do in various situations will the children pay much attention to the parents' moral opinions. This means that the parents have to be genuinely trying to live by the moral judgements which they make about their own (i.e. the parents') problems, and it also means that when they make moral judgements about their children's problems, they must make them as if they were their own problems—as if they themselves had to live with the results of accepting those moral opinions. It has to be understood on both sides that what one decides one ought to do is what one does. And that is what I mean by the prescriptivity of moral judgements; if one has not learnt that they have that feature, one has not really learnt to think or speak morally.

I now come to the other feature which I think moral language has. This is known in philosophical circles by the formidable name of 'universalizability'. The idea is not new: it goes back in essence at least to Christ's teaching, and was elaborated by Kant (1785, and see pp. 62 f. and 125 above); but it is far from being well enough understood. The simplest way I can think of to put this point is the following. When I say that I ought (or even that it is all right) to do a certain thing in my own situation, I thereby commit myself to the view that if the situation remained exactly similar, except that my own role in it was different (for example, I might play in the new situation the role of some other person whom I am contemplating hurting or robbing or killing), then the person who in the new situation occupies the role which I now occupy ought to act (or it would be all right for him to act) in the same way. In short, moral judgements are not tied to individual people as agents; they are tied to *features* of individuals and of their situations. I am not saying that what is sauce for the goose is sauce for the gander; for it might conceivably make a difference to the morality of the act that it was done by a gander, not a goose; but at least, what is sauce for the goose must be sauce for any precisely similar goose in any precisely similar situation. Suppose then that I, a gander, am thinking of maltreating my goose; before I can say that it is all right to do so, I have to agree that it would be all right for me, were I to turn into a goose just like this one, with the same desires and aversions, and in the same situation, to be maltreated in the same manner. I stress that in putting oneself in this way into other people's shoes, one has to put oneself completely into their shoes, including the places where the shoes pinch *them*; one is not allowed to say, for example, 'I don't mind this sort of treatment as much as she does.' The point is that, if you were in her situation exactly, you would mind it as much as she does, because the minding is part of the situation.

If this really is, as I think it is (though I shall not try to prove it here), a feature of the logic of moral language, then it is obviously of crucial importance for the practice of moral education. It may have seemed, as I discussed the other main feature, prescriptivity, that this by itself left us free to prescribe or to adopt absolutely any way of life we pleased. That is true. But when it is combined with the second feature, universalizability, the two together give us all that is essential to hold us in the path of a morality which is sufficient to make life liveable with others in society.

What I want to do now is to try and draw out some of the practical consequences for moral education of the fact that moral language has this second feature, just as I did in the case of prescriptivity. And the first consequence it has is really a very obvious one. Since one of the moves which has to be made in thinking about almost any moral question is to put oneself in the shoes of the other people affected by one's actions, it is an essential part of moral education to become able to do this. And this involves two abilities or skills which, though they have the same function in the logic of moral thinking, are psychologically such different things that they can conveniently be listed separately.

The first of these skills is the ability to discern and discover what the effects of our actions are going to be. The question 'What should I be doing if I did that?' is really the first question that has to be asked when we face any moral problem. And it is perhaps necessary to point out, because some philosophers have denied it, that what I should be doing includes the consequences that I should be bringing about. If the consequence of my pulling the trigger will be that a man dies, then in pulling it, I am bringing about his death, i.e. killing him. I said that to be able to discern and discover the effects of our actions is something that the morally educated man has to have learnt. If anybody wants to object that this has nothing specifically to do with moral education, I am not going to quarrel about words. All I wish to insist on is that all our moral education will be wasted if the products of it are so ignorant or so unperceptive that they do the most terrible things with the best of motives.

There is, however, an ability which falls into this general class, and which is so intimately a concern of moral education that, as I said, I am going to list it separately. This is the ability to discern the feelings of others and how our actions will impinge upon them. If someone cannot do that, at any rate to some extent, then his moral education really has been unsuccessful. If, for example, a boy is unaware that a girl— this particular girl—is unable to enter into and slip out of love affairs with the nonchalance which he himself can command, but is really being deeply hurt by his behaviour, then I would not call him a morally educated person.

It will be obvious how much, in saying these things, I owe to a book *Introduction to Moral Education*, by Wilson, Williams, and Sugarman (1967). The two abilities which I have just listed correspond to those which they call GIG and EMP. I think that there is no special problem about incorporating the production of GIG (general ability to know the consequences of our actions) into moral education.

Educators are already doing it with greater or less success by the ordinary methods of general education. I have, however, just one suggestion to make about this. If, while seeking to improve their pupils' knowledge of the world, schoolteachers were to try, as some do, to relate this information to choices that they will have actually to make in situations which raise difficult moral problems, they would both make the lessons more interesting and do something for moral education on the side. To take an obvious example, lessons on current affairs take on an added importance if they are related to the questions 'How ought one to vote?' or 'Ought one to allow oneself to be drafted to fight in one's country's wars?'

However, when we come to EMP (the understanding of people's feelings) there is here, perhaps, a special lesson for educators. It is commonly said, and with truth, that imaginative literature and drama and art in general can help people to learn to understand other people's feelings. So we have here a justification (a very important though not the only one) for the inclusion in the curriculum of both schools and families of the study of works of the imagination. But this is said so often that I do not need to stress it. Instead, since fiction has so many supporters (in some philosophical circles you lose caste if you fail to read a novel a week)—since fiction is in need of no advocacy, I should like to put in a word for fact. The writer of fiction has other motives (often excellent aesthetic motives) than the desire to portray the world as we are actually likely to find it. If young people get all their knowledge (so-called) of the world out of novels, they may not be fitting themselves in the best way for coping with the general run of human situations. This is especially so in matters concerning sex. For obvious reasons, and mainly because it makes their books more interesting, novelists tend to concentrate on the more unusual sexual situations. If these occurred constantly in everybody's life—which thank goodness they do not, or our moral education really would have failed—then there might be a lot to be said for getting people as they grow up to form for themselves moral principles primarily designed to cope with these extraordinary situations. But as it is, one hopes (and it should surely be an object of moral education to secure this) that most of our boys and girls will have the usual sort of happy family life; and to this end (as in other fields of morality) what they most need is a body of sound working moral principles which will do for ordinary situations. It would be a pity if they abandoned these because they might not do in situations which, we hope, they are never likely to meet. Indeed, if they do abandon them, it will make such situations much more likely, and thus, I am convinced, decrease the prospect of human happiness (for it is an almost universal truth that people in the best modern novels are never happy).

So really, I think, it is even more important to learn to sound the feelings of actual people in one's family and school than it is to explore the doubtless aesthetically more exciting feelings of people in novels. How is this to come about? I have one small suggestion among many that could be made. This is that parents, especially, should not try as hard as some of them now do to keep their children in the dark about their feelings. Many parents who have read or heard about the writings of popular psychologists have got hold of the idea that at all costs they must not be cross with their children. They have adopted a saintlike ideal of parenthood, which it is humanly impossible to realize, and perhaps not even desirable; according to this ideal, the parent loves his children constantly and never even feels angry with them—let alone shows it. The result in practice, with human parents, is that when their children do things which annoy them, they at first give no sign of this. Gradually, as time goes on and the offences—or perhaps other far more trivial offences—are repeated, the strain gets intolerable, and the parent comes out with some wild irrational outburst of rage over some incident which may be quite trivial and quite unrelated to the real cause of the annoyance. How much better it would have been if the parent, when he felt mildly annoyed by something the child did, had mildly shown it! Then, at least, the child would get to know how his (or her) actions affect other people's feelings in this kind of situation, whatever it is, and not be, as so many children are, utterly perplexed and at sea.

I could say a great deal more about this and kindred subjects; but space forbids. I want now to come to another quality that the morally educated man has to have, which, like the last two, is required directly by the nature of morality itself. Knowledge of the effects of our actions, even the most intimate and sensitive understanding of the feelings of other people, is not enough. The skilled torturer has a very thorough knowledge of just how his actions are affecting the feelings of those whom he is tormenting. To this knowledge has to be added love of our fellow men, or what Wilson calls PHIL. This requirement has received so many classical statements in Christian and other literature (I have already referred to two) that I will not dwell on it, beyond pointing out again that it arises directly from the nature of morality itself. To love men is to treat their interests (or ends, as Kant put it, 1785: BA69 = 430) as our own. Or, as Aristotle put it, it is to treat their good, and indeed their very existence, as of equal importance to our own good and our own existence ($1170^a25-{}^b8$). And this is required by the very logic of the moral words if we are thinking morally; for this logic forbids us to include in our moral principles any reference to individual persons as such; we cannot therefore, if we are thinking morally, prefer our own interests to those of other people. I emphasize that it is not that we *ought* not to do this; it is that, if we are using the word 'ought' correctly to make a moral judgement, we *cannot say* that we ought to do this—it would be an abuse of the word.

How is this love to be taught? This is what the psychologists ought to be, and to some extent are, working on. I have only one small lay suggestion to make, that it is most likely to be taught in actual situations in which people are in close contact with each other, i.e. not in the conventional classroom. I think that this question really is beyond my scope as a philosopher. But I know of a great many families in which it is taught; so these are what we should study. The most important thing of all in moral education is to have parents who love one another.

The picture of moral education which emerges from all this is, first of all, that of children learning to find their *own* moral principles to guide their *own* lives, with, of course, what assistance older people can give them; and secondly, of these principles being truly moral principles, which involves their being applicable whether you are the agent or the victim of the action which they enjoin. I am convinced that if parents first, and then children, understood better the *formal* character of morality and of the moral concepts, there would be little need to bother, ultimately, about the content of our children's moral principles; for if the form is really and clearly understood, the content will look after itself. So I would say to parents: 'Try to get your children to understand what morality is, which means first understanding this yourself; if they understand that, and you understand it too, you will not be displeased with the content of the morality which they adopt.'

I have not said anything about some virtues and other good qualities which have figured very largely in the classical discussions of moral education. I mean those qualities which one has to have if one is successfully and consistently to act on the principles which one has formed for oneself. This class includes, first, the intellectual and other skills needed to get done what we think ought to be done—such as prudence, foresight, and even gamesmanship. And it includes, secondly, what have always been thought of as peculiarly moral virtues (they figure prominently in Aristotle's list in books 2 to 4 of the *Ethics*): the virtues which give us the strength to do what we think we ought to do even when it is very, very difficult. These are the virtues of courage, endurance, self-control, and the like. They are obviously a very important part of moral education; and if I do not say more about them, it is only because I have not the space, and because, *for this generation*, what I have actually talked about seems to me to need more emphasis.

It is no easier in practice to impart these good qualities than the ones I spoke of earlier. In fact it is probably much harder, because they are so much matters either of temperament, which we cannot do much about, or of experience, for which we have to wait. For example, it is not typical of the young to be prudent; they will often, in the pursuit of laudable ideals, do things which later (if they survive) they will perhaps acknowledge to have been just silly. Parents and others can offer advice, but it may or may not be taken, and if it is not, there is often not much that the parent can do about it after the child has reached independence. The only thing he can do is to keep in communication, and hope. I do not think that parents should blame themselves very much if their children do things which seem to indicate a lack of circumspection; sometimes it is the parents who fuss too much. They should blame themselves more if they have not produced children who are able to think and act for themselves.

The present time is a very hazardous one for the young, because they are at the mercy of a great many dangers which most previous generations were spared. Most of these dangers are there in consequence of the activities of those in older generations who, seeking excitement in preference to rigorous thought, have filled the world with every kind of emotive rhetoric and propaganda, some of which is very skilfully presented and commands a huge audience through the media. The 'permissivists' have no monopoly of rhetoric and propaganda; but they *have* a near-monopoly of the attention of a great many of the young, who, as a result, get a pretty unbalanced diet of rhetoric. It is no use thinking that any kind of censorship could remedy this state of affairs; and it would not be desirable even if it could. The only remedy is for as many as possible of the young, and the old for that matter, to learn to sift the mass of rubbish which is poured out on both sides of these questions for the grains of truth which it may contain; and this is a thing which, if they can hang on to a common language in which they can communicate, and understand all the time what both of them are saying, young and old can do together.

Appendix: Rejoinder to G. J. Warnock

I can be brief, because Mr Warnock (now Sir Geoffrey) makes only two main points. The first of them he makes at such length and repeats so often as to give the appearance of thinking it an unfamiliar one, although it is one of the main themes of my first book, *The Language of Morals* (H 1952). This is that words like 'right', 'wrong', and 'ought' occur, used in much the same way, in many non-moral as well as moral contexts, and that their logical properties can be exhibited in all these uses. He has not, apparently, noticed something of which I was unaware when I wrote that book, but which has been forced on my attention during the process of having it and other writings of mine translated into foreign languages: that there are limits to the similarities between the moral and the non-moral uses. This can be seen by comparing, for example, the English original with the French translation of H 1960. The translator and I found it impossible to use the same French words throughout for 'right' and 'wrong' in their moral and non-moral uses. The same thing happened when this paper was translated into Urdu for a volume which never appeared; we found it best to use '*achchhā*' and '*burā*' in moral contexts, but '*durust*' and '*ghalat*' in non-moral. However, I do not think that the differences (which probably reflect real differences in meaning) affect the main logical properties which the moral and non-moral uses have in common. Having made so much of this theme in my first book I thought I might be excused for calling 'right', 'wrong', etc. *moral words*, instead of using such clumsier expressions as '*words having a central role in moral discourse*'. But the lecture he criticizes was addressed to an audience less meticulous, for the most part, than him.

The use which he makes of these similarities in his argument is as follows. Since children may be presumed to be familiar with some non-moral uses of these words, and since these non-moral uses, with which they are familiar, exhibit already the logical properties in question, it cannot be unfamiliarity with these logical properties that leads the children astray when they come to use the words in talking morally. Therefore, he argues, teaching the moral language cannot be, as I claimed, an important constituent in moral education (I

From *The Domain of Moral Education*, ed. D. B. Cochrane, C. M. Hamm, and A. C. Kazepides (Paulist Press and Ontario Institute for Studies in Education, 1979).

never claimed that it was the *whole* of moral education) because one would be teaching something that the children knew already.

A first and incomplete answer to this objection is that it does not follow, from the fact that children know how to use such words in one field, that they will unhesitatingly use them correctly in another. They will quite possibly not—especially if their knowledge of the use of the words in cricket, say, or in arithmetic, is a mere unformulated ability to use them correctly, unaccompanied by any clear logical understanding of the way they are used. Such an understanding may require a certain amount of philosophical penetration to attain. One of the ways, indeed, in which a teacher might help children to understand what they are doing when they are talking about morality would be to make them understand more fully what they are doing when they use the same words in talking about arithmetic and cricket. That was the tactic of *The Language of Morals*.

However, that is not the main point. 'Right' and 'wrong' are used in speaking, for example, of etiquette as well as cricket (we speak of the right way to hold a spoon, as well as of the right way to hold a bat). Morality might be like etiquette, or like cricket, or like neither of these. It might be like both, however, in that we could, if we wished, simply give up the aim of doing the right thing as determined by the rules of etiquette, or the rules for successful cricket-playing, or the moral rules (those accepted in our society, for example). Since Plato philosophers have sought for an answer to the question 'What is it that differentiates morality from other activities of which we use the same kind of language?' They hoped that the answer to this question would enable them to give a reason why we cannot simply without a qualm abandon 'the moral point of view', as we might abandon the rules of etiquette or the game of cricket.

Warnock has his own answer to this question, which he has expounded in his books (1967, 1971; see H 1968, 1972d). I should myself favour a different answer, namely that moral prescriptions are not merely prescriptive within a limited area of activity like prescriptions about cricket or etiquette, but *overridingly* prescriptive for the whole of our conduct (we cannot escape them by resigning from a particular activity, as we can resign from playing cricket even if we are in the middle of a cricket field and a game is in progress, or resign from our commitment to the rules of etiquette even if we are dining at high table). If we are not trying to play cricket or to eat with decorum, we cannot be reproached for not succeeding, except in so far as there may be a *moral* requirement in these situations to conform. 'Bad manners' or 'bad batting' by themselves cease to be open to reproach.

I wish to claim, therefore, that there is still something that the children have to learn about the moral language even after they have mastered the uses of the same words in these other areas. What this something is, is as yet unclear; but the failure to learn it may, it seems to me, account for many cases of the 'Wrong: so what?' syndrome (see p. 160). This is common enough for it to be surprising that Warnock does not seem to have encountered it. It may also account for many cases of the related failure to progress from moral heteronomy to moral autonomy (a failure discussed in the empirical literature, which Warnock does not mention). I am pleading, as I did in my paper, only for greater awareness of the linguistic factors (which are not the only factors), in such problems, and for greater efforts, both logical and empirical, to understand them.

No doubt Warnock is right in his books to stress that one of the things that makes moral discourse importantly different from discourse about these other activities is that good and harm to human beings feature very widely (though not, as he seems to think, to the exclusion of all else) among the considerations that make us reach one moral conclusion rather than another. I have given elsewhere (H 1972c: 92 ff.) my reasons why this should be so (reasons which, interestingly, do not rely on writing into the concept of morality itself any material stipulations to the effect that a judgement is not a moral judgement unless the grounds for it have to do with good or harm to human beings, but rely purely on the formal properties of words like 'right' and 'wrong' and on the facts of the human situation). However, there is one crucial point which he seems to me to have missed, and neglect of which comes out most clearly in the second main objection he makes to my paper. To this I now turn.

The point which Warnock misses is this. He agrees with me that the ability to discern the feelings of others, and the love of our fellow men, are required, besides the understanding of the language, before we shall be disposed to act in the way that we morally should. But he thinks that this discernment and this love are accomplishments wholly independent of the features of the moral language which I was stressing. It was, however, my main point in the passage he refers to that those features are intimately connected with these supposedly additional requirements. I amplify this elsewhere (H 1978b, cf. *MT* 197); but let me try here to state the connection baldly and perhaps more clearly than in my original paper. Russell once remarked that when Jesus said 'As ye would that men should do to you, do ye also to them likewise', he ought to have said that moral principles are not allowed to contain individual references. This logical feature of moral judgements makes them, in situations where the interests of others are affected, the natural expression of the kind of universal love which Jesus was preaching. We may even conjecture that the moral language has developed, with the features which it now has, *pari passu* with the spread of the ideal of *agapē* (see p. 62). As I said in another context (*LM* 50), 'To learn to use our moral language for the purposes for which it is designed . . . involves not merely a lesson in talking, but a lesson in doing that which we commend.' So to learn to use the universal prescriptive language in the sphere of interpersonal relations is something which cannot be done without at least adopting the ideal of love, though of course we all fail to live up to it.

I will now explain briefly why it cannot. If we are prescribing universally, we are prescribing for all exactly similar situations, including those in which we ourselves occupy the positions now occupied by those whom our actions affect. What we are prescribing is to do certain things, and what doing them would consist in is a function of what one would be doing if one did them, i.e. of the consequences of doing them. For example, if one pulled this trigger one would be killing this person. Thus it is an implication of prescriptivity that one cannot rationally prescribe anything without trying to ascertain its morally relevant consequences (for otherwise one would be prescribing one knew not what—see H 1979*a*). But because of universalizability one is prescribing (when prescribing morally) for cases in which one is oneself similarly affected; the morally relevant consequences, therefore, include consequential goods and harms to oneself, were one in the other's situation. If, therefore, one takes seriously the fact that one is prescribing universally an act which deeply affects the interests of another, one cannot avoid prescribing as if one were that other; and this is what Christ enjoins. There is obviously much more to be said in explanation of this; but that is all there is room for here.

I think it charitable to suppose that, when Warnock uses the word 'preposterous' of the claim which I have just expounded, he is using it in its etymological sense, given in the *Oxford English Dictionary*, of 'having or placing last that which should be first', sc. in importance. His objection to my views is that I give to the moral language and its logic (I beg his pardon: to the language we use when speaking morally and to *its* logic) an importance such as he does not think it possesses. He has not convinced me. I think, rather, that it has very great importance, not only because the understanding of it brings with it, essentially, the disposition to think universally (i.e. in a way which gives the interests of others an equal weight with our own), but because thinking in this universally prescriptive way leads to the corresponding actions; and also because thinking in this universal prescriptive way demands that we inform ourselves of what we are doing to the interests of those whom our actions affect, and whom we are required to treat as if we were they. The sensitivity and the love which Warnock and I agree to be criteria of a morally well-educated person are not (as he thinks) wholly independent qualifications, over and above the mastery of the moral language—qualifications which bear the whole weight of moral education, the learning of the language bearing none. Rather, the learning of the language *involves*, and cannot be consummated without, the acquisition of these qualities; and the process of coming to understand it therefore goes hand in hand with and *fosters* their acquisition. That is why moral philosophy has a relevance to moral education.

Platonism in Moral Education: Two Varieties

Plato can claim a pre-eminent place in the philosophy of education, for two reasons at least. The first is that he started the subject; the second is that he expressed with a force which has not since been surpassed a particular, seemingly authoritarian, view about it. Any liberal has to come to grips with this view, for which 'Platonism' is still the most appropriate name; and the first step is to determine more exactly what, in essence, the view is. This paper will not be concerned with the close examination of Plato's text; there are some prolegomena to this in H 1982. I shall say nothing about the quaint details of the educational curriculum in the *Republic* or (quainter still!) the *Laws*, which have distracted the attention of some commentators from more fundamental problems. What I aim to discuss is the question 'Can virtue be taught?', with which Plato introduces the subject in the *Meno*—the question which more than any other provides the incentive for his entire philosophical enterprise.

At the beginning of the *Meno* the question is posed: 'Can you tell me, Socrates, whether virtue (*aretē*, goodness) is a thing that is taught? Or is it neither taught nor learnt by practice, but comes to men by nature, or in some other way?' Socrates' reply (the transition to philosophy) is that he cannot answer these questions until he knows what goodness is. The implication of this reply is that the problem of the right method of moral education cannot be solved without a conceptual enquiry about what the end-state is which moral education is supposed to produce. It would be a waste of time to ask whether this conceptual enquiry is a linguistic or a metaphysical one; the notion that there is a difference between finding out what the thing called 'goodness' is and finding out what the word 'good' means can lead us into unhelpful

From *Monist* 58 (1974).

methodological wrangles, and away from Socrates' important question, which could be put in either of these two ways (H 1982: 27 f.).

I am going to sketch two possible answers to this question, and draw out the implications of each of them for the practice of moral education. Both answers are in a way implicit in what Plato says; through not being entirely clear on the subject (and why should he have been, because it takes much more than one man's lifetime for such a distinction to become clear?) he did not see that the two answers are not in the end compatible with one another—one has to choose between them. The first answer is the one which, I suppose, nearly everyone would attribute to Plato; but the second is also hinted at in his writings and in what he says about the views of Socrates. If Plato and Socrates were here with us, I would hope to persuade them that this second answer represents more nearly what they were trying to say; but I must admit that the first answer has more obvious support in the text. The first answer is the answer of authoritarianism and the closed society. The second is the answer of the man who is really, by his own intellectual and moral endeavour, seeking the *Form* of the Good. But that is a dark saying which will only become clear later. Let us call this second answer the *formal* answer (taking the word 'form' as Plato used it, and screwing up its formal character perhaps a little tighter than he did, following in this the lead of Kant). And let us call the first answer the *material* answer—the answer that is put in terms of the *content* of goodness or of morality.

The choice then is: When we try to answer Socrates' question and say what moral goodness is, do we define it in terms of the characteristics a man has to have in order properly to be called 'good'; or do we define it in terms of the logical properties of the expression 'good man'? The first sort of answer gives the content of moral goodness, the second its form. The first is the answer of the descriptivists, the second of the prescriptivists.

Let us explore the first kind of answer and its practical consequences. I will first state this answer in terms of the Platonic Theory of Forms in its most metaphysical guise, and show how it led, in Plato's thought, to the kind of authoritarian political and educational theory which we find in the *Republic* and the *Laws*, and which still has a great many adherents. I shall then strip away the metaphysical clothes from this descriptivist theory, and display it in its conceptual nakedness, as a modern descriptivist might expound it, and ask whether, as so stated, it still has the same authoritarian implications. I hope to show that it has; for the real source of the authoritarianism is the descriptivism, and not the metaphysical clothes.

Put in an old-fashioned metaphysical way, the first, material answer comes to something like this. There is, apart from this world of appearances, an eternally subsisting but unseen world of Forms, the Forms being arranged in a hierarchical structure with the Form of the Good at its apex. These Forms are the only possible objects of knowledge properly so called. We have had knowledge of these Forms in a previous existence; and by long dialectical training we can regain this knowledge (a process which Plato calls 'recollection'). Thus those who have the intellectual ability to undertake this dialectical enquiry, and they alone, can achieve knowledge of the Forms (which is the only true knowledge), and finally of the Form of the Good, the highest form.

The educational and political implications of this view are obvious, and have often been pointed out (for example, by Sir Karl Popper, 1945: i). If it is only this limited class of people that can ever attain knowledge of the Good, and if, therefore, they alone know how to tell good men from bad men (or for that matter good from bad specimens of any other class of things), the only thing we can possibly do, if we are to bring up our children to be good men, is to put the men of this gifted class (the only people who know what goodness is) in charge of the educational process; and if by 'in charge' we really mean what we say, this involves (as Plato saw) putting them in charge of the whole power structure of the State.

It must be agreed that Plato's metaphysical views do indeed have these consequences. But now let us see how much we can take away from these views without diminishing their authoritarian implications. Let us, in fact, take away everything but the descriptivism, and see what happens. The essence of descriptivism is this (and it is an essence which is shared equally by the two varieties of descriptivism called naturalism and intuitionism): it is the view that the rules which determine the meanings of the moral predicates (as indeed of all other predicates) are rules linking these words to things or features of things to which the words are correctly applied. To know the meaning of a moral word, then, is to know its correct application. Moral words in this respect are like the word 'red' or the word 'rectangular' (the former is a more apt analogy for intuitionists, the latter for naturalists). Just as, if we know the meaning of 'red' or of 'rectangular', we can tell by simple observation whether an object *is* red or *is* rectangular, so, the descriptivists hold, if only we knew what 'good' meant, we could tell by simple observation of his behaviour whether a man was a good man. The picture is over-simplified, but will do as a caricature.

It follows from this view that if somebody is able to observe a man's behaviour and its consequences, and knows the meaning of 'good', he cannot be in any doubt about whether he is a good man or not. Differences between different observers about the goodness of a man must be traceable *either* to differences about the meaning of the word 'good', *or* to differences about the facts. There is no other possible source of divergence in their judgements. The further possible source of disagreement that a non-descriptivist might postulate, namely an ultimate disagreement in evaluation which survived agreement about the concept and about the facts, cannot be admitted by the descriptivist.

From this, in turn, it follows that to discover the recipe for producing, by education, good men, what we have to find out are just two things: the meaning of 'good' and the relevant facts. These will be facts about the methods of education which do, in fact, produce the sort of man who is (according to the use of the word 'good' which the conceptual enquiry establishes) a good man. In order to know how to construct a rectangle, we have only to know what 'rectangle' means, and what we have to do with ruler and compass to produce something answering to this description. In order to know how to make a red dye, we have only to know what 'red dye' means, and what raw materials have to be submitted to what chemical processes in order to result in a substance having the properties determined by the meaning of the expression. Similarly, in order to know how to produce good men, we have, on this view, only to know what 'good man' means, and what kind of schooling results in the production of such men.

How do we find out these two things? We find out the meaning of the expression 'good man' by conceptual enquiry, i.e. by philosophical or by what Plato would have called dialectical enquiry (which means, literally, 'enquiry by talking'). If we are looking for a descriptive *definition*, the definition will have to be in the broadest sense a naturalistic one—i.e. one which defines the expression 'good man' in terms of the criteria for properly calling a man a good man. And it seems inevitable that the criteria we shall discover are the criteria current in the society in which we do the enquiry (see *LM* 109; *FR* 23). Thus our 'definition' (so called) of the good man will be not (as its proponents often think) an explanation of the meaning of the phrase 'good man', but rather what used to be called an 'essential' definition—that is to say, a synthetic statement disguised as a definition, which, so far from being merely the explanation of the meaning of the phrase 'good man', encapsulates the whole mores of the society and its ideas about what sort of men it admires.

If, on the other hand, the enquiry has the aim not of producing a definition of 'good man', but of giving a more easygoing account of its meaning, the situation may be even more dangerous, because the dangers are concealed. It is inevitable that a descriptivist, if he is seeking this kind of easygoing account of the meaning of the phrase, and (because he is a descriptivist) has to put his account in terms of the criteria for the application of the phrase, will come up with an account which encapsulates, as before, the current mores. The effect of this approach to the conceptual part of the enquiry upon the rest of it, and indeed upon the whole of educational policy and educational research, is not hard to predict. Indeed, we do not need to predict it, because we can already see it happening.

If we took a typical sociologist or psychologist and put him on to the job of researching into moral education, he would do something like this. He would first take as given some descriptive definition, or some more easygoing descriptive account, of the meaning of the expression 'good man', or of more fashionable evaluative expressions of the same sort. And he would then do empirical research into the correlations between certain kinds of schooling or upbringing and the production of adults conforming to the criteria specified in this definition or account. So, for example, if in the country in which he is working punctuality is highly valued, the account given of the meaning of 'good man' will include a clause saying that it is one of the criteria of a good man that he is punctual; and, accordingly, taking this as his starting-point, the researcher will find out what kinds of upbringing do, as a matter of fact, succeed in making people punctual. Then the powers that be will be very pleased with his work; they will take his results, apply them in practice in schools, and produce a much larger crop of punctual people.

This is, of course, a recipe for perpetuating the current mores. Fortunately our educational methods, judged by this standard, are still far from perfect, so that we are not uniformly successful (indeed not much more successful than the Athenians, whose failures in education Plato laments in the *Meno*) in minting people to the specification that society has laid down. There are exceptions: the armed forces, for example, which have a very clear idea of the virtues that they want in their men and officers, and take a lot of trouble to get them, do succeed to a remarkable degree in obtaining the kind of product that they want. But society in general is not so successful, partly because its methods are imperfect and its resources limited, and partly because it is not by any means of one mind about what mores it wants to inculcate. Psychology and sociology, however, are rapidly advancing disciplines; and although they have not yet succeeded in putting techniques into the hands of educators which can guarantee success in inculcating the desired mores, there is no reason why, if single-mindedly pursued, they should not gain rapidly in effectiveness. Coupled with a descriptivist moral philo-sophy, they will then make possible the realization of Plato's dream: the descriptive definition of the good man will be established, and men will be efficiently moulded to this specification. Perhaps we may see the Brave New World inaugurated at Walden New Town, if not in 1984, at any rate not long afterwards (see Huxley 1932; Skinner 1948). And the principal obstacle to this success, namely the diversity of mores current among different groups in society, will be progressively removed by this advance in educational technology; as more and more children are put through the machine, there will be fewer and fewer dissenting adults.

The type of 'good man' produced may vary from one society to another. It will be different in America and in Soviet Russia, for example; and different again in China. The virtue of conformity, however, will be stressed in all three places. If important differences remain between the types of 'good men' produced in these cultures, world conflict between the armies of the perfect will be the only way of resolving them, because (being descriptivists) the citizens of each society will be sure that those who have the qualities which they themselves have are good men by definition, and that the others, who deny this, are simply contradicting themselves. All this, I am convinced, would be the fruit of a descriptivist philosophy of moral education coupled with an efficient educational psychology.

It is against this sort of prospect that the young are at present conducting a more or less muddled revolution. I am glad that they are frightened, because the future lies with them, and if only one could make them clearer about the real source of the dangers that they fear, it would not be so difficult to avert them. The educational revolutionaries have at any rate an instinctive sense of what is going wrong. But moral philosophers spread at least as much muddle as clarity, and it is touch and go whether the educational revolution will get into the hands of people who have this clarity or not. If not, the revolution could easily make matters worse. All that would happen would be that a different descriptive definition would be used to programme the machinery of the 'good man' factory.

It is time now to turn to the other side of Plato's thought; for Plato, and for that matter Socrates and Aristotle, were at least as much prescriptivists as descriptivists. This will become apparent if, as before, we strip off the metaphysical coverings from their prescriptivism. It comes out clearly in the definition of the good given at the beginning of the *Nicomachean Ethics*

(1094ª1), which Aristotle attributes to persons unknown, but which goes back in essentials via Plato to Socrates. For its origins, the clearest place to look is in Plato's *Gorgias*, 467c ff. The definition of the good which Aristotle quotes with approval in the *Ethics* is this: it is what all things desire. The point of this is not a subjectivist one (namely, that what a thing desires is, for that thing, good), nor even that what everybody or everything desires, or thinks good, is good absolutely. Aristotle sometimes slips into this way of speaking; but his (and Plato's) distinction between the good and the apparent good was designed to avoid the dangers of subjectivism, and the matter is to a great extent straightened out in *Ethics*, book 3 (1113ª1 ff.). Aristotle's point is, rather, that to desire something, and to think it good, are one and the same thing; and this is a highly prescriptivist doctrine (though a false one, because it leaves out the universalizability of 'good'-statements). Like Hume's account, it insists on the motivative character of moral and evaluative thought.

The same idea comes to the surface when Aristotle says that practical wisdom (*phronēsis*) is *epitactic* (the Greek word actually *means* 'prescriptive'), and contrasts it with mere 'understanding (*synesis*)', in that the latter is concerned, not with prescribing, but only with judging (1143ª8). This distinction comes from Plato's *Politicus* (260a). But the clearest evidence of Aristotle's prescriptivism comes from his central doctrine of the practical syllogism, which was his basic account of the relation between thought and action (1147ª25 ff.). The first, universal, premiss of such a syllogism is always some evaluative proposition; to accept it is to have a motive. But from this premiss, when conjoined with a particular premiss stating a relevant matter of fact and thus subsuming some possible action under the universal premiss, the action itself necessarily follows (1147ª30). This is as much as to say that a person who accepts both premisses, and *can* act accordingly, will necessarily so act. And this, in turn, amounts to saying that, if he does not act accordingly, he does not really accept one or other of the premisses. In other words, we could say that, according to Aristotle, what makes the first premiss practical is that from it, in conjunction with the relevant particularizing or subsumptive factual premiss, the appropriate action follows. This could be regarded (though it would be anachronistic to do so, since Aristotle did not have this way of putting things) as a way of saying that the logical character of the vital evaluative words in these universal practical premisses (words like 'good' and 'should') is to be action-entailing, i.e. prescriptive. We might prefer to say 'imperative-entailing', but this would make no essential difference.

It is therefore not surprising that Aristotle, like Socrates and Plato, who held a similar doctrine, and like modern prescriptivists, got into great trouble over the weak-willed man, the acratic or backslider. This is the man who thinks that he should do something but does not do it. He is prima facie a counter-example to the doctrine that 'should' is a prescriptive word: and he was used as such against Socrates, as he is used against prescriptivists nowadays. People who do not understand Aristotle often speak as if in the famous passage on weakness of will (1145^b21 ff.) he was attacking Socrates and allying himself with the conventional descriptivist position of which the late Dr Ewing (1959, ch. 1) was perhaps the clearest modern exponent. Nothing could show greater misunderstanding of Aristotle. He is well aware that his own position, being a prescriptivist one, looks as if it were vulnerable to the same attack as had been made against Socrates. He therefore thinks himself bound to give an explanation of how he would deal with the case of the acratic. His explanation is, as Mr Robinson (1969: 144) puts it, 'very Socratic', and, as I would say, very prescriptivist. But this is not the place to say in detail what the explanation is (see H 1992c).

The notion that value-judgements are prescriptive is, then, deeply embedded in the Socratic-Platonic-Aristotelian tradition. The notion that they are, as I would call it, universalizable is not so deeply embedded—or at any rate not so clearly. It is, no doubt, implicit in the descriptivist side of their thought (whose existence I have already admitted); for if the moral words were descriptive, then moral judgements would be universalizable (see *FR*, ch. 2). The universalizability of moral judgements, however, surfaces only occasionally. We get it in the statement in 1095^a10 that the better sort of people 'desire and act in accordance with a principle', and in the doctrine, mentioned already, that rational thought leading to action starts from a universal premiss. We get it in the very important books on friendship or love (1155^a ff.), in which the great and fruitful paradox is introduced that the friend is 'another myself'. But the universalization is over only the very limited class of a man's friends; it was left to the Stoics and the Christians to extend it more widely, and to Kant to give it its general logical formulation.

There are, then, traces of universal prescriptivism in this old Greek tradition—though they have not often been noticed, because they are so heavily overlaid by descriptivist ideas. If, however, we accept for the sake of argument the view that moral language is a universally prescriptive language, and, with this in mind, look again at what Plato and the others say about moral education and development, we can, if we are bold, extract from them a very different view from that set out above. When they speak about finding the definition of the good, do we *need* to assume (as they seem to have assumed for most of the time) that it has to be a descriptive definition? Let us suppose, just for the sake of argument, that it is a universal-prescriptive one instead (and the definition of the good as the object of desire is at least half way to being prescriptive). What, then, will the philosopher-kings be discovering by their dialectic, and what will they be trying to teach their successors when they are morally educating them?

The answer is that they will be discovering and teaching the meaning and the logical properties of the universal prescriptive *language*—its concepts and the rules determining their employment (see pp. 86 ff., 163 ff.). Contrary to what descriptivists say, such discoveries will be purely formal—very like the discoveries in mathematics to which Plato compared them. And what the philosopher-kings would be teaching their successors would also be something formal. They would be teaching them to speak, and thus to think, in certain ways. But the ways they would be teaching them to speak would not be tied to a certain content of morality. They would not be inculcating the mores of the philosopher-kings themselves into their successors—though Plato in his dominant descriptivist mood often speaks as if this is what they would be doing, and

Aristotle follows him in this. Rather, they would be teaching them a certain moral vocabulary whose only rules are that the words have to be used prescriptively and universalizably. That is to say, one cannot, in this sense, think that one ought to do something without becoming disposed to do it and to prescribe that others do it in like situations.

It is my contention—whatever Plato would have said—that moral education, like mathematical education, and for that matter like other kinds of education, consists most essentially, or at any rate in large part, in learning a language (see pp. 154 ff.); and the language is, as I think, the universal prescriptive language. I share Plato's confidence in the content that our pupils will put into morality, if its form (the language, the concepts, the Ideas) be once fully understood. As in mathematics, having taught them the language, we can leave them to do the sums. And, if it is really a prescriptive language that we have taught them, we need not fear that they will fail to act on the conclusions of their reasoning from any other cause than weakness of will.

I shall not in this paper discuss the difficult question, which was very much in Plato's mind, of whether it is *possible* for everybody to learn and to use the moral language with a full attention to its logical properties. Plato thought that it was not; and if he was right, we have the problem of what to do about the many who can never 'thoroughly grasp' the language in this very demanding sense. Indeed, the problem is worse than that, for even the philosopher-kings themselves will have their off-moments, and an irrational part of their nature. Plato's solution to this problem is provided by his initial schooling of his philosopher-kings and their auxiliaries (and, though this is disputed, perhaps the rest of the population) in the moral virtues. The idea is that, since we cannot be rational all the time, and some of us never are, we need a strong backing of ingrained habit to keep us on the path which reason *would* decree if it were exercised. I am inclined to think that such a solution could be adapted to my second version of Platonism in moral education as well as to the first, without bringing with it the vices of the first; but that is too long a topic to raise in this paper.

We have to remember two important points. The first is the

Rylean point, perhaps not grasped by Socrates and Plato, that it is possible to know how to use a language, and avoid logical errors in its use, without being able to say how it is used or what its logical rules are (Ryle 1949: 27). The second is that there are two kinds of good habits which have to be acquired; habits of good moral behaviour, and habits of clear and logical thought. From the formalist point of view which I have been advocating, the latter is of especial importance. Plato, in an important passage (*Rep.* 503d), notices that *moral* qualities are required for intellectual progress; and modern teachers could learn from him the crucial importance for moral education of intellectual discipline. Loose thinking has corrupted more of the youth than loose living.

What are the practical consequences of my second version of Platonism for moral education and for educational research? They seem to me to be far-reaching. First of all, we are trying to teach a language. It is coming to be seen in other branches of education too that the acquisition of a language—of concepts and the ability to handle them—is at any rate a prerequisite for the educational development of a child. It is probably more than that. Probably the acquisition of the concepts and of the ability to handle them *is* the development. If this is so, then obviously the first task of educational research is to get to understand these concepts. And in the case of moral education this is the job of moral philosophy. It is therefore most important that psychologists and others who are working on the educational process and on the stages of child development should be clear about the philosophical issues. I blame philosophers for not paying nearly enough of their attention to these matters.

The next thing we need to do is to pursue actively the empirical study of the way in which the moral concepts of children develop. The work of Piaget, Kohlberg, and others cries out to be extended. The linguists and psycholinguists ought to be able to help here, especially in giving more precision to the investigation of the way in which children are using the moral *words* at different stages of their development: how one use develops into another; how many different stages there really are, and whether a child has to go through all of them or whether there are alternative paths; whether there are any snakes or ladders in this game, or any dead ends in which children get stuck. Could we characterize any stage as that of the *fully* morally developed man, and what is he like? By what kind of value-judgement do we characterize the later stages as higher?

It seems to me that one of the most essential tools in such research would be a way of distinguishing prescriptive uses of moral language from non-prescriptive uses. For example, when a child agrees that one *ought* not to lift goods from the super-market, does he think that this has any bearing on his actions— does he see any sort of logical inconsistency in saying this, and still taking the goods? This ought to be discoverable empirically. It would then be very interesting to investigate whether there is any correlation between prescriptive or descriptive uses of moral language and actual moral behaviour—what sort of people, respectively, are those whose moral language is predominantly prescriptive or predominantly non-prescriptive? I should guess that to fail to learn moral language in its prescriptive use is to remain at a low stage of moral development; but this needs empirical investigation.

Be that as it may, the chief lesson that I wish to draw from this discussion of Plato's thought is that, in order to get our moral education right, what is needed is co-operation between philosophers, psychologists, sociologists, and practising teachers. It is for the philosophers to make clear the logical properties of the moral language (both the language in which we discuss what we ought to do and that in which we appraise the results of moral education); for the psychologists to find ways of describing accurately what the results have been, so that the results of one type of upbringing can be compared with the results of another; for the sociologists to use these tools in order to determine what kinds of upbringing have what results; and for the practising teachers to make this research possible and to act on its lessons. I am not trying to tell any of the last three kinds of people how to do their jobs; they are on the right lines already. My plea is simply that unless these jobs are done with a good understanding of the moral concepts, which it is the task of the philosopher to seek, and unless the philosophical task is well done, these other admirable techniques will do more harm than good.

12

Why Moral Language?

In this paper (originally contributed to the *Festschrift* for Jack Smart), I take up a topic on which he and I disagree, and which at the same time gives me an opportunity to discuss the very important question of whether we could do without moral language. I shall take issue, not only with Smart's views, but also with those of Marvyn Zimmerman, whose paper of 1962 Smart (1984: 45) says is 'one of the most stimulating papers that have been written on moral philosophy for more than twenty years'. I shall also say something about a related topic, discussed by Peter Singer in another good paper (1973), namely 'Need we make a fuss about whether "ought" is derivable from "is"?' It is one of the many merits of Smart's book to have brought these questions again into the open.

As a preliminary to the discussion of these main issues, I shall first enter a complaint against Smart's use of the term 'pragmatics'. The triad 'semantics', 'syntactics', and 'pragmatics' was first put forward in a laudable attempt to make some distinctions within the rather general concept of 'meaning'. Unfortunately the terms are not now always used to mark the same distinctions, and some important distinctions escape this classification. For example, some writers (mainly linguists) seem to distinguish semantics as having to do with meaning in some quite general sense, and syntax as having to do with rules of sentence-formation not affecting meaning; but others (mainly philosophers) follow the original distinction and allow that there may be syntactic features which have to do with meaning. Thus the transformation which generates the imperative mood might be called in one sense a syntactical or grammatical transformation, but in

From *Metaphysics and Morality: Essays in Honour of J. J. C. Smart*, ed. P. Pettit, R. Sylvan, and J. Norman (Blackwell, 1987).

another it might be called a semantic change because it obviously affects the meaning of sentences.

This distinction need not here concern us. But the expression 'pragmatics' has created enormous confusion in moral philosophy which, since the work of J. L. Austin (1962: 100), there is no excuse for prolonging. The same confusion has sometimes resulted from the indiscriminate handling of the Wittgensteinian expression 'the use' of words and sentences. Austin distinguished between illocutionary and perlocutionary acts, and within the former between different kinds of illocutionary force. The word 'pragmatics' might have been designed to blur these distinctions, and, as is well known, it confused the emotivists. When Stevenson called part of his book *Ethics and Language* (1944) 'Pragmatic Aspects of Meaning', he treated what were perlocutionary features of moral language as if they were constitutive of its meaning, and as a result became an irrationalist, because perlocutionary acts are not subject to logical rules.

But illocutionary acts *are* so subject (see e.g. Searle and Vanderveken 1985). It is perfectly in order to claim, as the emotivists did, that moral judgements have a different sort of illocutionary force from that of ordinary 'constative' speech acts, but yet, as they did not but as I have done, to claim that they are subject to rules of consistency and other logical rules, and that rational moral argument is therefore possible (*LM* 15 f.). Talk about pragmatics obscures this possibility, because it leads people to say, as Smart does (1984: 64), that his chapter 3, which I am going to discuss, is concerned with the pragmatics of 'ought' and not with its semantics; and this might be thought to imply that the questions discussed by Smart in that chapter, following Zimmerman, have nothing to do with logical consistency. It also implies that what is discussed in chapter 4, the semantics of 'ought', does have to do with logical consistency. But, as I shall show, although some of the issues raised by Zimmerman have to do with the perlocutionary effects that we produce by making moral judgements, it is impossible to sort out these issues without an understanding of the *logical* properties of the illocutionary acts which we perform in making them. As we shall see, through neglecting these logical properties, Zimmerman is led to underrate grotesquely the importance of having such a language, and thus totally misconceives even its 'pragmatics', in the sense of what we can achieve by using it, and what we would fail to achieve if we did not have it. What we can do *by* saying things must depend on what we are doing *in* saying them, and this is to a large extent determined by the logical properties of the words we use.

I will try to summarize Zimmerman's thesis, which Smart accepts, as accurately as I can in a few sentences. He thinks that we could do without the word 'ought', and thus avoid the tiresome disputes which have arisen about whether 'ought'-statements are logically derivable from 'is'-statements. We could, he says, make do simply with 'is'-statements. By 'make do' he means 'achieve our object'. He takes it for granted that the object of making 'ought'-statements is to persuade people to do things. But we could persuade them just as well, he thinks, by making the 'is'-statements which give the reasons why doing those things will bring about what *they* want to bring about. If these reasons do not persuade them, then saying to them that they ought to bring about those things will not persuade them either. So why not dispense with the 'ought'-language and just give the reasons, using only 'is'-statements?

As Kenneth Hanly sees (1964), the word 'want' which occurs in this argument is crucial (perhaps more crucial than even he realizes). To want something to happen is to be in a state of mind which, if it had to be expressed in words, could be expressed by saying that one accepts the prescription that it happen. The acceptance does not have to be itself verbalized (dumb animals can want things); but if it *were* verbalized, that would be a way of doing it. So Zimmerman's contention amounts to this, that instead of persuading people by saying something prescriptive ('You ought'), we could persuade them by showing them that *they*, in wanting something, accepted a prescription. The most essential item among the 'is'-statements that Zimmerman says will do instead of the 'ought'-statement (which is a prescription) is thus a statement that somebody (the addressee) accepts a prescription.

Suppose I say to the judge in Zimmerman's example (1962: 53), not 'You ought to sentence the prisoner', but 'You want (or will want when I have given the facts about the case which will make you want) to sentence the prisoner' I am then attributing to the judge the acceptance of a prescription, or predicting that he will accept one, instead of issuing one to him. And Zimmerman is quite right in thinking that to get the judge to act as I intend, *he* has to accept the prescription. This way of putting Zimmerman's point may not please him, but it begins to make clear how the logical properties of prescriptions are important.

It may become clearer still if we consider a simpler kind of prescription, the ordinary imperative. Zimmerman could equally well have said that we could do without this. For if (as so many people wrongly think) the meaning of imperatives is constituted by their function of getting people to do things, one can more successfully get someone to shut the door by giving him (in indicative sentences) the reasons which will lead him to want to shut the door than by saying to him 'Shut the door'. So is not the imperative mood dispensable too?

There are two things wrong with this argument. The first is that it relies on the 'verbal shove' theory of the meaning of imperatives. I have explained at length elsewhere why this is wrong (*LM* 13, H 1971*a*). We have here the same confusion between illocutionary and perlocutionary acts. A schoolmaster has said the same thing, *in* saying 'Keep quiet' to the boys in his class, whether his object is to get them, *by* saying this, to keep quiet, or to get them to make a noise so that he may have the pleasure of thrashing them. What makes the utterance of the imperative *that* illocutionary act is nothing about what the speaker is trying to achieve by saying it, but the fact that compliance with it would consist in keeping quiet. His intention *in* saying it is to make it the case that the boys will not be complying if they make a noise. *In* saying what he says, he makes this the case; and *by* thus making it the case he may achieve the object of getting the boys to expose themselves to his eccentric, but now authorized, amours.

It is thus the logical properties of the speech act, in the sense of what it implies, or what compliance with it would have to consist in, which give it the perlocutionary effect that it is intended to have. If the boys did not know that they had to keep quiet in order to comply, their natural inclination to mischief would not cause them to make a noise. They would not know what, in this situation, mischief would consist in. (Suppose, for example, that they thought that 'Keep quiet' was not a command addressed to them, but a way of trying out the acoustics.) Thus we see that to perform the illocutionary act of commanding is a means to performing the perlocutionary act of getting the boys to keep quiet or to make a noise (as the case may be); but the two acts are not identical. As the example shows, they can come apart.

I have used an uncommon example to illustrate the difference between illocutionary and perlocutionary acts. But if we ask, by analogy with Zimmerman's and Smart's question, whether we could do without the imperative mood, we can think of ordinary examples without limit to show that it would be very awkward. The basic reason (which applies to sentences in the indicative mood too) is that we do not want to, and indeed cannot, give reasons for everything that we say. If asked for reasons we can normally provide them; but a programme that required us always, *instead* of saying something, to give the reason for saying it would be impracticable.

Just as we need a means of making statements without then and there giving reasons for them, so we need a means of giving instructions, making requests, praying, issuing invitations, and an enormous variety of other prescriptions, without on each occasion supplying the reasons. It would be not merely inconvenient but in practice impossible to do so. The kinds of situation in which we need the imperative mood are much more various than some philosophers, who concentrate their attention on military orders, seem to realize. There are cases, for example, where the speaker is an acknowledged expert ('Take two pills three times a day'); cases where *someone* has to be in charge ('Take in the jib sheet'); cases where we just want to know what somebody wants us to do and are disposed to do it ('A double pink gin on the rocks, please'); cases where we *hope* that somebody is disposed to do our bidding ('Give us this day our daily bread'). This list could go on for a long time. The imperative mood is a very useful and in practice necessary part of our language, and if somebody told us we could do without it we should be unlikely to believe him, and should think he had some philosophical axe to grind.

The usefulness of the imperative mood lies in the fact that we can use it to communicate prescriptions without going into the reasons for them. It is interesting, also, that the prescription that is communicated may be complied with for different reasons by different hearers. The Fabric Committee chairman says to the College Meeting 'Our recommendation is: Reface the Old Library in Clipsham stone'; one fellow may vote in favour because he thinks that otherwise stones will start falling on people's heads from the decayed façade; another because he likes the look of new stonework; another because he has shares in the Clipsham quarries. But the recommendation (which is a kind of prescription) to which all three assent is the same. If the chairman had had to dispense with the imperative form he used and its equivalents, and actually give the reasons, no single motion could have been put before the College Meeting which would have secured the votes of all these three people. The virtue of the form he actually used was that it made clear what the recommenda- tion was (i.e. what would be involved in complying with it) without having to give a lot of reasons. No doubt in the committee's report a lot of reasons would be given; but the fellows did not have to accept *those* reasons in order to accept the recommendation.

Returning to the case of the more complicated prescriptions which 'ought'-sentences express, we can now appreciate the possibility that the perlocutionary effects of moral language are brought about because it has the logical properties that it has, and therefore can be used to perform the illocutionary acts called moral judgements. If this were so, it would be less likely that moral language was dispensable.

It is paradoxical if someone who thinks he is talking about 'pragmatics' pays as little attention as Smart does to the actual perlocutionary effects of the use of moral language in our society. I am going to list some of these. The most basic is that it serves as an engine for producing agreement on how people should behave. This is the truth after which contrac- tualist theories are groping. If we had only plain singular imperatives but nothing equivalent to 'ought', agreement would be harder to reach. What makes people agree on the moral principles that most of us accept is that we are looking for prescriptions which we can all universalize; they have to cover cases, both actual and hypothetical, in which we ourselves occupy the positions of those affected by the adoption of, and therefore at least partial compliance with, the prescriptions. This is the essence of the Kantian argument that I have used in constructing a system of moral reasoning (*MT*). If we had only singular imperatives available, and not the universalizable 'ought', we should have to look for very large sets of singular imperatives, directing in detail how each of us should behave; and how could we easily agree on these? But if what are proposed to us are much simpler universal prescriptions, it may be that we can agree on them as a compromise, when we see what the effects of adopting them would be—that is, the effects of cultivating *these* moral principles.

It may be said that we could do this without using 'ought'; we could just use universal imperatives, which certainly exist. But they would not serve. In order to conduct the argument we have to consider hypothetical and past actual cases; and in the ordinary imperative mood we cannot talk about the latter, and would find it at least difficult to talk about the former. We need a language in which properly universal prescriptions can be framed, applicable to all logically possible cases identical in their universal properties, no matter what individuals occupy the roles in them. Otherwise there will be loopholes in the argument (for example, somebody may say 'I can readily accept that principle, because I am powerful enough to protect myself against the evil consequences for some others of its adoption'—see *FR* 188 ff., *MT* 112 f.). If, to overcome these difficulties, we set about expanding the imperative mood to cover the past tense and all persons, as I once tried (whether or not successfully) to do (*LM* 187 ff.; H 1979*b*), what we shall be doing, in effect, is to reinvent the word 'ought'. This can hardly be an argument for saying that we can do without it.

One of the advantages, then, of having 'ought' in our language is that it reveals, to anyone who cares to look, the logical basis of the general agreement, which undoubtedly exists, on a standard set of moral principles that has been found serviceable. It also enables us to revise these principles by mutual discussion. In order to secure agreement on moral principles, all kinds of arguments are needed, relying no doubt on the production of a lot of 'is'-statements, above all about people's desires or preferences. But the reasons for the proposal are not the proposal itself. We adopt a moral principle because of the consequences of having it; but it is not itself a statement of those consequences. And if we had to do without the principle and just catalogue the consequences, we might never reach agreement. To start with, we should not know what the proposal was that we were trying to agree on. Next, the catalogue of facts would not itself carry with it the logical requirement that the principle agreed on had to be a universal prescription; and this, as we have seen, is an essential part of the argument by which we can reach agreement. Further, different people may have slightly, or even radically, different reasons (in the form of different facts) for agreeing on the same principle.

But this is only the beginning of the benefits we get from having in our language a form of words with these logical properties (prescriptivity combined with universalizability). Once we have the agreed principles, we can set about propagating them. Here we must avoid a trap set for us by Zimmerman. He seems to argue: The use of 'ought' is to 'persuade' or 'get' people to do things; but there are better ways of doing this; so we do not need 'ought' (1962: 54–6). But the *illocutionary* use of 'ought' is not to persuade or get people to do things; it is to express universal prescriptions. Persuading or getting people to adopt them is another matter. Maybe there are more effective ways than just saying 'You ought'. Adducing reasons in the form of facts about consequences is only one of these.

What we are talking about here is moral education in a broad sense. Part of this, no doubt, is teaching people the reasons for the principles (which involves their understanding, not just the facts, but the logical properties of moral judgements). But normally this comes much later than the inculcation into our offspring of moral principles which we ourselves think sound (and perhaps can even defend in argument, if we have prepared ourselves to do so). Later they will themselves, we hope, come to appreciate the arguments. But the process could never have begun unless we started by teaching them the word 'ought', which, as we have seen, expresses a universal prescription *without* giving the reasons for it. Children can be got (indeed have to be got) to internalize *some* universal prescriptions before they are given the reasons for them; and different parents and teachers may have quite different reasons. Later the children will come themselves to examine these reasons, and decide between them, or even amend the principles themselves if they see good cause. But to start with they have to understand what it is to follow universal prescriptions without having the reasons for them. And for most of our day-to-day adult lives the same applies to all of us. That is why we need the level of thinking which I have called 'intuitive'.

Very few of the advantages of moral education could be realized if we did not have a language for pursuing and later defending it: a language with the logical properties which 'ought' has. So the effects of a genuine abandonment of 'ought' from our language (and not just the substitution of some equivalent expression) would be catastrophic for our society. We can actually see the beginnings of such a development; but I am old enough to have seen this happen before (*LM* 72 ff.), and optimistic enough to believe that they will never be more than beginnings, because 'ought' and similar words are too essential to our survival for us to succeed in giving them up.

In recent years (in fact just when Zimmerman was writing his paper) it became quite common to advocate the abandonment of morality. Zimmerman has not been the only philosopher to echo, wittingly or not, this popular trend among intellectuals. The argument was that we can get along without morality if only we attend to our own and other people's feelings and especially desires (see pp. 108 ff.). If there is enough love around, what need for justice?

Aristotle (1155^a26) was familiar with this move, which was made in ancient times too. He seems to have agreed with it, but was percipient enough to see that it was not enough as a basis for good living, which involves 'desiring and acting in accordance with a [universal] principle', instead of being, like children, 'guided in life by feeling and following particular whims' (1095^a7–10). And, even if each individual could

reconcile his own disparate and conflicting feelings, the snag
for society is that interests, and therefore desires, of different
people diverge and conflict, and something other than
attention to them is needed to produce the kind of *modus
vivendi* that makes living in one society tolerable or even
possible. This something is morality. If attention to others'
feelings were to be widespread enough to achieve this, it
would have become a morality. The anti-moralist movement,
and other similar ones before it, only started because people
had forgotten this conciliatory purpose of morality, and
thought of it as *nothing but* a set of rules for which no reasons
could be given. In this they were abetted by some deontologist
moral philosophers who were acquainted with only the
intuitive level of moral thinking. Against such a background of
ossified morality (*LM* 149; H 1960), both the anti-moralist
movement and the arguments of Zimmerman are easy to
understand.

Is it an obstacle to the process of rational agreement I have
been describing that 'ought' cannot be logically derived from
'is'? Zimmerman might affect to think so. He has in his paper
(1962: 53) a straw man who, on hearing that it cannot be
derived, says 'Disaster! We can never justify ethics and
morality!' I say 'might affect', because I do not think that this
is Zimmerman's real view. His real view is the same as mine,
that we can get on perfectly well without *such* a justification of
morality. He goes further than me, and implies that we can do
without morality altogether, and therefore without a justification of it; but that is a mistake, as we have seen. He is quite
right, though, to think that 'is'–'ought' derivations have
nothing to contribute to the avoidance of disaster.

The thought of the straw man is this: If nobody ever
believed anything that could not be supported by 'is'-
statements, and nobody believed that 'ought'-statements
could be supported by 'is'-statements (i.e. that 'is'–'ought'
derivations were possible), then nobody would believe any
'ought'-statements, and morality would collapse. But we can
see how absurd this is if we consider the analogous case with
imperatives. If we believed, as most people do, that imperatives are not derivable from 'is'-statements (*LM* 78), would
we therefore give up using imperatives (ordering, instructing,

asking, inviting, urging, begging, or praying people to do things)? It seems that the imperative mood has a use in language which does not depend on the derivability of imperatives from 'is'-statements; so why should not the same be true of 'ought'-statements, if they, like imperatives, express prescriptions?

Is it irrational to voice requests etc. without being able to derive them from 'is'-statements? The thought that it is so stems from a misconception about reason-giving which I have exposed before (H 1979a). Suppose I say 'Give me a double pink gin on the rocks, please', and somebody is impertinent or philosophical enough to ask me 'Why?' I may come out with some 'is'-statements. Let us avoid the pitfall of supposing that I could make do with 'want'-statements. If I said 'Because I want it' (or even 'Because it would be to my liking'), I should be missing the point; my desire or wish for it is precisely what I was expressing when I said 'Give me . . . please'; it does not give the reason for saying it. The questioner would go on 'But why do you want it?' I would then have to answer, as I should have answered before, with a more helpful 'is'-statement: 'It would taste like *that* (if you don't know what cold gin and angostura tastes like, you can try one yourself); and the degree of intoxication that a double gin produces, which is my second reason for wanting it, is like *that* (you can try that too). I am assuming that your taste-experiences and susceptibility to alcohol are much the same as mine. If they aren't, then I can't tell you what it is like for me, but that is an old philosophical problem we needn't argue about now; at least I have produced as my reason a conjunction of "is"-statements which *I* know how to support.'

If I say 'Give me . . . because it will taste and feel like *that*', I am not *deriving* the imperative from the 'is'-statement. The 'is'-statement gives my reason for voicing the request, but does not entail the request. We often utter sentences of the form '*q* because *p*', even when both constituents are 'is'-sentences, without the statement that *q* being *derivable logically* from the statement that *p*. For example, I can say 'It is poisonous because it contains cyanide', although the statement that it contains cyanide does not *entail* that it is poisonous (H 1963b, s.f.). It would entail it if conjoined with the premiss that everything containing cyanide is poisonous; but that premiss itself is not logically nor even analytically true.

So, if I can say 'Give me . . . because . . . ' without there being derivations of imperatives from 'is'-statements, why cannot the judge say 'I ought to sentence the prisoner, because . . . ' without there being a corresponding derivation? The 'cyanide' example yields a clue here. There is, no doubt, a universal, synthetic, *prescriptive* premiss which the judge accepts, namely that he ought to sentence prisoners who have been found guilty by due process. If this in turn were questioned, the kind of reasoning which I invoked earlier would provide a means of justifying it (*FR* 115 ff., 124 f.). This kind of reasoning does not involve 'is'–'ought' derivations. What it involves is asking judges and others to choose one of a set of alternative prescriptions to accept, on the condition that they be universal (and therefore applicable whatever role the chooser were to play—of a judge, or a prisoner, or one of the many victims of crime), and in full knowledge of what that would be like (a knowledge expressible in 'is'-sentences).

What is in evidence here is a fundamental mistake about rationality (H 1979*a*). To have a reason for what we say does not involve being able to derive it logically from an 'is'-statement which does not entail it. It involves having something in mind which is our reason. This could, but need not be, expressed in an 'is'-sentence. That it is a reason is another way of saying that there is some universal synthetic premiss which we accept, and which, in conjunction with the aforementioned reason, *does* entail what we said. All this applies to imperatives, moral statements, and factual statements alike. Even the man who asks for the gin because it would be like that to drink it must be accepting, at any rate for the time being, the premiss that he should, *ceteris paribus*, on occasions like this, when he is in this kind of mood, take drinks which would have that effect on him. He is being incontinent, as Aristotle put it, 'in obedience, in a manner of speaking, to a principle coupled with a factual belief' (1147[b]1). The justification of the universal premiss is an entirely different matter. I have dealt with it as regards moral arguments (*MT*), and I leave it to philosophers of science like Smart to deal with it as regards factual statements.

The next question that Smart will want to ask is about my use in the last few paragraphs of the analytic–synthetic distinction. Because he likes Quine's views on this (1951) more than I do, he might think that I shall be in trouble because I use these suspect terms. But I am in no trouble at all. The first thing I wish to say about this (which is worth saying, although it could be accused of being rhetoric) is that I do not think it profitable to argue with people who deny that there is a distinction between analytically and synthetically true statements. The reason why I do not think it profitable is this: 'Analytic' is one of a set of expressions (others are 'synonymous', 'consistent', and 'follows from') which are essential to the assessment of arguments. For example, if somebody does not know the difference between one statement following from another and its not following, what could ever be achieved by arguing with him? And since 'analytic' and 'follow from' are interdefinable, if he is prepared to use one he must be prepared to use the other.

Perhaps that was just rhetoric. So, for the sake of argument, I am going to assume that the word 'analytic' *is* suspect, and try to see what would happen in my own moral philosophy if I dispensed with it. It seems to me that I should not suffer much; and the reason for this is important. It is that the method of moral reasoning that I advocate is entirely formal. It can make use, therefore, of the notions '*logically* true', '*logically* follows', and the like, and does not have to use the suspect expression 'analytic'. Those who like completely formal systems can construct a system of deontic logic having the same properties as I say ordinary moral language has. In this formal system the sign corresponding to 'ought' will be defined in terms of the universal quantifier and the imperative mood-sign (as I do for 'must' in *MT* 23), and will not need to import any notions of the kind that Quine wants to ban. If the formal logical relations between statements in this system are as I say the formal relations between statements in English are (and I can see no reason why they should not be), then I could in principle do all that I want to, by way of introducing the system of reasoning, without using the notions of synonymy between statements in English and of their analyticity. Of course the English-speakers that I am trying to communicate with and help would have to learn the new language; but they could as easily do this as they can learn any other formal language. Personally, because I do not have the fastidious scruples that Quine has, I prefer to go on talking English; but it makes no fundamental difference.

Actually, it is not I but my opponents in moral philosophy who are likely to be in trouble. They really do need to claim, at any rate if they are naturalists, that certain expressions are synonymous as used in ordinary English (for example, 'good' and 'satisfying basic human needs'); or that certain statements made in ordinary English are analytically true (for example, that the gratuitous infliction of pain is wrong). By all means let them try out those on Quine: my withers are unwrung. If I were a follower of Quine, I would say that the synonymy or analyticity cannot be established, because the notions themselves are shaky. Not being a follower of Quine, what I shall actually do is to challenge the naturalists to show that they *are* analytic or synonymous, in the confidence that they will fail. But I myself can take refuge in the safety of a system of reasoning which does not need to use such suspect notions.

If, for the sake of argument, we accept Quine's thesis that there is no hard and fast line between the analytic and the synthetic, we shall still have a spectrum with deeply entrenched theses at one end and easily discardable ones at the other. In terms of such a view, we can ask the naturalists where on this spectrum they would put their favoured moral judgements. Obviously they will try to put them at the entrenched end. But on any controversial question of morality, what is at issue is precisely whether such-and-such an opinion *should* be so entrenched. So a naturalistic theory can never be used to settle any controversial moral question. Like intuitionism, it may seem to work for questions to which we all think we know the answers, but not with those which really bother us. The fraudulence of both these theories consists in trying to make out that questions are settled by our intuitions, or by an appeal to language, or by some Quinean entrenchment, when they are not.

I can usefully end by dealing with a difficulty raised by Peter Singer (1973), which, though not discussed directly by Smart, is relevant to matters that he does discuss. Singer uses an argument very similar to one that I remember using myself in early lectures to show that we cannot derive 'ought' from 'is'; but he turns it on its head. I used to argue, and would still argue, that since the main point of moral judgements is to guide actions, and since they cannot do this without having imperatives as their consequences, they cannot themselves be derivable from pure non-moral 'is'-statements, since *these* do not have imperative consequences. If statement *R* does not follow from statement *P*, but does follow from statement *Q*, then *Q* also cannot follow from *P* ; for if it did, then *R* could be made to follow from *P* via *Q*, which is contrary to hypothesis. So if *P* is an ordinary statement of fact, and *Q* a moral judgement, *Q* cannot follow from *P*.

Though this argument is valid, I gave up using it because objectors tended to deny one of its premisses, namely that moral judgements entail imperatives. I still think that they do, if used prescriptively (this is indeed a tautology); but the matter obviously needed more discussion, which I duly gave it (*LM*, ch. 11; *FR* 26 ff.). Singer's argument is very similar, but in reverse. He accepts that what we need to have is something to guide actions. He accepts that non-moral facts do not by themselves do this, in the sense that there is no logical bar to agreeing with the facts and not acting. So there is a 'gap' between the factual statements and the decision to act. The question is whether a moral statement or judgement put in between the two can bridge the gap; and Singer argues that it cannot, because whatever view we take of the status of the moral judgement, a gap will still be left one side of it or the other.

He distinguishes two extreme views about the logical character and relations of moral judgements, and then goes on to consider an intermediate view, which he attributes not unfairly to me. None of these views, he says, will bridge the gap. At one extreme we have what he calls the form-and-content neutralist, or for short the *neutralist*, position. (Since my own position is content- but not form-neutralist, the abbreviation might mislead, but I will accept it.) The neutralist holds that 'there are no limits on the kind of principle which can be held as a moral principle' (1973: 52). This cannot be what Singer really means, because nobody would want to maintain that sentences of absolutely any kind could express moral principles. For example, 'No pigs have wings' could not. What Singer means is rather that, as he says a few sentences further on, according to the neutralist 'to count as a moral principle, a principle does not have to satisfy any of the formal requirements *that have sometimes been proposed*, such as being able to be willed as a universal law, being acceptable to an impartial observer, being able to be formulated without the use of proper names, personal pronouns, or other singular terms' (1973: 52, my italics).

So Singer's 'neutralist' is not exempting moral principles from *all* formal restrictions. In fact Singer goes on to say that it is a strength of neutralism 'that it provides a very close *logical* connexion between the moral principles a man holds and the way he acts' (1973: 53, my italics). This is to say that moral principles have to be prescriptive, which is a formal property. He has also said earlier that they have to be overriding according to the neutralist; and this too is a formal requirement.

The descriptivist, on the other hand, makes no such formal connexion between moral principles and decisions to act. But he does (at least if he is a naturalist) make a *logical* connexion between moral judgements and the facts which are the reasons for them. This is because he puts on moral principles restrictions of both form *and* content. For example, he may say that 'moral judgements are logically tied to suffering and happiness' and that they must not 'arbitrarily place more importance on the suffering and happiness of a particular person or group of persons than on the suffering and happiness of any others' (Singer 1973: 53). The first of these restrictions is on the content, the second on the form. In virtue of the first, the descriptivist should be able in principle, once someone has agreed that to give money to famine relief would prevent more suffering than spending it on a new Mercedes, to compel him to conclude that he ought to give the money to famine relief.

The two extreme positions exhibit, as Singer shows, symmetrically opposite weaknesses. The descriptivist can get the reluctant donor to agree that he *ought* to give the money, but has no way of bringing him to the decision actually to give the money. The neutralist, on the other hand, can bring him to this decision once he has accepted the moral judgement that he ought to give it, because of the neutralist's logical link between moral judgements and action; but the reluctant donor remains at liberty not to accept the moral judgement, even though he has agreed on the non-moral fact that a gift would relieve more suffering. So neither the descriptivist nor the neutralist can get all the way by logical means from non-moral facts to decisions to act; for both of them there is a gap: for the descriptivist between values and actions, and for the neutralist between facts and values.

Singer concludes that the dispute between these extreme positions is of no practical importance; and he supports this conclusion by pointing out that, faced with the reluctant donor, both would use essentially the same means of getting him to go all the way, though they might use different words. The reluctant donor would say to the descriptivist that, although he agreed that he ought to give the money, that was no reason for giving it. The descriptivist's next move would be to try to get him to 'take notice of morality' by 'appealing to the feelings of sympathy and benevolence which, in common with most of mankind, he probably has to some extent' (Singer 1973: 53). The neutralist, on the other hand, will seek to overcome the gap, though it is in a different place, by appealing to the same feelings. He knows that the reluctant donor, *if* he accepted the moral principle that one ought to relieve suffering, would give the money; and therefore he will use the very same appeal to human sympathy to get him to accept the principle.

The similarity is obvious between Singer's conclusion and Zimmerman's thesis which I discussed earlier and which attracts Smart. Singer, however, does not go to the extreme length of denying that we need to use 'ought' at all; he merely says that we need not make so much fuss about whether it is derivable from 'is', because that is a trivial, verbal question which depends merely on how we define the moral words, or the word 'moral'. I agree with both Singer and Zimmerman that some of the reasons sometimes given for worrying about the gap between 'is' and 'ought' are bad ones. We do not need to worry, so much as to give an account of how, although 'ought' is not logically derivable from 'is', we can still reason about moral questions. This I have tried to do.

Zimmerman's contention is that we can do without 'ought' and appeal instead to desires. Singer's argument, if pursued to its limit, would have the same consequence. For if, in the argument from 'is' via 'ought' to action-decisions, there is going to be a gap on one side or other of the 'ought', and the gap can be bridged only by an appeal to sympathetic and benevolent feelings (which are a kind of desires) then why not dispense with the 'ought' and just appeal to the desires, as Zimmerman suggests? Singer still differs from Zimmerman, because he would appeal to a special kind of feeling, which one might even dignify by the name of 'moral feeling'; and nobody could deny that this is from the moral point of view an improvement. But both writers make it look as if we should stop worrying about the logic of moral language and whether 'ought' is derivable from 'is'.

I am going to counter Singer's argument in the same way as I countered Zimmerman's; and I can best do so by considering what he says about the 'composite' or 'middle' position (1973: 55), which is my own. This is content-neutral but not form-neutral. That is to say, it puts formal restrictions on what can count as a moral principle, but no restrictions of content. As we saw, even what Singer calls 'neutralism' puts some formal restrictions on this, namely prescriptivity and overridingness. I only need to add to these a requirement of universality or universalizability. Singer expounds this position very fairly, and I have already sketched it in this paper, so I will not explain in detail how universalizability helps bridge the gap, but will simply consider Singer's objection to the manœuvre. I must add that Singer's paper was written some time before my *Moral Thinking*, and that our positions are now much closer to each other (Singer 1979, 1981, 1988). In what follows I shall not be trying to controvert Singer's present views, but only to deal with the difficulty raised in his paper.

His objection consists in producing the character whom in my books I have called the 'amoralist'. This is 'a person whose overriding principle of action is non-universalizable—for instance a person who acts on the principle of pure egoism'. I dealt with the amoralist at some length in *MT* 182 ff. and *FR* 100 f. My tactic was to admit that there can be amoralists, and that I cannot refute them by logic, provided that they are consistent in their amoralism; but then to produce prudential reasons why we should not be amoralists. In particular, I argued that if we were educating a child with only the child's interest at heart, we would be well advised not to bring him up as an amoralist, but to give him a normal moral education, and in so doing both teach him the moral language with its logic, and cultivate in him the firm intuitive principles which would be most likely to make him both happy and an acceptable member of society.

Into this argument I shall not go at length. But I do want to emphasize, as I did when answering Zimmerman, the importance for moral education of having a moral language. It is very hard to imagine what moral education would be like if it had to be conducted without one. I discussed earlier the recent (indeed recurrent) tendency among intellectuals to say that we could do without morality. If we tried to do this, we should have to reinvent it under another name. The same holds for the moral language; for it would be hard to practise morality without some way of expressing moral opinions. These opinions are, after all, one of the things that we are trying to get people to have when we are educating them morally. They will have in addition to acquire dispositions to act on these opinions; but before they do this they have to have the opinions.

As both Singer and Zimmerman see, we could not do without some appeal to people's feelings or desires. Singer adds to this, but Zimmerman does not, that the desires will have to be sympathetic and benevolent ones. Suppose we ask, then, how such feelings or desires will be expressed. The words we use in moral discourse are designed for this very purpose. That is why I said that the project of doing without morality would lead to its reinvention.

But there is more to it than that. To acquire impartially benevolent desires is to come to accept one kind of universal prescriptions (not the only kind, because there can be fanatical universal prescriptions which are not benevolent— some are even malevolent (*FR*, ch. 9, *MT*, ch. 10)). Moral judgements are the way language provides of expressing these prescriptions. But it goes further; it also provides them with a logic. Moral education, which, I have argued, it is in our interest to have, brings this logic with it. The logic is based on the features of prescriptivity and universality. It has these features just because it is designed to express the impartially benevolent feelings that Singer wishes to appeal to. If we assume that people are nearly always at least benevolent to *themselves*, and therefore prescribe what they think is for their own good, and if we then require them to universalize their prescriptions, they will have to treat the good of other people as if it were their own and prescribe for others as if they were prescribing for themselves. It is crucial for this argument that moral language has the features both of prescriptivity and of universality.

If this is so, then we can see why, in spite of what Singer says, it does matter very much that 'ought' is not derivable from 'is'. For prescriptivity is a necessary part of the argument. If moral judgements were not prescriptive, one move in it would be barred, namely the move which asks whether we are prepared to prescribe that what we are proposing to do to somebody else should be done to us were we in his position. But if moral language is prescriptive, and prescriptions are not logically derivable from non-moral facts, then moral judgements are not derivable from them either; and conversely, if they were derivable, they could not be prescriptive. So it is very important whether they are derivable. We have come back to my original early argument.

The importance is not merely theoretical. If moral judgements were derivable from factual statements, and therefore not prescriptive, morality would lose its grip on people's conduct. We would have, as we have already in some quarters, a 'So what?' morality (H 1971*c*: 113; see also p. 160). By this I mean the morality of those who can say 'Yes, I know I ought; but so what?' Singer uses such people as an argument against the descriptivist, quite rightly, and says that this prescriptivity is the strength of the neutralist position. It is one strength of my own sort of neutralist position too. If morality is universally *prescriptive*, one cannot say 'So what?', because to accept the moral judgement is already to accept its bearing on our conduct. In order to avoid the bearing on our conduct, we have to stop making the moral judgement. I have not denied that it is possible to do this, and become an amoralist. But I have argued that there is a price to be paid for it—a price which we would be imprudent to pay.

In his latest writings (cited above) Singer has arguments to show why the scope of morality gets extended beyond the tribe and the race to the whole of humanity, and beyond the human species to other sentient creatures. I hope that these arguments will be successful. As I have argued in reviewing one of his books, moral language, and its natural tendency to extend the range of universalization, plays an even bigger part in this than Singer suggests (H 1981*b*).

What would Smart say to all this? I hope that he would agree that the 'pragmatics', as he calls them, of moral language extend a good deal further than he has followed them in his book. Once we start looking at the process of moral education, and see how difficult it would be in default of a language with the logical and illocutionary features which alone make the pragmatics possible, we can see that the whole cohesion of our society depends on having such a language.

Opportunity for What? Some Remarks on Current Disputes about Equality in Education

In the past few years a great many heads have been broken in many places in disputes about equal rights; and of these disputes that about equality in education has been one of the most violent in some countries. It is my belief that at least some of these heads would not have been broken if some clearer thinking had been going on inside them. Not that everything can be achieved by clear thinking; firmness of purpose and other moral qualities are also required. But if more clarity were introduced into these disputes, some of the violence might be replaced by co-operation, when the disputants discovered that there were principles (perhaps a bit less simple than the slogans on their placards) upon which they could agree. That, at any rate, is the hope with which I, as a philosopher, approach this question.

Nearly all disputes about equality are expressed in the language of *rights*. This is a pity; for out of all the concepts in our moral language that of rights is one of the least clear, and the efforts of philosophers have attained less success here than perhaps they have elsewhere. It would seem that rights have something to do with *justice*; but that too is a very unclear concept. It, in turn, has something to do with what we *ought* to be doing or what it is *right* to do; but the relation is as yet unexplained. I shall spend the first part of this paper examining these concepts and the relations between them; and then in the rest I shall go on to apply what I have said to some practical issues of some importance. If any reader finds the analysis dry or remote, I ask him to be patient. I shall not be able to make it very long or thorough; I have tried elsewhere (H 1978*a*, *MT*, ch. 9) to give a fuller account of

From *Oxford Rev. of Education* 3 (1977).

justice, and shall have to limit myself to a summary treatment here.

Rights are the stamping-ground of intuitionists—of those who think that they just know the answers to moral questions, without argument or the use of reason. I have tried in *MT* 149 ff., following Hohfeld 1923: 36 ff., to distinguish and clarify the different senses of rights, both legal and moral, and to show how we can establish what moral rights people ought to have.

These distinctions are important, and perhaps fewer heads would be broken if they were understood; and there are many more complications into which I should have to go, if my purpose were not something different. The problem, however, to which I wish to direct attention is one common to all these senses of 'rights', or kinds of rights. It is this: in the legal case we think that we can get it decided whether a person does or does not have a certain right by going to the courts or the legislature; but what happens when not a legal but a moral right is claimed? For example, suppose that in a certain country there is no *legal* right to universal education—i.e. no law has been made requiring the authorities to provide it— but that some people wish to claim that it *ought* (morally) to be provided, or that it would be *unjust*, though not contrary to the existing law, if it were not. They might very well express this claim by saying that everybody had a *moral right* to schooling. But there would not be, as in the legal case, a clear way of determining whether this right existed; those who said that it did not could not be taken to court, nor could the legislature pass a law establishing this *moral* right, though it could indeed establish, by passing a law, a *legal* right to education.

The failure to distinguish between moral and legal rights is one of the sources of the doctrine of natural law and natural rights, which are a kind of confused slurry of legal and moral rights all mixed up. I shall not now set foot in this quagmire, except to say that, in my view, everything that natural-law theorists wish to say about rights could be said much more clearly if they spoke of moral rights instead of natural rights. The distinction between rights which are claimed on moral grounds and those which are claimed on legal grounds would then be kept clear, as it now often is not, even in the courts.

Although moral rights are not the same as legal rights, there is an analogy between them which can be helpful if we do not press it too far. Just as legal rights have their basis in laws, so moral rights have their basis in moral principles. There is a difficulty about establishing moral principles which is more perplexing than that about establishing laws; but the analogy at least helps us to *locate* the difficulty. *If* we could settle what are the right moral principles as easily as we can settle what the law is, or what it is to be, then the *rest* of the argument about moral rights would go more swimmingly. So one, at any rate, of the difficulties which face us has been pin-pointed: it is the old problem of how we are to select our moral principles. Into this problem, since I have devoted most of my philosophical writings to it (see *MT*) I shall not go in this paper—I think I have an answer to it, but it would take too long to explain. A few hints as we go along will have to suffice.

But even if we had a method for choosing our moral principles, our difficulties would not be at an end; for not *any* moral principles will do for determining people's rights, but only principles of a certain kind, namely principles of *justice*, which are only one kind of moral principle. And the word 'just' too is ambiguous (see H 1978*a*). There is one sense of it in which justice is more or less coextensive with the whole of morality; the '*justus vir*' of Horace (*Odes*, 3. 3) and his counterpart in the Bible (Wisdom 3: 1) are simply those who do what they ought—the righteous or upright. But, as Aristotle explained (1130^a14), there is also a narrower sense of 'just' in which it means 'fair'. Confusion between the two senses is another cause of broken heads. In the more general sense of 'just' it seems self-evident that we ought to do what is just; and this is indeed so, if the just act *means* the right act, the act that we ought to do. But in the narrower sense it can be the case that we ought not, in some unusual situation, to do what is just. The man who said 'Let justice be done, though the heavens fall' was perhaps confusing the two senses. Sometimes it is impossible to be absolutely fair in this imperfect world, without transgressing some even more important duty. It is unfair to the man with Lassa fever to keep him in quarantine for weeks; it was not his fault that he got it and we are inflicting real and unmerited harm on him to protect the public from greater harm. It may not be fair to parents who have moved house at great expense simply in order to be able to send their children to a good school, to have them bussed away to another school. It may not be fair —that is one of the disputes which concern us—but people claim, and they could be right, that we ought to do it all the same.

The principles of justice, in the sense of fairness, are a kind of moral principle which holds only in general, and admits of exceptions; they are what philosophers call prima facie principles. That means that, even if someone is right in claiming that children have *in general* a right to equal education, there may be other overriding moral reasons why we ought not to give it them—suppose, for example, that the money which it would cost could be used instead to prevent some other people from starving. The problem reduces then to this: How do we select these prima facie principles of justice, and how do we decide when a case has arisen which is so exceptional that we ought to contravene them? These are questions on which, perhaps, some light has been cast by more general philosophical discussions about the selection of moral principles.

It is the great merit of John Rawls (1971) and his disciples (e.g. Richards 1971) to have recognized what was already known but not clearly: that the argument about what it is just or fair to do has to proceed in two stages. There is first the stage at which we select *principles* of justice or fairness; and then the stage at which we apply these principles in order to determine what *particular acts* are just or fair. Rawls's way of selecting the principles of justice relies too much on intuition; though he may have got the formal properties of his procedure right, his excessive use of intuition may have made him think that these formal properties have consequences which they do not have (H 1973). But the general idea is right, namely that we have to have some method of selecting principles of justice; it makes no sense, in default of them, to ask what individual acts are just.

My own view (H 1978a) is that the principles can be chosen on a utilitarian basis. This, indeed, is the only just way, in yet another sense of 'just', to choose them. The sense in question here is that called by philosophers *formal justice*. Moral judgements are generally agreed by most philosophers to have a logical property which we call 'universality' or 'universaliz-ability' (see *MT* 21). This is not the same as the feature of generality which I mentioned just now as possessed by prima facie principles. It comes to this, that one cannot without logical inconsistency make different moral judgements about cases which one agrees to be otherwise similar. This is the basis of the Golden Rule (the foundation of morality) and also of the principle of the utilitarians that everybody is to count for one and nobody for more than one (Bentham, cited in Mill 1861, ch. 5). That certainly sounds just. But if we count everybody for one and nobody for more than one, we have to treat equal benefits or harms to different people (two or more) as of equal weight in our decision-making. This formal principle does not take us very far; it does not solve all moral problems for us. But at least it serves to establish on firm logical foundations a certain kind of utilitarianism (there are many other kinds, some of them quite wrong). As applied to the choice of principles of justice, and indeed of other prima facie moral principles too, this has the consequence of requiring us to choose those principles of justice which have, as philosophers say, the highest acceptance-utility—that is to say, the principles whose general acceptance in a community will confer the greatest benefits, all in all, on the members of the community, at the cost of the least harms. It goes without saying that the acceptance of *some* principles of justice or other is of benefit to a community; a community without *any* principles of justice to determine how its members are to conduct themselves towards one another in respect of the division of goods and other matters governed by such principles is unlikely to be a happy one. I hope to illustrate in the rest of this paper, after this theoretical introduction, with reference to the dispute about equality in education, how the method which I have just sketched helps us in choosing principles of justice, and shall make some specific suggestions.

Notice, first of all, the enormous step which we have taken, if we agree with what I have just said, away from what has been a commonly accepted dogma for almost all those who have discussed the problem of educational equality, on both sides of the political fence. They all speak as if education were a benefit to the recipient, and no more. It is in the child's interest to receive an education, and therefore fairness requires that this benefit should be justly distributed between children—which for the egalitarian means that no child ought to receive more of it than any other child. I am going to call this approach to equal rights to education the *cake theory*. Education is, however, not like a cake that has to be divided fairly (that is, in most people's opinion, equally). If it were, then the sole or chief moral problem would be one of fairness as between the children; and that has often been thought. No doubt there would be subsidiary problems about our duty to avoid various undesirable side-effects if the insistence on equality leads, for example, to frustrations for those children who could have deployed their talents to better effect if some extra attention had been given to them. But these problems will be, on this view, of quite minor importance compared with the main problem of securing distributive justice.

But education is not quite like a cake that has to be divided fairly between the children. The theoretical considerations which I have just been summarizing make this very clear. If they are correct, then the principle of justice which we should select in this area is one which does the best not just for the children, but for *all in the community* whose welfare is affected by the acceptance of the principle, treating each as one, i.e. fairly. Since many people besides the children themselves are affected, this alters the picture vastly. Education is less like a cake that has to be divided up than it is like ammunition or weapons which have to be shared among soldiers. I ask the forgiveness of pacifists who do not like military examples if I use this analogy, which is the clearest I can think of; if they find it distasteful they can substitute any other kind of equipment or supply. Let us call the alternative theory which I wish to consider the *equipment theory*. It may be that to have ammunition and weapons is in the interest of everybody in a battle, at any rate for self-defence. But obviously nobody is going to argue that therefore we ought in fairness to distribute them equally. For the point of having ammunition is to use it in order to win the battle. And with this in mind we may have reasons for distributing it unequally. We may give more to those who can shoot straight and will not waste it, for example.

While I am speaking of armies, let us think a little about military (or, if pacifists, about any other kind of vocational) training, which, if denied the name of education in the purest sense, is at least like it in many respects. Does anybody say that everybody in the army has an equal right to training? To basic training perhaps, because they will be unhappy and at a loss and useless without it. But what about specialist forms of training which not everybody can master? Is it unfair if somebody is taught to be an artillery surveyor or even a staff officer when others are not? No doubt when there are two equally well-qualified officers who might go to the Staff College, it is unfair if one can go and the other not. But no one thinks that, because not everybody can go to the Staff College, nobody should. The reason why nobody thinks this is that training at the Staff College has a purpose, namely to produce officers who will fulfil well their duties on the staff and provide from their ranks a supply of good generals who will help to win battles in the future. This is the prime consideration; it takes precedence over questions of equal distribution between the candidates.

When we turn from vocational training to education in general, both the cake theory and the equipment theory can be seen to be too one-sided; the truth lies in some kind of combination of them. The considerations about fairness between the children put forward by cake-theorists have, indeed, a great deal of force; but they need to be balanced by an admixture of equipment theory.

With this in mind, let us ask what I say is the main question: What principles of justice as regards the provision of education will have the highest acceptance-utility? In other words, if we were choosing what principles of justice to recommend to a community, and had the good of the people in the community at heart, and were impartial between them, what would we recommend? We can if we wish try to imagine that we are God, the impartially benevolent Creator, choosing principles of justice to impose on his creatures; or, if that is too much of a strain, we can think of ourselves as what we all are, educators at least of our own children—and ask, What are the principles of justice which, if we bring up our children to hold them and everybody else does the same, will produce the greatest good for their generation as a whole and for their successors?

This means that we have to ask what are the various interests affected, and how the different policies that we might pursue would affect those interests. Our object is that the things we shall actually be doing (and it is difficult in this uncertain world to be sure what we are actually doing, because what we are doing is to bring about certain consequences, some of them long-term, and predictions about these are hard to make)—that the things we shall actually be doing shall be as fair as we can make them between all those interests. What we shall be doing is inculcating the principles in question—i.e. principles of justice or fairness which our children, and other people whom we influence, will accept; and our object will be to choose those principles whose acceptance will serve those interests as fully and as fairly as possible. As we have seen, this is achieved if, counting each of the persons affected for one and nobody for more than one, we give equal weight to the interests of each and then maximize the satisfaction of them in total.

What then are the interests involved? According to the cake theory, the only interests we have to consider are those of the children to be educated. But although those interests are certainly important, it would be an astonishingly gross over-simplification to suppose that they are the sole interests affected, or even, all in all, the dominant ones. One idea which has persuaded people that they are may be mentioned in passing: it has often been thought that there is some kind of pre-established harmony between the interests of children in acquiring education and the interests of the community (i.e. of its members generally) in getting them educated. This would be so if the amount and quality of education which it is most in the interest of the children to have is identical with the amount and quality which it is in the interest of the community that they should have. This is true only to a certain degree. Up to a point, it will profit the children if they acquire the sort of education which will make them useful members of society. But it is easy to think of attainments which it might be in the interests of the children to acquire, but whose acquisition by them may not do much good to anybody else. Suppose, for example, that a child can become a very bad musician, but one who gets immense satisfaction from his bad performances. Suppose that his instrument is the voice and that he cannot be taught to sing in tune, but is so unmusical that his singing, though excruciating to everybody else, gives him huge pleasure. How much in the way of educational resources is it right to expend on teaching him to sing like this? This sort of problem arises acutely in the case of handicapped children, who can be, at great cost, taught certain minimum attainments which will help them to find a place in society and thus make them happier; but the good that they do to themselves and others by exercising these attainments may be far less than the cost of teaching them. The problem is eased if we remember that even if the handicapped person becomes just barely self-supporting, society is relieved of the burden of supporting him, and that this can be set against the cost of his education. But even so there is a balance to be struck. And we must remember that we are all handicapped in various respects relatively to the really high achievers.

I take it as established, then, that the community has an interest in children's education which is over and above, and may conflict with, the children's own interest in getting educated. This is very important when we come to consider the question of educational equality. It is often debated whether children of talent should be given more of our educational resources, or less, or an equal amount to everybody else. The argument for the last course is simple unthinking egalitarianism, which supposes that equality in distribution of anything one cares to name is always fairest. The argument for giving them less is also an egalitarian one, but more sophisticated: they already have an advantage in being more talented; true equality will therefore be restored if we make it a handicap race and give to the less talented compensating advantages which will enable them to compete on equal terms with the talented. The argument for giving the talented more of our resources is that they will be able to make better use of what they get.

If we are followers of the cake theory and are egalitarians we shall embrace one of the first two answers: the first if we are naïve; the second if we are more sophisticated. If the only interests to be considered are those of the children, then the question becomes one of distributive justice simply between *them*; and if we think a little, the second answer has an obvious appeal. But if we are not confirmed cake-theorists, the position is less simple. Let us recur to the analogy with the military academy, and remember that our ordinary academies share with it at least this feature, that their products are expected to contribute better to the needs of their fellow men and women than they would have if not educated. Does anybody think that when one is training potential generals one should place a handicap on tactical and strategic geniuses, in order that those of mediocre talent may compete with them on equal terms? An army that followed such a policy would make it certain that it would be defeated in future wars.

This, then, is a strong argument for giving to our talented children as much in the way of educational resources as they can use. I shall come in a moment to arguments on the other side. For the benefit of Marxists who claim to be egalitarians, I may perhaps mention that this fostering of talent seems to be one of the cardinal features of educational policy in the Soviet Union and its imitators in Eastern Europe.

At this point voices will be heard murmuring 'élitism', 'meritocracy', and other such bad words. We must certainly discuss these notions, and the best way to discuss them is to raise the issue of equality of opportunity and its relation to plain equality in distribution. These two sorts of equality were once thought to be allies; now it is more common to find them treated as enemies. They were thought to be allies when the principal obstacle to equality in the distribution of educational opportunities and all other good things in life was hereditary privilege. 'Open careers to talents', it was said, 'and these inequalities due to hereditary class will disappear.' It was the achievement of the antimeritocrats to point out that this may not be the end of the story. If one opens careers to talents, those with greater talents will get the pickings. A policy of complete equality of opportunity will therefore result in gross inequalities in the distribution of money, power, and all other sought-after things.

It has therefore come to be seen that in order to secure equality in distribution one has to place very severe restrictions on equality of opportunity. If we went to the extreme in this direction, we should afford opportunity in inverse proportion to talent, so that achievement was equalized. Since some cannot achieve much, however much they are given in the way of opportunities, this would result in confining the achievement even of the talented to the same low level. Thus, if a complete moron cannot learn to read even if given the undivided attention of a tutor all to himself and the most expensive apparatus, we must not try to teach anybody to read, because that would give them an unfair advantage over the moron. Nobody is such an egalitarian as that; but elements of this kind of thinking appear in the most respectable places. It would seem that a cake-theorist who is also an out-and-out egalitarian is indeed committed to this absurdity.

It is less likely now than formerly that somebody will want to say at this point that I have failed to distinguish between *native* talent and those abilities which are the result of privileged educational and family backgrounds. It used to be said that anything a child could achieve by his own native ability, given the opportunity, he had a right to achieve. It was fair, that is to say, to compensate children who were disadvantaged by poor family backgrounds by giving them a head start over children of equal ability from more favourable backgrounds, even if it could only be done (as is indeed the case) by diverting educational resources away from the latter to the former. But in the case of children with different *native* endowments, such compensation was not called for. But now it has become a commonplace to say that talent itself, whether due to heredity or to early environment, is an unmerited advantage, for the lack of which those who lack it should be compensated.

Up-to-date egalitarian cake-theorists are therefore not likely to save themselves from the absurdity just mentioned by distinguishing between native talent and favourable family backgrounds as sources of unfair advantage. They will have to save themselves, if at all, by abandoning either the cake theory or their egalitarianism. I would recommend them to try, first, abandoning the cake theory and see how far that gets them. I must mention in passing that I have been talking about the distribution of educational resources as such, not about the rewards which are allotted to success in climbing the educational ladder. If it were claimed that an egalitarian could agree with all that I have said about distribution of educational resources, but demand that all should get equal rewards at the end of their education, that would raise a wider social question which is not the subject of this paper. It would have to be discussed in the light of, among other things, the difficulty of getting children to put out effort in learning without any incentive in the form of a reward for the successful. If, on the other hand, it is claimed that the vice of giving more resources to the talented is not the unfair distribution of resources in itself, but the effect it has in producing inequalities in the advantages enjoyed by the children for the rest of their lives, then we have to ask, about the total social effects of the educational arrangements which we adopt, the same questions as now face us in any case as a result of our abandonment of the cake theory.

If we abandon the cake theory, we are allowed to consider, in addition to the advantages to the children of being educated, the advantages to the community of having them educated. As a change from my military example, let us consider the situation of a developing country. Let us suppose that this country badly needs doctors and engineers. Relatively few children have the ability to become first-rate or even competent doctors and engineers. Will anybody be found to say that in the interests of fairness those children who have this ability should be held back, and the limited resources which could have been used for their higher education devoted instead to educating the others, until all have reached the minimum standard of which all are capable? Shall we not be more likely to say that *for the good of all*, who need doctors and engineers, extra resources should be devoted to medical schools and schools of engineering? This, so far, is just intuition, not argument; but the arguments are to hand and I have already indicated what they are. If we are trying to be fair to all, the all that we are trying to be fair to include not merely the children but all those whose interests the children may be able to serve when they grow up.

This provides an argument for pursuing equality of opportunity in such countries. But the developed countries are no different. All societies need to make the best of the talent available to them. And doctors, engineers, and other technicians are not the only products of education that we have to consider. Even more important are the people Plato referred to as 'guardians' (i.e. rulers)—among whom we may, in deference to Marx, include the wielders of economic as well as political power. And that is where meritocracy comes in.

The argument about meritocracy would have been a great deal clearer if more attention had been given to the possible meanings of the word 'merit', or, to be more accurate, to the possible criteria of merit. The 'crat' part of the word 'meritocrat' means one who rules or wields power. We are unlikely, however democratic or egalitarian our polities become, to avoid being ruled, or having power exercised over us, by somebody (the power struggles between so-called egalitarian Maoists in communist China testify to this disagreeable fact). So we can perhaps pass by the 'crat' part of the question; we are going to have 'crats' of some kind, whether we like it or not, and whether they are politicians, bureaucrats, executives, union bosses, or whatever. The more pressing part of the question, as Plato saw, was how to get good ones; and, we might add in deference to Popper (1945, vol. i, ch. 7), how to see to it that they do not get corrupted by power and are restrained even if they are, and can at worst be got rid of without violence.

Education plays a very big part in securing good rulers. No country will be well governed which does not possess a large reservoir of able people educated so as to enable them to make the best of their abilities. If to say this is to be an élitist, then that is what I am. But it becomes at this point crucial to explain what one means by 'merit'. Merit is not the same thing as the ability to get to the top by whatever means. A genuinely meritocratic system is one in which the qualities which are desirable in a ruler are sought for in the education of those with a talent for ruling, and in the selection of the actual rulers from among their number. Such a system can be democratic if the method of selection is democratic; but this demands a fairly high quality of education and percipience in the electors.

Moral education is therefore, to say the least, a very important part of education—for otherwise how will they know merit when they see it? It is in danger of being neglected. And we have to decide what qualities constitute merit; and in doing this, moral philosophy may be a help, though that is not the topic of this paper. What I have been doing so far is to produce arguments for equality of opportunity in education, by showing that the opportunities which we are thereby providing are opportunities for children, not simply to advance their own interests, but to fit themselves to serve other people in whatever capacity. That was the point of my title 'Opportunity for What?' So far, we have an argument for giving to talented children the opportunities which will enable them to do this best. And inevitably these will also be opportunities to turn themselves into meritocrats, and thus the resulting distribution of power and advantages will be unequal. So far, therefore, we have a highly inegalitarian argument, based, paradoxically, on the principle that the equal interests of all affected by a policy are to be given equal weight.

But we must not be content with stating just that side of the case. If the arguments for educational equality based on rather general principles or slogans about fairness, and ultimately on mere intuitions or prejudices, are mostly bad ones, there are perhaps some good ones too. A utilitarian like myself can, in fact, produce some good arguments for a surprisingly high equality of distribution of all goods, *in most actual societies*, though if we try to extend these arguments to unusual or fantastic conditions of society, trouble at once results. All this I have tried to show in the paper about justice referred to earlier; and comparable arguments can be adduced in the area of education.

One very important such argument is concerned with *envy*. The exercise of power by one person over others leads easily to envy and its near kin resentment, whether justified or not. This is mitigated in most societies by various means. It needs to be if they are to survive; and, even if envy does not lead to the collapse of society, it is in itself an evil. The most sinister of these means is the oldest. If those in power can make their subjects not merely *do* what the rulers want but *want* what the rulers want, envy and resentment may be enormously reduced. Whether in the form of traditional authority or of modern methods of propaganda, this expedient is made less effective by the spread of any kind of education that is more than mere indoctrination. It is unlikely, therefore, to be available to the rulers of a well-educated society, and its place will have to be taken by more democratic means of reducing envy. The chief of these are, first, the ability of the ruled to select their rulers, to turn them out if they are dissatisfied, and to participate, themselves, in the processes of government to the extent that they can understand the questions at issue. All these have an immediate bearing on education; for they all presuppose that the ruled have some common ground of understanding with the rulers; and this they can only acquire if to some extent they have had a common basic education.

The second means of reducing envy goes a good deal deeper. The common education that I have just mentioned will, if properly organized (and that cannot be taken for granted), induce mutual respect. The British 'public' (i.e. private) schools are often said to be socially divisive, and so are the academically élitist grammar schools which the Labour Party wishes to absorb into a comprehensive egalitarian system. To some extent it is true that they are socially divisive. If some children, whether through their own talent or the wealth of their parents, are educated in different schools from the rest, they may come to think of the rest as less worthy of respect, and social divisions are thus accentuated. This, then, is another good reason for a common and to some extent equal education, though it is no reason for holding back the talented. Mutual respect may even be increased if everybody is known to be going to the place in society for which he is best fitted, and if the rewards which he then receives are proportionate to his services. Nearly everyone has something that he can do well, be it ruling or putting on thatched roofs, and we ought to be able to respect one another for our different attainments. That educational system will most reduce envy which is best at finding out children's peculiar talents and enabling them to exercise these. But we cannot abolish (except by better education of the envious) the kind of envy which, if it is deprived of one object, at once finds another. The important thing is, not to give an exaggerated prestige to certain roles in society at the expense of others (not even to that of ruler). The more people say that they do not envy the Prime Minister (as most sensible people say now) the better.

These, then, are good social reasons for affording equal opportunities for all in a common system of education, which should at the same time provide variety of curricula to suit different children. They are very much better reasons than those based on abstract principles of distributive justice. They amount to saying that things will go better in society if that is the way we arrange our education—and that is a very strong reason. However, these social reasons for providing equality of educational opportunity *can* be counterbalanced, in certain situations, by other social reasons for not trying to bring it about too fast. When we are talking in these practical terms and not in terms of abstract principles of distributive justice, we have to strike a practical balance. To pursue equality in education at the cost of its overall quality may not be justifiable on utilitarian grounds. Abrupt changes which impair the education of a particular generation of children, and provoke their parents, as they have in some countries, even to violence, are seldom wise (though the State should not always give in to violence, or the result will be more violence). It will depend on the situation. We have, in determining our educational priorities, to try to be fair to everybody, including those who are likely to get their heads broken.

REFERENCES AND BIBLIOGRAPHY

References are to the date and page-number, unless otherwise indicated. References beginning '*LM*', '*FR*', and '*MT*' are to *The Language of Morals* (H 1952), *Freedom and Reason* (H 1963*a*), and *Moral Thinking* (H 1981*a*) respectively. References beginning with 'H' are to the first part of the bibliography; the rest, beginning with the author's name unless this is clear from the context, are to the second. Full bibliographies of the writings of R. M. Hare are to be found in H 1971*a* (to 1971), *MT* (1971–81), and H 1988 (1981–7).

1. Writings of R. M. Hare

1952 *The Language of Morals* (Oxford UP). Translations: Italian, *Il linguaggio della morale* (Astrolabio-Ubaldini, 1968); German, *Die Sprache der Moral* (Suhrkamp, 1972); Spanish, *El lenguaje de la moral* (Mexico UP, 1975). Also Chinese and Japanese.
1955 'Can I be Blamed for Obeying Orders?', *The Listener* (Oct.). Repr. in H 1972*b*.
1960 ' "Nothing Matters": Is "the Annihilation of Values" Something that could Happen?' (in French). English version in H 1972*b*.
1963*a* *Freedom and Reason* (Oxford UP). Translations: Italian, *Libertà e ragione* (Il Saggiatore, 1971); German, *Freiheit und Vernunft* (Patmos, 1973; Suhrkamp, 1983); also Japanese.
1963*b* 'Descriptivism', *British Academy* 49. Repr. in H 1972*c*.
1967 'The Lawful Government', in *Philosophy, Politics and Society* 3, ed. P. Laslett and W. G. Runciman (Blackwell). Repr. in H 1972*b*.
1968 Review of G. J. Warnock, *Contemporary Moral Philosophy*, *Mind* 77.
1971*a* 'Wanting: Some Pitfalls', in *Agent, Action and Reason*, ed. R. Binkley *et al.* (Blackwell). Repr. in H 1971*b*.
1971*b* *Practical Inferences* (Macmillan, London).
1971*c* *Essays on Philosophical Method* (Macmillan, London).
1972*a* 'Principles', *Ar. Soc.* 72. Repr. in H 1989*a*.
1972*b* *Applications of Moral Philosophy* (Macmillan, London).
1972*c* *Essays on the Moral Concepts* (Macmillan, London).

1972*d* Review of G. J. Warnock, *The Object of Morality, Ratio* 14 (English and German edns.).

1973 Critical Study: 'Rawls' Theory of Justice: I and II', *Ph. Q.* 23. Repr. in *Reading Rawls*, ed. N. Daniels (Blackwell, 1975), and in H 1989*a*.

1975 'Abortion and the Golden Rule', *Ph. and Pub. Aff.* 4. Repr. in H 1992*b*. German translation in *Um Leben und Tod*, ed. A. Leist (Reclam, 1990). Italian translation in anthology ed. by S. Maffettone (Liguori, forthcoming).

1976*a* 'Ethical Theory and Utilitarianism', in *Contemporary British Philosophy* 4, ed. H. D. Lewis (Unwin). Repr. in *Utilitarianism and Beyond*, ed. A. K. Sen and B. A. O. Williams (Cambridge UP, 1982), and in H 1989*a*. Italian translation in *Utilitarismo e óltre*, ed. S. Veca (Il Saggiatore, 1990).

1976*b* 'Some Confusions about Subjectivity', in *Freedom and Morality*, ed. J. Bricke (Lindley Lectures, U. of Kansas).

1978*a* 'Justice and Equality', in *Justice and Economic Distribution*, ed. J. Arthur and W. Shaw (Prentice-Hall). Repr. in H 1989*b*. Original Polish version, *Etyka* 15 (1977).

1978*b* 'Relevance', in *Values and Morals*, ed. A. I. Goldman and J. Kim (Reidel). Repr. in H 1989*a*.

1979*a* 'What Makes Choices Rational?', *Rev. Met.* 32. Repr. in H 1989*a*.

1979*b* 'Universal and Past-Tense Prescriptions: A Reply to Mr Ibberson', *Analysis* 39.

1981*a* *Moral Thinking* (Oxford UP). Translations: Italian, *Il pensiero morale* (Il Mulino, 1989); German, *Moralisches Denken* (Suhrkamp, forthcoming). Also Chinese and Japanese.

1981*b* Review of P. Singer, *The Expanding Circle, New Republic* (7 Feb.).

1982 *Plato* (Oxford UP).

1984 'Rights, Utility and Universalization', in *Utility and Rights*, ed. R. Frey (U. of Minnesota P.). Repr. in H 1989*b*.

1986 'Punishment and Retributive Justice', *Ph. Topics* 14, ed. J. Adler and R. N. Lee (U. of Arkansas P.). Repr. in H 1989*b*.

1987 '*In Vitro* Fertilization and the Warnock Report', in *Ethics, Reproduction and Genetic Control*, ed. R. Chadwick (Routledge). Repr. in H 1992*b*.

1988 'Possible People', *Bioethics* 2. Repr. in H 1992*b*.

1989*a* *Essays in Ethical Theory* (Oxford UP). Italian translation, *Saggi nella teoria etica* (Mondadori, forthcoming).

1989*b* *Essays on Political Morality* (Oxford UP). Italian translation, *Saggi sulla moralità politica* (Mondadori, forthcoming).

1989*c* 'A Kantian Approach to Abortion', in *Right Conduct*, ed. M.

D. Bayles and K. Henley, 2nd edn. (Random House). Repr. in *Soc. Th. and Pr.* 15 (1989) and (abridged) in H 1992*b*.
1992*a* 'Could Kant have Been a Utilitarian?' (in German), in *Zum Moralischen Denken*, ed. G. Meggle and C. Fehige (Suhrkamp, forthcoming). Italian translation in *Materiali per una storia della cultura giuridica* 21, 1991. English version in *New Studies in Kant in Honor of W. H. Werkmeister* (Proc. of conference at Florida State University, 1991), ed. L. B. Brown and R. M. Dancy (Reidel, forthcoming).
1992*b* *Essays on Bioethics* (Oxford UP, forthcoming).
1992*c* 'Weakness of Will', in *Encyclopedia of Ethics*, ed. L. Becker (Garland).

The date 1992 is conjectural.

2. Other Writings

ANSCOMBE, G. E. M. (1958), 'Modern Moral Philosophy', *Philosophy* 33.
ARISTOTLE, *Nicomachean Ethics* and *Poems*. Refs. to Bekker pages.
AUSTIN, J. L. (1962), *How to Do Things with Words* (Oxford UP).
BAUDELAIRE, C. P. (1857), 'Le Vin de l'Assassin', in *Les Fleurs du mal*, ed. E. Starkie (Blackwell, 1942), 112.
BECK, THE MOST REVD G. A. (1964), 'Aims in Education; Neo-Thomism', in Hollins 1964.
BERLIN, SIR ISAIAH (1958), *Two Concepts of Liberty* (Oxford UP).
BRAITHWAITE, R. B. (1955), *An Empiricist's View of the Nature of Religious Belief* (Cambridge UP). Cited from J. Hick, *The Existence of God* (Macmillan, 1964).
BRANDT, R. B. (1979), *A Theory of the Good and the Right* (Oxford UP).
BROWN, S. C., ed. (1975), *Philosophers Discuss Education* (Macmillan, London).
BRYANT, A. (1957), *The Turn of the Tide* (Collins).
BUTLER, JOSEPH (1726), *Fifteen Sermons* and *Dissertation on Virtue*. Selections in *British Moralists* 1, ed. D. D. Raphael (Oxford UP, 1969).
BUTLER, SAMUEL (1903), *Ernest Pontifex; or, The Way of All Flesh*. Cited from Florin Books edn. (Cape, 1945).
COLLINGWOOD, R. G. (1940), *An Essay on Metaphysics* (Oxford UP).
Congregation for the Doctrine of the Faith (1987), *Instruction on Respect for Human Life in its Origin and on the Divinity of Procreation: Replies to Certain Questions of the Day* (Vatican City).
DEARDEN, R. F. (1975), 'Autonomy as an Educational Ideal', in Brown 1975.
DRYDEN, J. (1637), *The Hind and the Panther.*

ELLIOTT, J., and MACDONALD, B. (eds.) (1975), *People in Classrooms* (U. of E. Anglia).

ELLIOTT, R. K. (1975), 'Education and the Development of the Understanding', in Brown 1975.

EWING, A. C. (1959), *Second Thoughts in Moral Philosophy* (Routledge).

FERRIS, PAUL (1971), 'Teenage Sex: The New Dilemma', *Observer Review*, 18 July.

FLEW, A. G. N. (1950), 'Theology and Falsification', *University* 1. Repr. in Flew and MacIntyre 1955 and elsewhere.

——(1964), Review of H 1963*a*, *Rationalist Annual*.

——and MACINTYRE, A. (eds.) (1955), *New Essays in Philosophical Theology* (SCM).

GAUNT, WILLIAM (1945), *The Aesthetic Adventure* (Cape).

GLOVER, J. C. B. *et al.* (1989), *Fertility and the Family* (Fourth Estate).

GORDON, E. (1963), *Miracle on the River Kwai* (Collins).

HANLY, K. (1964), 'Zimmerman's "Is–Is": A Schizophrenic Monism', *Mind* 73.

HOBBES, T. (1651), *Leviathan*.

HODGSON, P. (1969), 'Modern Science', *The Tablet* 223 (21 June).

HOHFELD, W. (1923), *Fundamental Legal Conceptions* (Yale UP).

HOLLINS, T. C. B. (ed.) (1964), *Aims in Education* (Manchester UP).

HUME, DAVID (1739), *A Treatise of Human Nature*.

——(1748), *An Enquiry concerning Human Understanding*.

HUXLEY, A. (1932), *Brave New World* (Chatto & Windus).

KANT, IMMANUEL (1781), *Kritik der reinen Vernunft*. Refs. to pages of earliest editions, as given in translation by N. Kemp Smith (Macmillan, London, 1929, rev. 1933).

——(1785), *Grundlegung zur Metaphysik der Sitten*. Refs. to pages of earliest editions and of Royal Prussian Academy edition as given in margin of translation by H. J. Paton, *The Moral Law* (Hutchinson, 1948).

——(1797), *Metaphysische Anfangsgründe der Tugendlehre* (pt. II of *Metaphysik der Sitten*. Refs. to pages of first edition and of Royal Prussian Academy edition as given in translation by M. Gregor, *The Doctrine of Virtue* (Harper & Row, 1964).

LAMB, CHARLES (1818), 'The Old and the New Schoolmaster', in *Essays of Elia*, cited from 1899 edn. (Macmillan, London).

MACINTYRE, A. (1964), 'Against Utilitarianism', in Hollins 1964.

MACKIE, J. L. (1977), *Ethics: Inventing Right and Wrong* (Penguin).

——(1982), *The Miracle of Theism* (Oxford UP).

MEDAWAR, P. (1961), Review of T. de Chardin, *The Phenomenon of Man, Mind* 70.

MILL, J. S. (1861), *Utilitarianism*.

MILTON, J. (1667), *Paradise Lost*. Cited as *PL*.

NEWMAN, J. H. (1834), 'Lead, Kindly Light', *British Magazine* (Mar.). Repr. in most hymnbooks.

——(1865), *The Dream of Gerontius*.

PIPER, MYFANWY (1955), Libretto of Benjamin Britten, *The Turn of the Screw* (Boosey & Hawkes).

PIUS XII, POPE (1957), Allocution in *Acta Apostolicae Sedis* xxxxix, pp. 1027–33.

PLATO, *Euthyphro, Gorgias, Meno, Politicus, Republic*. Refs. to Stephanus pages.

POPE, ALEXANDER (1734), *An Epistle from Mr Pope to Dr. Arbuthnot*.

POPPER, SIR KARL (1945), *The Open Society and its Enemies* (Routledge).

QUINE, W. V. (1951), 'Two Dogmas of Empiricism', *Ph. Rev.* 60. Repr. in his *From a Logical Point of View* (Harvard UP, 1953).

RAWLS, J. (1971), *A Theory of Justice* (Harvard UP and Oxford UP).

RICHARDS, D. A. J. (1971), *A Theory of Reasons for Action* (Oxford UP).

ROBINSON, JOHN (1967), *Honest to God* (SCM).

ROBINSON, RICHARD (1969), 'Aristotle on Acrasia', in his *Essays in Greek Philosophy* (Oxford UP). Originally published in French, *Rev. Philosophique* 1955.

ROSS, W. D. (1930), *The Right and the Good* (Oxford UP).

RYLE, G. (1949), *The Concept of Mind* (Hutchinson).

SEARLE, J. R., and VANDERVEKEN, D. (1985), *Foundations of Illocutionary Logic* (Cambridge UP).

SINGER, P. (1973), 'The Triviality of the Debate over "Is–Ought" and the Definition of "Moral" ', *Am. Ph. Q.* 10 (1973).

——(1979), *Practical Ethics* (Cambridge UP).

——(1981), *The Expanding Circle: Ethics and Sociobiology* (Oxford UP).

——(1988), 'Reasoning towards Utilitarianism', in *Hare and Critics*, ed. D. Seanor and N. Fotion (Oxford UP).

SKINNER, B. F. (1948), *Walden II* (Macmillan, New York).

SMART, J. J. C. (1984), *Ethics, Persuasion and Truth* (Routledge).

STENHOUSE, L. (1969), 'Open-Minded Teaching', *New Society*, 24 July.

——(1970), 'Pupils into Students', *Dialogue*, Schools Council Newsletter, no. 5.

——(1971), 'The Humanities Curriculum Project: The Rationale', *Theory into Practice* 10.

STEVENSON, C. L. (1944), *Ethics and Language* (Yale UP).
TELFER, E. (1975), 'Autonomy as an Educational Ideal', in Brown 1975.
THORNTON, J. C. (1966), 'Religious Belief and Reductionism', *Sophia* 5.
VAN BUREN, P. M. (1963), *The Secular Meaning of the Gospel* (SCM).
VERNEY, S. E. (1964), *Fire in Coventry* (Hodder & Stoughton).
WARNOCK, G. J. (1967), *Contemporary Moral Philosophy* (Macmillan, London). Also in *New Studies in Ethics*, ed. W. D. Hudson (Macmillan, London, 1967).
——(1971), *The Object of Morality* (Methuen).
WARNOCK, BARONESS M. (1975), 'The Neutral Teacher', in Brown 1975.
——(1984), *Report of the Committee of Inquiry into Human Fertilisation and Embryology*, HMSO Cmnd. 9214. Repr. with additions as *A Question of Life* (Blackwell, 1985).
WILSON, J. (1964), 'Education and Indoctrination', in Hollins 1964.
——WILLIAMS, N., and SUGARMAN, B. (1967), *Introduction to Moral Education* (Penguin).
WISDOM, J. (1944), 'Gods', *Ar. Soc.* 45.
YOUNG, J. Z. (1951), *Doubt and Certainty in Science* (Oxford UP).
ZIMMERMAN, M. (1962), 'The "Is–Ought": An Unnecessary Dualism', *Mind* 71. Repr. in *The Is–Ought Question*, ed. W. D. Hudson (Macmillan, London, 1969).

INDEX